CONTEMPORARY BLACK THOUGHT

SAGE FOCUS EDITIONS

CONTEMPORARY BLACK THOUGHT

Alternative Analyses in Social and Behavioral Science

Edited by **Molefi Kete Asante**
and **Abdulai S. Vandi**

 SAGE PUBLICATIONS   Beverly Hills   London

For information address:

SAGE Publications, Inc.
275 South Beverly Drive
Beverly Hills, California 90212

SAGE Publications Ltd
28 Banner Street
London EC1Y 8QE, England

Printed in the United States of America

Library of Congress Cataloging in Publication Data

Main entry under title:

Contemporary Black thought.

    (Sage focus editions ; 26)
    Bibliography: p.
    Includes index.
    1. Afro-Americans–Addresses, essays, lectures.
2. Blacks–Addresses, essays, lectures. I. Asante,
Molefi K., 1942-   II. Vandi, Abdulai S.
III. Series.
E184.6.C66   305.8'96073   80-15186

ISBN 0-8039-1500-4
ISBN 0-8039-1501-2 (pbk.)

FIRST PRINTING

Dedicated to
Eka, Hota, and Djifa,
who know the truth

CONTENTS

PREFACE

The conscious attempt of the editors and authors in this volume is to present the alternative views to the Eurocentric conceptualization of behavioral and social sciences. No longer operating from a pathological view of the world in respect to Africans, these scholars assert in clear, decisive ways the integrative dimension of the human experience. Our aim in making this volume available is instructive in both a theoretical and a practical manner. In the first place, there has never been a collection of original manuscripts of this nature; second, the coalescence which brought about its inception is truly remarkable when it is understood that in different places of the world, at about the same time, these authors saw the need to do research which reflected a more authentic aspect of the social and behavioral problems of the world.

It was especially discouraging when we noted that numerous scholars of African descent in almost every field wrote scholarly manuscripts from the Eurocentric point of view, that is, as if the only audience were a white, Western one. More particularly, the theoretical base or beginning point of their research was a white theoretical foundation, whether it was linear, evolutionary, fragmented, or particularized according to discipline. Thus, we found writers eagerly explaining the abnormality of blacks by white norms, or the pathology of blacks by standards of white health, or African history through the eyes of Europeans, or the communication patterns of black families by comparison with those of white families. Such a situation created whole generations of misled scholars and miseducated students. Thus, in this book we have assembled some of the more valuable critiques of the social and behavioral problems of the world to counteract the prevalent and erroneous model that sees Europe as a teacher and the African world as pupil.

The manuscripts are not polemic, unless in the sense that their theoretical and philosophical assumptions allow them to derive nontraditional results. We have edited these manuscripts in such a way that the analytical methods are clear and precise. It is not the desire of the authors or editors to see a volume which would beg any scholarly questions or issues. Therefore, the work presented here represents the best tradition of fair and open analysis and evaluation. In assembling this group of original essays we wanted to challenge our authors to prepare manuscripts which would stand not only the immediate test of keen observers but the long-range test of permanence as a way to view the world.

Because of the wide range of social and behavioral topics covered, it is our belief that readers will come back to the book many times for reflection, discussion, and examination. It is a volume which reports more theoretical issues than it does research findings, but it will serve as the base from which research interested in alternative paradigms will draw much support. Necessarily, the first marks must be theoretical marks to give guidance to the research works which will flow from these sources. All research follows some theoretical plan, deliberately or unconsciously. Our intention, then, is to lay the groundwork for a more productive scholarly development. It should be a development which will eventually influence scholars in all parts of the world.

To provide the maximum amount of exposure to all theoretical views, it is necessary that new explorations be presented so that researchers who have not yet been so thoroughly inbued with a one-dimensional perspective may find other paths and different methods. We see this happening already in the communication field, where several of the scholars writing for this volume have explored new angles to human communication which take into consideration the behavioral characteristics of African people or the cultural characteristics of African Americans. Their results, of course, are different from that communication because of the veil of Eurocentricism. Instead they deal with the alternative models of communicating; we say "alternative" only in the sense that many people assume the European model to be the only one, just as the European model would be called an alternative model to the African model if the African model were the prevalent paradigm. Each has value in its own context. It is when writers mix the context or do not know which model to employ that we have conceptual confusion. For example, to speak of communication on the continent of Africa and not to understand the role of communication the ancestors play within the community in traditional societies, would be to give an erroneous view of communication in a total sense. Yet numerous authors, black and white, have so spoken and written in the past. To speak of a public speech as an interrupted spoken public discourse is to miss the meaning of the speech in the African-American church, for instance. The problem is that whenever a scholar begins with a certain perspective, it is that perspective which will determine the outcome. We understand that the preacher and any other speaker speaking before a black audience expects certain "interruptions" from the audience. Yet we would be hard-pressed to explain this phenomenon in a white model, because there are no interruptions anyway; the only thing that is happening is audience "affirmation" of the speaker.

Perhaps with the publication of this book we will begin to redress the confusion which has surrounded the social and behavioral dimensions of human life. Our new explorations are meant to be the foundation upon which others will build the edifices which will reflect the values, culture, and thought of African and African-American peoples.

—Molefi Kete Asante
Abdulai S. Vandi
Howard University
Washington, D.C.

PART I

COMMUNICATION AND CULTURAL DIMENSIONS

Frantz Fanon has said that the media of information and communication are the carriers and preservers of a society's culture. Paulo Freire, however, warned that acculturation, if distorted, may subjugate a society's masses by keeping them under constant ignorance, fear, and dependence. Information and communication are, perhaps, the only strategic weapons now available to humanity for combating exploitation, ignorance, and oppression. The United States has an edge over its most contemporary adversary, the Soviet Union, only because it enjoys a slight superiority in satellite communications. Hence, whoever controls the scarce orbital space locations in the twenty-first century, will dominate the rest of the world.

No longer is humankind intimidated by the arsenal of weaponry or great military might, as is demonstrated by Iran's "blatant violation of every conceivable diplomatic protocol," and the arrogance of the Ayatollah in face of a possible annihilation of his country and people by the giant U.S. military might is a classic example of this in the contemporary world crisis. Our authors, cognizant of alternative dimensions in communication and culture, have painfully provided a fresh approach to our troubled world. This new knowledge is bound to revolutionize the entire communications discipline and rejuvenate human relations in general.

Asante explains how the communication era has nullified primitive notions of the person, such as the managerial person, one-dimensional person, bureaucratic person, and organizational person. He contends that the communication person is the only viable description of the truly contemporary person. Vandi, of the new Third World scholars, has thoroughly discussed new explorations in global information and communications, and called for an alternative plan of action: the New International Political Order (NIPO). His radical argument is that there must be a fundamental change in the world political and ideological order in any attempt to bridge global barriers in the proposed policy contexts of the New International Information and Communication Order (NIICO), and the New International Economic Order (NIEO). He launches a profound attack on the symptomatic Eurocentric scholarship in global information and communications. Asante explores the Afrocentric perspective on intercultural communication, suggesting that the approach of most social analyses is Eurocentric and thereby restrictive. An Afrocentric view of culture is open, flexible, not given to absolutistic views. Richards's compelling argument is that in the communication of ideas, the European notion of progress has been the dominant element of change. She shows that the concept of progress as communicated in European thought is self-validating. Awa clearly has demonstrated how cultural the dimension is significant in the debate surrounding the "right to communicate" controversy. These articles are provocative and original.

1

THE COMMUNICATION PERSON IN SOCIETY

Molefi Kete Asante

The chapter is concerned with nothing less than human maturity. It is my intention to address in a systematic way the pragmatics of communication, particularly with respect to the way we are affected by our environment. Such a task undertakes a reorientation of the enterprise of social science, a reformulation of assumptions, and a more thorough response to the diversity of human experiences in communication. Some writers have begun to see a crisis in the field of social sciences. I see no such crisis, because those who profess belief in the system are inclined to continue their faith. Perhaps what we see is a need for a new world view. Those who do not believe in the system are the ones expressing difficulty; we are concerned and disturbed. The historical epoch of social science has its own bases, its own prophets, and its own holy places. We cannot question the integrity of what that system does, merely by charging a crisis; we must demonstrate a more righteous way to explore human issues. It is therefore the purpose of this present enterprise to present a clarifying portrayal of human beings in the generic sense, as they exist in contemporary society.

What I propose is a comprehensive plan for analysis rather than the legitimation of any political, economic, or social system. The communication person is at the center of all systems, receiving information from all equally, and stimulating all with the power of his or her personality. Based upon the assumption that the material and spiritual are really parts of the same system, the communication person thrusts him- or herself into the world of the unknown, knowing at all times that messages, symbols, and signs are the influences penetrating his or her every action. Thus, there is no quest here to establish any orientation toward social science based upon a materialistic view or a spiritualistic view. The view expressed in this chapter is harmonious, holistic, and full.

It is hard to escape the fact that the ideal of social science is rooted in the grounds of materialism. In the works of Europeans, from Plato and Aristotle, from Locke and Skinner, we have the full flowering of a material consciousness which led to the compartmentalization of social sciences into sociology, psychology, economics, political science, ad nauseum; the process is not yet finished, although social science seems near its end. Even though we find these antecedents in history, the idea of social science as an autonomous field is relatively recent. In fact, in many other parts of the world, outside of Europe and America, it was unheard of until the advent of academic imperialism. Its lateness as a historical phenomenon, however, has not prevented it from exercising a strong influence in the development of human studies. What concerns me is the position which has led us to accept this limited view of reality, and the disastrous effects our acceptance has had on the events of the world. The discovery of "society" as a concept did not really occur until the eighteenth century, although societies, organized groups of people, had existed thousands of years before. Thus, the special characterization of living arrangements as "societies" meant that it became possible for people to be studied in numerous ways. The philosophical roots of the works of the Europeans were the same; Europeans all attested to the emergence of societal man on their continent. Hence, Hegel wants the world to know that there is no society unless all are free. The special character of this view as it related to freedom, even in a European sense, had been possible, to a greater degree even in Africa. At the same time that we see the rise of "society" as a concept in Europe, and at the same time that European scholars insisted on the "freeness" of those within the society, most European societies held either indentured servants or slaves. A different world would have been created if "family sciences" had become the core of analytic studies.

There have been studies of economic, sociological, and political science dimensions of society for a number of years now. They have inquired into the nature of origins, determinants, norms, potentialities, spheres of influence, and categories of production. But what the European authors have failed to reckon with is the vagueness of their use of the term *society*. If they have wanted to speak of New Guineans, Africans, or certain groups in South America they have forced themselves to use the term without meaning what they mean when they use it in a Eurocentric sense. This ambiguity is the cause of much analytical difficulty. But it grows naturally out of a myopic perspective on the world. The balkanization of academic studies as was done with the development of the social disciplines is anathema to the African world view, except where that view is following or adopting a European view. Some Europeans themselves, however, have pointed out the inherent problems in the conceptualization. One may point to the work of Heinrich von Treitschke, whose work really centers on the importance of the state. Left to von Treistschke, we may be discussing a form of "state sciences," inasmuch as he believed that no society could exist apart from the state. Yet the argument he makes is one that we could easily make for communication or "family sciences" in the African sense. Social science cannot be separated from political science, but neither can it be separated from communication, either as art or science. Indeed the very gluon of society is communication. While politics may regulate how and where people will live, communication provides the substance of their living together within certain territorial boundaries.

Understanding the context of this rise of society is important to our view of the communication person, a person at once free, collective, global, and aspiring; a person no longer bound by state sentiments, no longer encapsulated by political structures, no longer one-dimensional; a person becoming, potentializing, and establishing him- or herself. This is not to deny that the social attitude was at one time unprecedented, dynamic, powerful, and controlling. It has not always been so, and will not always be so. We so easily fall into the trap of believing that what is will always be; that is a serious analytical fallacy. We live in an era, or rather an epoch, and already the new epoch is approaching, bringing with it new concepts, terms, and challenges. Growing from the field of human liberation sentiment, the concept of society was a responsible concept, perhaps in its initial formulation even a positive one. This contextual discussion demonstrates the response of scholarship to the changes within the environment. Our present situation calls for a new formulation which will place communication squarely in the middle of any theoretical and philosophical discussion on the nature of society.

COMMUNICATION CHARACTERISTICS

The characteristics of communication which relate to this new epoch are based upon these postulates: (1) A systematic understanding of human interaction across cultures is basic to an effective critique of societies; (2) the potential of human communication resides in the creative development of personality; (3) communication is itself the new social environment; (4) a social situation that distorts human development is illegitimate; and (5) the communication person is holistic. There are a few, but only a few, scholars who have even fully understood these premises. Some have, like McLuhan, seen only the viability of communication as analogue; others, like Berlo, have misunderstood the creative development of culture and personality as a part of human communication. It is left, however, to more recent scholarship to capture the true essence of the communication person. Appiah (1979) sees in the *Okyeame* an integrative function of communication, because it is this person who holds the Akan society together, even though the *Okyeame* serves the state in an official capacity. The *Okyeame* is not the state; neither is he the people. The *Okyeame* is the integrator, bringing both the state—in this instance, the king—and the people together. In just this manner, communication serves as the gluon of the society, binding all its parts. Nhiwatiwa (1979) subscribes to the same view as Appiah, arguing that the communication is the source and end of interaction; it is a creation, a collective production. She notes that until we expand the horizon of communication thinkers beyond European models, we will not be able to grasp the holistic nature of the communication person. Support for these positions will continue to gain ground because we are fed up with fragmentation and particularization. Ancient Africans believed in the unity of the universe and demonstrated in their daily work the continuity of the sacred and secular, spiritual and material; it is this holistic view, characterized by a strong sense of personalism, which establishes the communication person.

I think it is clear that the social science model we have been living with is not able to produce viable patterns of holistic science, nor is it able to transcend the immanent normative characteristics of Western models. This lack has been evident whether the user of the model has been European or not. The problem is not in the person but in the model, inherently so. Thus, the more well trained, and without intervening training, an individual is in the European model, the more likely he or she is to interpret the world through inadequate eyes; so we get strange social science from African-American and Chinese-American social scientists, because they have been encapsulated by the European social science model. Stranger still is the fact that they cannot see the problem because they are so closely tied to it, adopting the same justifying phrases, upholding the same positions, and arguing on the same pathological grounds, without knowing the origin or the cause of the model; they embarrass themselves. Fortunately, such intellectual deviance has been seen more in sociology, psychology, anthropology, and economics than in communication.

Under the present social science model, the potentialities of the academic devoted to a full explication of contemporary society will only be partially realized, because society does not allow the academic to place communication at the center of the analysis. Unable to fulfill the intellectual needs of the scholars who seek a holistic approach to the world, the compartmentalized model forces everyone into frozen blocks. It does not take much imagination to see what happens to the society because of this unnatural arrangement. Sociologists argue in terms of psychologists taking over their territory; anthropologists do not want to be confused by communicationists who insist that they who are not political scientists are not economists, and so on. On the practical side, jobs, orientations, prophets, and textbooks are particularized; they allow one to know one side of the knowledge but not others. Indeed, you may not know all about the particular discipline you choose to know about. The complexity of the field may prevent you from knowing anything but your specialty. Unfortunately, this means that you probably know very little about the nature of humankind. The communication person repudiates cryptic views of humanity. Our attempt is to find a just place for integrative knowledge and to enthrone the communication person, trained to have substantive reasons and to provide good choices. The elevation of communication to its proper position in the micro- and macroanalysis of society will eliminate the feuds between disciplinary areas; communication serves as the arbiter of all social science disciplines through messages, information, and persuasion.

NATURE OF MAN

Until the present epoch, communication theory has been unaware of the age's assumptions about the nature of man and the universe. Almost no communicationist has postulated a concept of humanity. Indeed, I do not believe that any theorist in the past thought that he or she should formulate a clear view of humanity and the universe; so many things were given that the communicationist merely followed the formula already established by the Europeans who articulated the concept of social science later defined more precisely by the Americans. Nevertheless, not even the American communicationists refined the place of humanity in the universe for those interested in studying about the processes which impinge upon people acting and people behaving. It is as if we were playing out the music already set down by some Ellingtonian master, without finding our own way. There is, however, nothing wrong with following what others have done, so long as it can be determined that what they have done is consistent with what one must do to make an adequate analysis of the place of humanity in the universe. All our predictions in communication rest upon certain foundations which, if they did not exist, would render the whole process questionable. We cannot take any theoretical formulations for granted; they must be questioned in the light of our conceptualizations of humanity. To suggest that people communicating was a universal phenomenon but that how they communicate was a specific historical manifestation, would have caused the early communicationists considerable difficulty. They were seemingly unable to raise their sights any higher than the European frame of reference which had nurtured, stroked, and comforted them. Thus, it is only in this epoch of communication history that the total enterprise of a philosophical foundation for the study of communication can be properly placed. A theory cannot forever remain innocent of its assumptions about human nature, because it runs the risk of being pocketed by the interests of a given system and of failing to be a true instrument for optimizing the human condition. It is not surprising that rhetoricians like Bryant and Brigance saw communication as a servant of democracy. For them, the adjustment of ideas to people and of people to ideas was the full adventure of human beings communicating. Such a view made any theory of persuasion and information a captive of vested interests. To maximize human resources, a theory of communication needs to break away from the boundary of specific social or political systems and reach for universal assumptions which can then be tested by those interested in applying them to particular situations.

Communication theory, as developed by contemporary scholars, tends to become like psychology, whereas in the past what communicationists did was often modeled, methodologically, along the lines of a historical approach. This is itself a moment in the history of social science. Since the 1950s, communicationists have been turning more and more toward the empiricism of psychology in an effort to raise the stature of the discipline and to combat all of those who criticize communication for not being able to make predictions. This fact alone has pushed communicationists to consider psychology valuable. Therefore, the postulates that are presented here are indeed a new chapter in the philosophical underpinning of communication. As social science grew out of a certain climate, social and political, in Europe, the development of the various models of communication, that is, in terms of method, coincided with certain historical pressures. But even such coincidence was not enough to drive the early communicationists to formulate a view of humanity. An increase in awareness—even more, a revolution in consciousness—occurred in the classrooms and in the streets, but it was largely ignored by theorists who were trying to perfect their newly discovered psychological formulas for application to communication. They were hell-bent to walk in the ruts already created for them without ever once giving thought to what contribution they could make to the understanding of society. Thus, as history lost its ability to hold the communicationists in a methodological vise, psychology was tightening its own vise around the necks of a whole generation who never raised their eyes from the statistical chart. In the present epoch the dominant methodological motif of communication research derives from psychology. We have no complete formulation of communication as a social science, although we have numerous treatises on how certain aspects of psychology relate to communication. Models of humanity are needed to shed some light on the nature of our whole communication enterprise. It may be of some value to explore the models which have been offered by others, to see where communicationists can make worthwhile contributions. Models of humanity have been given by many scholars in the social sciences. The psychological types seem to predominate, even when the discipline is organization theory. Thus we have the organization person, the adjusted person, the upwardly mobile person, the encapsulated person, the indifferent person, the manipulator, and the one-dimensional person. There is also the psychological person, the technological person, the historical person, the global person, the parenthetical person, the protean person, the temporary person, the post-Christian person, the irrational person, the multivalent person, the fallible person, the transparent person, the deliberate person, the unitary person, the hopeful person, the transcendent person, the phenomenological person, and the mozartian person. All these models attempt to address the major problems of human existence. The authors of these models are concerned with diagnosis, description, and prescription for human illness; they all assume that something is seriously wrong with the way we approach the question of human beings in the universe, and each seeks to provide a solution by giving us a method of analyzing ourselves. Frustration, particularly as it figures in keeping people from doing their best work, is the key psychological problem confronting all of these models.

The formualtion of a framework for a sound conceptualization of the communication person is the most urgent task of this discussion. I am indebted to both social scientists in a general sense and to black scholars in a particular sense for their background contributions to this quirk in my mind. As I have said previously, the idea of the communication person involves an integrated system; the human being stands at the center of the communication environment, acting as organizer of messages. The communication person is a sensory being, responsive to images, sights, and sounds, addicted to urban settings with their inexhaustible supply of visual and auditory stimuli, comfortable with electronic media, at one with computer technology and yet in harmony with the manifestations of humanism, untrapped by any one political doctrine but open to all human possibilities. Unlike other profiles of humanity, that of the communication person reveals the human being as singularly master of all he or she surveys without becoming a dictator over others; although the communication person possesses the power of information, he or she is checked by a creative belief in the human personality. Communication people are in charge of their own wills because they coordinates from their own centers the information they receive, and at the same time produce and send messages. You may say that communication people are right in the middle of the action, making it logical to themselves and to those who are around them. They sit in board meetings, serve as public relations consultants, study architecture, collect your taxes, and for all practical purposes you may even be one of them. This view of humanity is in opposition to those views that hold the standards of normality to be the norms of any one social system. Most of the models which have been developed have assumed certain individual norms from the society of the model's author, and therefore have been compromised in their true value as an analytical tool. Thus, the "normal" person is the one who conforms to the norms of whatever social or political system the author is highlighting. In such a situation it would be hard for the Chinese scholar to hold the same standards of normality as the person from England. Furthermore, in terms of psychology it may be that to the African the European's quiet expression when he greets a long-missed friend is abnormal. This would be a system-based normality. We must reject system-based normalities for those which cut across or rise above specific systems. Communication man by his very nature is a creature apart from the narrow confines of a limiting view of the world. Our researchers have been blind to the inherent fallacies in a system which bases its criteria of normality on those which are immanent in existing social arrangements.

David Berlo's *The Process of Communication* and Hugh Duncan's *Symbols in Society* constitute two of the best examples of efforts by communicationists (in the case of Duncan, a sociologist-turned-communicationist) to tackle the problem of the nature of humanity. In both cases, however, we get the system-trapped normality which I have been criticizing. Berlo, to be fair to him, never really gives a view of humanity in any clear sense; he implies and infers certain things about the nature of human beings. His linear approach to communication sets him up as a defender of a point of view, a perspective, and some immanent criteria which are indefensible. Berlo is a victim of the social science methodological school which sets criteria for all systems and places by appealing to Eurocentric models. His linear approach to communication, the sender-message-receiver-feedback paradigm, is one-dimensional. It is a historical development not unlike that which brought in the social science paradigm in the first place. Hence, what David Berlo really articulates is a view of communication similar to the prevailing views of humanity in disciplines such as psychology, sociology, anthropology, economics, and political science. Inasmuch as these disciplines in their present form originated in the Western world, it is not so farfetched to conceived of Berlo's entrapment as natural; to do otherwise would be to ask Western scholars to transcend their own cultural and social situations in ways that few people have ever done in history. We could think of a Martin Luther King, a Gandhi, and, perhaps, a John Brown. None of these people were in any strict sense scholars, though all possessed that unique ability of great people to analyze situations and to cast their eyes in a visionary way toward the general good of humankind. Berlo's perspective, although closest to that of a communicationist, is still far away from a developed perspective on the nature of humanity.

Duncan, on the contrary, approaches communication from the standpoint of society, and, as a sociologist gathering strength from the critique of Durkheim and Weber, shows that symbols function to create order and disorder in societies. By establishing the link between sociology and communication through society and symbols, Duncan becomes the essential bridge between the fields. His view of human nature, however, is also difficult to discern, unless, of course, one wants to suggest that Duncan is interested in the dramatic person. Following Kenneth Burke even more closely than he follows the sociologists, Duncan sets up his own dramatic stage for analysis of symbols in society. What we must ask is whether or not he has any view other than that of Burke. The answer seems obvious from a reading of both of his major works. Duncan was a prisoner of Burke. He could not get out of the second European world war. It defined for him the whole nature of humanity; this was his most telling flaw. Berlo, on the other hand, was content to allow his views to emerge from his treatment of the processor of communication; Duncan based his views of humanity on a dramatic metaphor. This metaphor was itself faulty inasmuch as it was only a slice of life. Having seen the disorder created by the displacement of symbols and signs during the war, he could hardly see what was beyond the boundaries of Europe. What Duncan did must be accepted and applauded, on the one hand, because no one had done for sociology what he did for it by showing the connectedness between drama and life. Although George Herbert Mead must be credited with touching on the area as a fruitful intellectual enterprise, it was Duncan who explained how the symbol worked to destabilize and to stabilize societies. His view of human beings was obviously that they are manipulatable creatures, capable of being molded by the drama being played out on the stage of life. On the other hand, however, Duncan's unawareness of the richness and vastness of the varieties of communication in the African

world left his theories pallid and limp when faced with the world communication society. There is a school of communicationists, mainly represented by the likes of Frank E.X. Dance, Samuel Becker, and Gerald
Miller, that seems to indicate that the person is less of a factor in
communication than, say, the message. Others have contended that a
person-centered perspective is most rewarding for the study of communication. They argue from the notion of person-centeredness. But in neither
the case of the first group nor that of the second have we had any
consistent speculations about the nature of man from a communicationist's point of view. It was as if no systematic formulation could be
derived from the field of communication. This was, of course, not the
case; it was only an appearance created because, until recently, communicationists have acted like second-class citizens in the world of social
science. Those who were able to escape that appearance have often sailed
in different waters. Thus, Schramm, McLuhan, Rogers, and Klapper are
said to have mixed loyalties. However, it is not so much that their loyalties
are mixed as that what they study keeps them away from the personal
dyads of the communication situation.

Communication is today's most powerful field. Its expansion as an art
and science has not been equaled in the history of American academics.
Almost everything in our contemporary society is influenced by communication; it is truly the "becoming" environment. Nothing is extraneous to it
as a field of inquiry. The growth of media industries has had an expanding
impact on the discipline. Students in universities want to learn about
media influences, media development, presentation of messages, development of audiences, and interpersonal communication. The rising degree of
international trade and commerce has opened new possibilities for intercultural communication and diplomatic communication. New arrangements in organizations have called into question our understanding of
communication in organizations. These are only a few of the areas to
which communication as a field of inquiry is now committed. However
communication cannot succeed as an area of inquiry if it makes systematic
commitment, that is, political or social commitment, to any established
social order. The reason for this is that certain communication analyses
may end up demonstrating in communication terms the nonviability of a
given organization or international communication set-up. All systems
must remain available for communication analysis.

NEW PERSPECTIVE

The methodological posture which the communication field must take
is that all sectors of a society and all societies can be explored, analyzed,

and questioned on the basis of their contribution to the human personality. Any society that distorts, hinders, or damages the human personality must be called into question. No value-free attitude toward communication situations is possible; indeed, it is an existential impossibility. Unfortunately, too many communicationists have tried to make the discipline respond to the framework of existing social systems; the results have been dismal examples of poor and irrelevant research. They have made the field of communication nothing more than a mimic of the prevailing ideology and, as such, they have been unable to effect any real changes in the condition of the human race. Communication must transcend what is defined as its purview. Only in this transcendence can it really become the field that it should be for the scholars of this and the next country. Aboaba, in her brilliant study (1979) of the Nigerian press under military governments, has demonstrated how freedom of the press was a culturally determined term and, in fact, proved that the Nigerian press was perhaps "freer" under military rule than it had been under civilian rule; at least, she showed that the press still had the ability to criticize the government and its policies to as a degree equal to or greater than that existing under prior to military rule. Furthermore, she contended that the press of the Western nations was hopelessly controlled by commercial interests. Here it is necessary to suggest that no press is absolutely free of external constraints, although some may be economically constrained and not politically constrained. Aboaba could not have done this study without looking beyond the narrow confines of traditional perspectives, which would not have allowed her to argue that freedom of the press was not objective but relative. In this sense, she becomes one of the most clarifying critics of the overextended concept of freedom of the press, as well as of the idea that the press is some special preserve for objective advocacy for the people. What she does for the field is to question some of the holy cows, and when she is done we are directed to the fact that those cows are merely chewing different grass or grazing in different meadows. With her critique of the idea of press advocacy, she states profoundly the cultural connectedness of all institutions within societies. Thus, in Nigeria, where the press is a creation—rather, a development which came with the Europeans—one must look to the traditional cultural relationships in order to determine precisely how the people, the readers, and the audiences view the work of the press. Perhaps, she argues, in the cultural pattern of the society we will be able to find the answer to the press's role in contemporary Nigeria. Since the traditional court announcer or news carrier or drummer was attached to the palace, we have some idea of what the people expect. It is not too much to understand that the audience may very well not comprehend the role of a press that attacks government when the traditional cultural patterns emphasize harmony and dictate that the propagation of news speak for the royal court. Surely the leaders of a government in a society where this has been the traditional pattern would be disturbd by a press taking an antagonistic stance. Aboaba does not propose that we act one way or the other; she simply lays out the cultural peculiarities of different societies and tells us that we had better look at the patterns within a society before we start to make prescriptions. Her views are controversial and they are certain to receive some stiff criticism from those who believe that communication is the defender of particular world views. In the final analysis, such people will continue to hide behind their self-perpetuating, defensive mechanisms. If the human personality is not being elevated, exalted, and healed, then our role as communicationists and as communication people is not being fully realized.

All communication begins with the self. The basis of any general view of communication in society, regardless of the particular emphasis—mass, interpersonal, rhetorical, intercultural, or organizational—is the degree to which the individual has minimized his or her message contradictions. One definition of neurosis is a discrepancy between one's potential and one's actual achievement. Sometimes the neurosis may be due to external factors; indeed, this may be the general and common state of neurotic people. They have not been able to achieve their potential because of their environments. Nevertheless the person who seeks to minimize communication contradictions must do so willingly and with the idea that all communication begins with the self. The ability to find in oneself the source of one's own communication problems is only part of the truth. It is only when an individual remains ineffective as a communicator in spite of favorable environmental conditions and good natural gifts that we have to question that individual's functional ability. What people can communicate to others effectively, they should communicate if it will contribute to the development of their human personalities. A true view of the communication field must rest on what human beings can be as communicators. The field must come alive, make a difference in our lives, as the messages with which we are bombarded influence each of us. In one sense, the field of inquiry has yet to live up to the vast dimension of communication in contemporary society.

Edward Hall gives popular voice to the concerns of the masses who are affected by the growth of communication in every sphere, by demonstrating how anthropologists can make some sense out of the cultural messages each of us receives. He deliberately addresses the same subjects that we would expect a communicationist to address. He does not defend the indefensible. Some scholars believe that a certain type of communication world view must emerge and be supported as the only possible outcome. Hall is content to show that different societies have different ways of expressing themselves and that this has nothing to do with inferiority. We have not had any popular works by communicationists to compete with Hall's viewpoint, either in a supportive or a questioning manner. This is not because we do not have ideas or do not know the facts, but rather because we are intoxicated by psychological and physical science methods and have almost abandoned good common sense in our research. Thus, it is not an accident that in our field we are forever questioning ourselves, and others are forever questioning us, because what we do is often not derived from systematic concern with human development. Hall at least gives the impression that his research is concerned with making life better for human beings, whether they are capitalist business-men or Marxist proletarians; he feels that he has something to offer the person who wants to improve his or her communication. He is one of the few European-American scholars to come close to the intellectual thrust of the Afrocentric scholars.

Put simply, the communication person, as reflected in the best thinking of the age, is now closer to the African than at any other time in history. This is because of the congruence of African society with the demands of a person's inner self for harmony. A total environment of symbols where the communication of needs, wants, and desires operates to maintain the equilibrium of the village is very much upon us. Quite frankly, there exist numerous villages rather than one single global village. We, as individuals within the various villages, are instruments of the natural harmony. Despite runaway media technology and our insertion into the postmodern communication system, we have emerged and will emerge more concretely as keepers of the society. Our theoretical view must not emphasize the Western conflict view, but the more humanistic view which is based on harmony. It is not the tradition of African societies to see conflict as a method of progress; in fact, societies are made livable and kept that way by removing and keeping out conflict as much as possible.

Communication is the key ingredient in such a world view because it is only through symbol that harmony can be restored once it is lost. If it is not regained during one communication event, it is continued at another, perhaps with different players, until it is worked out. In the event of a disagreement between persons the problem is discussed, and if no solution is forthcoming the talk is joined by others who may play the major role in devising a solution. In the United States such a system would probably prove practical where all kinds of disputes arise over social and behavioral problems. Consider the fact that in a dispute between labor and man-agement in the United States, the aim is usually to achieve a different synthesis, whereas according to the model suggested by harmony the aim would be to achieve a justness based upon the relationship between the persons involved in the dispute. Relationship is the operative value in the communication person view of the world. How do we become mature in a world where relationships are spurious, nonpermanent, and shaky? The communication person is a relationship person. In the sense that relationships are meaningful, the gluon that holds society in place, they are also the source of harmony. When we can learn from the engineer, computer programmer, mailperson, chemist, entertainer, or lawyer with whom we happen to have a relationship, we are secure in a harmonious situation. Individuals who lack relationships are anathema to the new maturity of the communication age; it is too fleeting, too changeable to be caught without relationships. Permanence resides in the maturity of the relationships we possess.

I recognize that this essay has raised a lot of questions, answered some and left others open for discussion. However, it has done precisely what it set out to do by providing an alternative focus to that propounded by social scientists who see only from a Eurocentric viewpoint. The communication person repudiates fragmentation and stretches toward a full holistic harmony.

REFERENCES

ABOABA, D. (1979) "The Nigerian press under military rule." Doctoral dissertation, State University of New York at Buffalo.
APPIAH, M. K. (1979) "Okyeame: an integrative model of communication." Doctoral dissertation, State University of New York at Buffalo.
BERLO, D. (1960) *The Process of Communication*. New York: Holt, Rinehart & Winston.
DUNCAN, H. (1968) *Symbols in Society*. New York: Oxford University Press.
GRANT, E. (1979) "An Afrocentric communication environment for Black mental health care." Doctoral dissertation, State University of New York at Buffalo.
HALL, E. (1976) *Beyond Culture*. Garden City, NY: Doubleday.
——— (1966) *The Hidden Dimension*. Garden City, NY: Doubleday.
——— (1959) *The Silent Language*. Garden City, NY: Doubleday.
McLUHAN, M. (1965) *Understanding Media: The Extension of Man*. New York: McGraw-Hill.
NHIWATIWA, N. (1979) "International communication between the African and European worldviews." Doctoral dissertation, State University of New York at Buffalo.

2

GLOBAL INFORMATION AND COMMUNICATIONS: NEW EXPLORATIONS

Abdulai S. Vandi

INTRODUCTION

We have seen great advances in international communications in our time. We are destined to see countless more in the future. As one indicator, government policy makers began in the 1970s to take greater interest in telecommunications. The new activity was focused on gaining the greatest possible benefit from modern technology. The thrust was toward mapping guidelines for the future.

Can reasons for the heightened interest be isolated? It is important that awareness was growing that many technologies—not simply communications, economics, and information—were converging and promising revolutionary improvements in means of passing information to and among people. In the world of the 1980s, computers and telecommunications will work even better together. They will significantly increase the flow of information among the users of the information (Maddox, 1972; McLaughlin, 1979; Richstad, 1977).

POLITICAL DEVELOPMENTS IN THE WORLD OF 1980s

Political developments in the world of the 1980s will be dominated by nonaligned independence movements (Van Dinh, 1979). Nonalignment has deep roots in the concepts of anticolonialism, antiimperialism, peace, and equality. As Van Dinh (1979: 75) noted, "since its official birth [nonalignment] has gradually but solidly moved to the front line in its fight for a new economic and information order without which there is neither freedom nor lasting peace."

The world of the 1980s will also continue to see spectacular successes by national liberation movements opposing colonial rule. National ibera-tion as a concept represents a political expression "either of bourgeois forces or of . . . proletarian forces" (Magubane, 1977: 89). Conceptualized liberation is destined to increase concern regarding human rights, both political and economic.

NATIONAL POLICIES AND INTERNATIONAL DEBATES

Many developing countries have begun to grapple with the political, legal, economic, and social ramifications of the new information society (Pipe, 1979). In the debates on data flow, national interests have been expressed in different ways: both in print and at international meetings. However, charged language and unsupported assertions, rather than facts or solutions, have characterized this debate, according to Pipe (1979: 118), who writes:

> Empirical analysis has been lacking because proponents of measuring the quantities (bits and bytes) of data streaming across frontiers are vigorously opposed by those who claim that data flow is a qualita-tive matter. Those arguing the qualitative side stress that it is not how many data cross a national border but what is done with them.

In developing countries of the world, the potentials of computerized information systems, especially as they apply to public administration and planning, have received major attention only recently. A recent Intergov-ernmental Bureau for Informatics (IBI) investigation indicated that sixty countries have already adopted some form of official informatics policy. But the formulation and establishment of adequate national policies for dealing with informatics still have a long way to go. The political, eco-nomic, social, and technical issues involved in international data flows are only now being recognized for their far-reaching implications and impact.

IDEOLOGICAL PERSPECTIVES: PROBLEMS AND PROSPECTS

In the second half of this century, self-conceptions and world views have been in flux. People have been groping for ways in which to interpret their emergent perceptions. Thus, the times have been, and continue to be, ripe for ideologies, those relative systematic doctrines that articulate group perspectives and provide a basis for collective action.

All the ideologies of First, Second, and Third World nations profess to be true as devices for upholding certain values. Ideologies help provide a picture of what the world is like. Only a few, however, have gained wide acceptance. To be effective, the beliefs must fit with the shared perspectives of many people and must make sense in terms of historical experience (Magubane, 1977; Nordenstreng and Schiller, 1979; Singham, 1977; Smythe, 1979).

Socialism stands out as one of the few systems that have gained wide acceptance. Socialist societies now embrace some 30 percent of the world's population. The advent of such societies, as Smythe (1979: 99) has pointed out, has raised questions regarding an appropriate view of the notion of individual dignity. In addition, these societies have challenged the role of the marketplace as an arbiter of taste, particularly with respect to information dissemination and communication.

The nonalignment movement has been criticized steadily, and even ridiculed, by major Western mass media (Van Dinh, 1979). Powerful multinationals and transnationals of the information industry feel threatened by the movement and its underlying ideological perspectives. The reason for their fear is clear, according to Van Dinh (1979). They not only recognize that the Third World countries in general and the nonaligned countries specifically have just cause on their side; they also know that these nations have been responsible for bringing a special awareness to the international forum for the first time. That awareness is related to the problems of neocolonialism, on the one hand, and the new economic order, on the other.

AN OVERVIEW OF CAPITALISM, SOCIALISM, AND MARXISM

The world business system centers today on the American economy. This economy binds together the market systems of Canada, Japan, and Western Europe, among other areas of the world. Thus, the capitalistic mode continues to dominate the global economic and political order through the activities of the multinational and transnational corporation—in shorthand, MNC and TNC.

It is true that transnational corporations operating directly in the field of mass communications have made important contributions to the revenues and profits of private industry. However, capitalism continues to ignore the needs and desires of the masses. Socialism and Marxism have tried to remedy this capitalistic inadequacy.

Marxism, for one, has shown that colonialism was the way of capitalism. Colonialism survived as a means of guaranteeing a continuing supply of raw materials and maximum profits. As Singham (1977: iv-v) has pointed out,

> Marx and Lenin show quite clearly how the institutions of capitalism were not confined to specific national entities, but that capitalism and imperialism utilized the individual stare mechanisms to expand and thus to create not a dual economy within a given society but

rather a single economic system with a division of labor. . . . The
phenomena of underdevelopment [are] thus merely the result of the
persistence of the phenomena of the order of primitive accumulation
for the benefit of the center.

Against that background, individual freedom has never been fully protected, not even by the pluralism of capitalistic enterprise. Although the
individual stands to benefit when large organizations compete and bid for
his or her support, a world of large organizations leaves many people
defenseless against powerful leaders.

Marxism and socialism have attempted to overcome this inadequacy as
well. The two ideologies have also pointed up a negative factor: that
pluralism is compatible with, and indeed has an affinity for, the so-called
elitist theory of democracy.

Lenin, following Marx, explained that capitalism is based on the constant absorption of economic loss by political entities. Economic gain is
distributed into "private" hands (Singham, 1977). But only now, today,
can we observe the first serious challenge to the dominant capitalist mode
of production. The challenge has matured into a fully-fledged movement,
especially among Third World nations, to subordinate the capitalistic focus
on an elite group to the needs and desires of the masses.

BRIDGING GLOBAL BARRIERS

The politicoeconomic revolt of the late 1970s has taken concrete
forms. The New International Economic Order (NIEO) and the New
International Information and Communication Order (NIICO) represent
two of the important developments in international relations that have
emerged in recent years. The search for and the subsequent emergence of
both orders, according to Singham (1977: xi), has been based in "a
demand by the Non-Aligned nations to rectify the . . . imbalance that
exists among states."

Galtung (1977) has noted that the founding instrument and related
resolutions and conventions of NIEO have an international character; they
do not deal simply with the intranational order. The task of NIEO in
direct action and related measures is to prepare the external conditions of
a given country while its internal structure is changing. Thus, more
equitable sharing will be ensured. But there will also be more to share.
Specifically, NIEO will bring about internal changes in Third World countries that will lead indirectly to a higher standard of living for the masses
and decreased inequality.

NIICO also seeks to establish relations of equality among developed and
developing countries. But this agency works in the areas of information

and communication (Masmoudi, 1979; Teheranian et al., 1977). The aims of the proposed order, again, are greater balance and justice. NIICO proposes to ensure that the principles of freedom are applied fairly and equitably in all nations (Logue et al., 1979).

According to a number of authorities (Galtung, 1977, 1978; Nordenstreng and Schiller, 1979; Singham, 1977), NIEO and NIICO have great significance for Third World countries—conceptually and in terms of social justice and basic norms. The base target is a more equitable distribution of wealth. Clearly, the two new international orders represent potential solutions to the already tense world economic and communications information problems. As Hamelink (1979: 144) commented,

> The redressing of global inequalities and injustices requires information which will fight preconceived ideas, ignorance, and alienation, and facilitate the conscientization of citizens to ensure their control over decision-making.

TRANSNATIONAL STRUCTURES AND SYSTEMS

Before global barriers can really be bridged, however, the major aspects of the two orders—the flow of technology and the investment required—must converge. Jussawalla (1979) has pointed out that the private sectors of developed countries have been most responsible for the move toward conversion. That means that the private sectors have engineered the diffusion of modern technology for industrialization. Transnational corporations have served as the vehicles for diffusion.

Technological innovation can, however, spread from one nation to another in two major ways, according to Mowlana (1975: 77). Innovation becomes reality "either through transfer by imitation of production functions or new goods, or transfer by corporations that establish the innovation operation as a subsidiary." Multinational corporations usually become both the channels of technological diffusion and the bankers of industrial profits.

Too often, however, transnational corporations monopolize communications hardware and news media. Thus, the multinationals have been viewed with suspicion and hostility in host countries (Jussawalla, 1979). What is therefore needed are national policies for the diffusion of technology. Such policies would ensure that "the multinational corporation as communicator with other business enterprises can stimulate, even create, new consumer markets" (Mowlana, 1975: 87).

In the effort to bridge global barriers, it will also be crucially important to assess and effectively manage the system within which the process of technological diffusion occurs. Too little attention is directed at present to structural influences and the determinants of the communications effect (Mowlana, 1975; Said and Simmons, 1975).

MEDIA TRAFFIC: FREE AND BALANCED FLOW OF INFORMATION

The free and balanced flow of information is yet another way effectively to bridge global barriers. The predominant concept of today's order is, in fact, a free flow of information; that principle is embodied in such national and international documents as the Universal Declaration of Human Rights and the United Nations Constitution (Harms, 1979). The overarching structural form of the order, as Richstad (1977) has pointed out, had its foundation in mass-media systems. But these systems encountered basic contradictions to the free-flow principle:

> These contradictions and changes in ways of thinking about communication, a broader global political base, and development of new technology have all led to the move toward a new communication order.... The concept of communication today is viewed as a multi-way, interactive, participatory, horizontal process, rather than a one-way, sender-receiver, vertical transfer of information [Richstad, 1977: 2-4].

Clearly, the new order has not yet evolved to its final form. However, the factors that will significantly influence this evolution have become evident: a greater willingness among developed nations of the world to share communication resources, employment of satellites to break previously established patterns of vertical communication, the establishment of news pools and exchanges in developing countries, and increased sensitivity on the part of transnational news agencies regarding news about the Third World (Homet, 1979; Richstad, 1977; Snow, 1979).

INTERCULTURAL AND TRANSRACIAL COMMUNICATION

In the field of information communication, a Third World news agency, the Inter-Press Service (IPS), has been established in recent years to take into account the continuing realities of Third World societies. A news and information communication service has been established under the agency's aegis to communicate, specifically, intercultural and transracial information. Harris (1979: 5) has noted that, encompassed within this approach that focuses on realities, there exists "the conviction that information provides a unique vehicle to inform the world about steps being taken toward amelioration of the 'quality of life' of various peoples, particularly in the Third World."

A number of other suggestions have been advanced regarding the building of bridges for cross-cultural, intercultural, and transracial communication (Schramm, 1977). Some of these deserve recognition. For example, a growing sense of interdependence is held to be essential. Second, there must be an end to near-monopoly control of transnational media. Third, there must be a replacement of direct service from international news agencies by cooperative arrangements with national agencies. Finally, there must be an end to the "market orientation" of transnational news and entertainment.

Language planning and policy represent yet other aspects of bridge-building in the area of intercultural and transracial communication. The Marxist-Leninist theory of mass media and the Leninist theory of the new type of press offer outstanding approaches to honest, scientifically objective planning in this area. As a starting principle for a new theory of mass-media research, the character and social role of mass media in the process of mass communication must be accepted:

> The intentions of the communicator, his features, and all the elements conditioning his activities are cognizable; the message itself with all its explicit and implicit contents is cognizable; the specificity of every channel and its influence on the reception of the message are cognizable, as are the needs and interests of the recipients; . . . cognizable also are all the direct and indirect, primary and secondary functions performed by mass media [Pisarek, n.d.: 22].

Arrangements for effective international understanding and world harmony must consequently be based on a theoretical approach that is oriented toward the needs of the majority—that is, of the working class. It is a known fact that the socialist mass media represent the point of view and the interests of this majority class (Pisarek, n.d.). Thus, this perspective for bridge-building in the area of language planning and policy must be recommended.

INTERNATIONAL COMMUNICATIONS POLICY AND NATIONAL DEVELOPMENT: THE NEW GLOBAL BALANCE

At present, over 140 political units in the world are organized as nation-states and act as such on the international scene. National development for countries that have made the historic transition from agrarian to industrial societies has been found to involve three fundamental revolutions: economic, political, and communications (Maddox, 1972; Teheranian et al., 1977). What is needed today is a uniform international communications policy that will parallel and guide national and international development in the economic and political sectors. In short, what is now needed is a new global balance and a convergence of the major characteristics of all three revolutions.

INFORMATION COMMUNICATION AND DEVELOPMENT: THE PARAMETERS OF THEORY AND POLICY

Developmental theories of modernization fall into one or a combination of the following categories: stage, index, differentiation, and diffusion

(Teheranian et al., 1977). The keynote approach to development theories during the 1960s was called the "Dominant Paradigm" (Hudson et al., 1979). Definitions of development focused on rates of economic growth. Gross national product and gross national product per capita became statistical, absolute indicators of levels of economic development. As a result, the distribution gaps between rich and poor widened rather than narrowed.

Nations thus became aware of the inadequacies of the Dominant Paradigm thesis. The existence of telecommunications facilities has led to different forms of political development and thus to different policy perspectives. Goldschmidt (1978), for example, has reported on the impact of communications and subsequent citizen participation in such remote areas as Itka, Alaska.

The role of mass media in the national communications and socioeconomic development of less technologically advanced countries has been the subject of considerable debate (Nordenstreng and Schiller, 1979; Teheranian et al., 1977). No one can deny, however, the impact of communications development on national theory and policy. From a dialectical perspective, every idea or experience transmitted by the mass media has its counterpart in social reality. Thus, the effects of the media, and of communications overall, in the process of national development depend on "how closely the media work with or against opinion leaders who are safeguarding traditional ideas and institutions or pioneering new ones" (Teheranian et al., 1977: 46).

FREE AND BALANCED FLOW OF INFORMATION, TECHNOLOGY, AND KNOWLEDGE

We can move toward end-postulations. A new global balance depends on the free and unimpeded flow of information, technology, and knowledge. For example, to realize their greatest potential, computers must be linked to users in remote locations. Computers must be so integrated with other computers, strategically placed, to realize their optimal potential. To complete such an undertaking, computers must open and unify their data banks while increasing their stores of information. In return, computer traffic will add a valuable new source of business for the suppliers and users of communications services.

An encouraging sign appearing in the 1970s was that world governments began to realize the importance of advance planning in telecommunications. The continued growth of this kind of communication could not, as a result, be stifled as it had been in the past—by a lag in policy-making. Many nation-states publicly recognized the need for free and balanced flows of information, technology, and knowledge.

Furthermore, the disparity in the distribution of the world's telephones between the northern, southern, and eastern hemispheres, based on need rather than the so-called market demand, is noteworthy. According to Hudson et al. (1979), 80 percent of the world's telephones are in North America and Europe. The capitalist or First World countries have by far the largest share, with 86 percent of the world's telephones for a total population of 759 million, while the socialist or Second World countries account for 7 percent for a population of 1.3 billion, and the Third World or oppressed countries have only 7 percent for a population of over 2 billion.

POLICY-MAKING PROCESSES: ORGANIZATIONS
AND REGIONAL ORGANIZATIONS

One of the first organizations to address the need for a new global balance in the area of telecommunications was the International Telecommunications Union (ITU). During the early 1970s, membership in ITU increased to 138 with the accession of Equatorial Guinea to the International Telecommunications Convention (Nordenstreng and Schiller, 1979). In 1970 alone, nearly 600 documents concerning radio communications were discussed and approved. Subjects included the use of satellites for the transmission of telephony and television, the use of computers to improve the reliability of forecasts and frequencies likely to be usable between various points on earth, the reliability of radio services, and technical and economic factors related to the broadcasting of both sound and vision programs by means of satellites. Of special interest were means of facilitating participation in the work of the International Consultative Committee for Radio (CCIR) by new or less developed countries.

ITU, however, had developed its purpose, policy, and structure long before the advent of the United Nations. According to Wallenstein (1977: 138),

> as one of the oldest functional-purpose international organizations, the ITU is dedicated to voluntary agreements. These concern allocation of a scarce, internationally shared resource, the radio frequency spectrum; standardization of telecommunications services and systems; and joint planning.

Among other organizations, the International Telecommunications Satellite Consortium has become a policy-making force. INTELSAT is in some ways quite different from ITU and UNESCO and in other ways fairly similar. For example, it was established as a commercial enterprise, but is owned by governments or designated representatives. Although technology-specific, it has developed a complex decision-making structure rivaling that of the ITU. Finally, although INTELSAT is a commercial enterprise, its existence has great meaning in the debate over the New International Communication Order (Levy, 1975; Mowlana, 1977).

International communications up to the present have been regulated with remarkable consistency and smoothness through INTELSAT and other organizations like it. But competition for geostationary orbital locations has been increasing in recent years. Russia is currently establishing several Statsionar satellites in geosynchronous orbit for global distribution. According to Mowlana (1977), ten of these satellites were to be launched by 1980. Thus, the next few years will decide what the relationship will be between the Soviet Union and INTELSAT. As Levy (1975: 655) commented,

> the question arises whether technological imperatives or political considerations will guide the activity and determine the structure of regimes that support the use of technology on an international scale. In the case of communication satellites, the establishment of such a regime involves the search for structures that could satisfy technology and still remain responsive to political forces that desire to affect the decision-making process.

The question of interorganizational jurisdiction will become even more complicated with the creation of the International Maritime Satellite Organization (INMARSAT). Rule-making for intersystem coordination is destined to be affected. INMARSAT is expected to utilize some of the same international resources as other satellite systems. It is hoped that UNESCO will deal with the questions of distortion and regulations in the new international information order.

ROLES OF ITU, INTELSAT, AND UNESCO IN THE TRANSITIONAL ORDER

Collective purposes are not simply defined according to universalist and technologically imposed imperatives (Levy, 1975). This has been well demonstrated in the case of the Interim Arrangements for INTELSAT. The role of INTELSAT, as well as those of ITU and UNESCO, focuses on the issue of global versus regional systems. INTELSAT agreements provide specific evidence that "this collective enterprise expresses the unilateral goals of its members" (Levy, 1975: 675). As a result of the creation of INTELSAT, there now exists a single operating system for public telecommunications by satellites.

The British preference for a separate system dedicated to maritime applications, it should be noted, comports with Britain's own program to develop a maritime satellite capability. Great Britain would underwrite over half of the costs of development of the Marine Operations Technology Satellite—or ESRO-MAROTS—hardware program for maritime communications and navigation. However, this system now challenges the roles of both INTELSAT and ITU. The Marine Operations Satellite has placed limitations not only on the scope of communications services, but also on INTELSAT's ability to provide services of a specialized nature under contractual arrangements with outside parties.

Some global—in the sense of overriding—considerations must influence us. INTELSAT, ITU, and UNESCO were established for the general purpose of enhancing world peace and understanding. How well the various organizations serve in this capacity will be determined in the near future by how many separate systems outside their jurisdictions will be established and become operational.

THE NEW INTERNATIONAL POLITICAL ORDER (NIPO): AN ALTERNATIVE

Absolutely fundamental changes are required in our current world political infrastructures. We have today to issue a call for a new order.

Why is change necessary? A New International Political Order (NIPO) could guarantee equal access to politics, resources, communications, and knowledge on a universal basis. Tensions could be ameliorated—including those arising out of Cold War rhetoric, the East-West nuclear armaments debate, North-South political and economic differences, and the issues of cultural hegemony and domination. In addition, such problems as the scarcity of resources and the monopoly of natural resources by the Organization of Oil Producing and Exporting Countries (OPEC) could be resolved.

The refusal of Western-oriented, First World scholars to address the issue of this fundamental change in the world's political order undermines their credibility. That refusal also gives rise to mounting tensions related to the already inflated problems of economic and communication/information controversies.

COMMUNITY OF INTERDEPENDENT NATIONS

International interdependence is hardly a new notion. In Sewell's (1979: 46) words, "Adam Smith and David Ricardo analyzed the gains to be made from international trade; and the development of the United States was largely funded by capital from foreign banks and governments."

Only recently, however, has there developed an awareness of the need for an effective new statecraft for the 1980s. A number of reasons may be cited for the continuing lack of a coherent policy, according to Grant and McLaughlin (1979). First, uncertainty colors the question of whether the current pattern of relatively high inflation and slow growth in the industrial democracies is temporary. Second, the dispute continues regarding the relative importance of these new trends for the United States. Third, one must note the enduring differences on the question whether other-than-real political values should be reflected in foreign policy and, if so, which values should be given precedence. A fourth reason is a divergence of views about what is politically feasible.

Various authorities (Grant and McLaughlin, 1979; McLaughlin, 1979; Sewell, 1979) agree that we need a new consensus in some new forum. The issue: whether both developing and developed countries can meet to establish broad policy guidelines. It would seem, in fact, that much of the world is calling for the New International Political Order. Clearly, it will take some time to establish broad policy guidelines for such as order. The effort will be worth it in the long run, however.

According to Sewell (1979: 87), the issue of international information exchange "has greater potential for bringing about an unexpected explosion in the North-South dialogue than almost any other issue." The same might be said, regarding unexpected explosions in the East-West political dialogue, of the potential establishment of a network of scholars/ researchers from First, Second, and Third World nations.

THE EROSION OF CULTURAL DISTINCTIONS

A community of interdependent nations will certainly bring about an erosion of cultural distinctions and the emergence of rootless homogeneity. Now is the time for such initiatives.

According to Hamelink (1979), the problem of establishing a community of interdependent nations focuses on another problem: current management of international information structures. The basic principles involved are the sovereignty and equality of states; the rights of states to adopt appropriate economic, political, and cultural systems; full, permanent sovereignty over national resources; full and effective participation by all states in international decision-making; the right to formulate a model of autonomous development geared toward the basic needs of the population; and the right to pursue progressive social transformations that will enable the full participation by all peoples in the developmental process. These principles give new meaning to the concept of interdependence:

> In the present international order, interdependence is actually equated with a hierarchical relationship between independent and dependent nations. The new . . . order, however, proposes a relationship between independent nations that is based on sovereignty and equality [Hamelink, 1979: 145].

NIPO transcends the two existing new orders, NIEO and NIICO, because it embodies the base principles of both orders. NIPO also calls for the concrete establishment of a community of interdependent nations, along with the elimination of cultural distinctions that have in the past formed a detrimental influence.

The new global balance associated with international communications policy and national development can only be developed according to radical new parameters of informational, communications, and development theory and policy. The roles and structures of such organizations as ITU, INTERSAT, UNESCO, and IMARSAT must be highlighted in terms of their impact on the new global situation. Only in this way can the needed fundamental changes in current world political infrastructures take place.

REFERENCES

GALTUNG, J. (1978) "Grand designs on a collision course." *International Development Review* 78 (March-April): 43-47.

——— (1977) "The new economic order in world politics," pp. 158-174 in A. W. Singham (ed.) *The Nonaligned Movement in World Politics.* Westport, CT: Lawrence Hill.

GOLDSCHMIDT, D. (1978) "Telephone communications, collective supply, and public goods: a case study of the Alaskan telephone system." Doctoral dissertation, University of Pennsylvania.

GRANT, J. P. and M. M. McLAUGHLIN (1979) "Global forces on the North-South stage: Can a new statesmanship guide their interaction?" pp. 15-44 in M. M. McLaughlin (ed.) *The United States and World Development: Agenda 1979.* New York: Praeger.

HAMELINK, C. J. (1979) "Informatics: Third World call for new order." *Journal of Communication* 29 (Summer): 144-148.

HARMS, L. S. (1979) "A note on the evaluation of communication orders." Paper presented at the Advanced Summer Seminar on International Communication Policy and Organizations, July 5-August 4, Honolulu.

HARRIS, P. (1979) "The international information order: problems and responses." Inter-Press Service, Rome, January.

HOMET, R. (1979) "Goals and contradictions in a world information order." *Intermedia* 7 (March): 2.

HUDSON, H. E., D. GOLDSCHMIDT, E. B. PARKER, and A. HARDY (1979) *The Role of Telecommunications in Socio-Economic Development: A Review of the Literature with Guidelines for Further Investigations.* Washington, DC: Academy for Educational Services. (Report prepared by Keewatin Communications Group for ITU.)

JUSSAWALLA, M. (1979) "Bridging global barriers, two new international orders: NIEO, NICO." Paper presented at the Advanced Summer Seminar on International Communication Policy and Organizations, July 5-August 4, Honolulu.

LEVY, S. A. (1975) "INTELSAT: technology, politics, and the transformation of a regime." *International Organization* 29 (Summer): 655-680.

LOGUE, T., S. RAHIM, J. RICHSTAD, and M. JUSSAWALLA (1979) "UNESCO, ITU and INTELSAT: international communication policy and organizations."

Paper presented at the Advanced Summer Seminar on International Communication Policy and Organizations, July 5-August 4, Honolulu.

MADDOX, B. (1972) *Beyond Babel: New Directions in Communications.* Boston: Beacon.

MAGUBANE, B. (1977) "Non-alignment and the na'ional liberation movements," pp. 88-90 in A. W. Singham (ed.) *The Nonaligned Movement in World Politics.* Westport, CT: Lawrence Hill.

MASMOUDI, M. (1979) "The new world information order." *Journal of Communication* 29 (Spring): 172-185

McLAUGHLIN, M. M. [ed.] (1979) *The United States and World Development: Agenda 1979.* New York: Praeger.

MOWLANA, H. (1977) "Political and social implications of communications satellite applications in developed and developing countries," pp. 124-142 in J. N. Pelton and S. Snow [eds.] *Economic and Policy Problems in Satellite Communications.* New York: Praeger.

——— (1975) "The multinational corporation and the diffusion of technology," pp. 77-90 in A. A. Said and L. R. Simmons (eds.) *The New Sovereigns: Multinational Corporations as World Powers.* Englewood Cliffs, NJ: Prentice-Hall.

NORDENSTRENG, K. and H. I. SCHILLER [eds.] (1979) *National Sovereignty and International Communication.* Norwood, NJ: Ablex.

PIPE, G. R. (1979) "National policies, international debates." *Journal of Communication* 29 (Summer): 114-123.

PISAREK, W. (n.d.) "Marxist-Leninist theory and methodology of mass media research."

RICHSTAD, J. [ed.] (1977) *New Perspectives in International Communication.* Honolulu: East-West Communication Institute.

SAID, A. A. and L. R. SIMMONS [eds.] (1975) *The New Sovereigns: Multinational Corporations as World Powers.* Englewood Cliffs, NJ: Prentice-Hall.

SCHRAMM, W. (1977) "Cross-cultural communication: suggestions for the building of bridges," pp. 14-21 in J. Richstad (ed.) *New Perspectives in International Communication.* Honolulu: East-West Communication Institute.

SEWELL, J. W. (1979) "Can the North Prosper without growth and progress in the South?" pp. 46-76 in M. M. McLaughlin (ed.) *The United States and World Development: Agenda 1979.* New York: Praeger.

SINGHAM, A. W. [ed.] (1977) The Nonaligned Movement in World Politics. Westport, CT: Lawrence Hill.

SMYTHE, D. W. (1979) "Overview of capitalism and socialism," pp. 99-114 in K. Nordenstreng and H. I. Schiller (eds.) *National Sovereignty and International Communication.* Norwood, NJ: Ablex.

SNOW, M. S. (1979) "Policy and planning problems in international telecommunications: the case of satellites." Paper presented at the Advanced Summer Seminar on International Communication Policy and Organizations, July 5-August 4, Honolulu.

TEHERANIAN, M., F. HAKIMZADEH, and M. L. VIDALE [eds.] (1977) *Communications Policy for National Development: A Comparative Perspective.* London: Routledge & Kegan Paul.

VAN DINH, T. (1979) "Nonalignment and cultural imperialism," pp. 261-275 in K. Nordenstreng and H. I. Schiller (eds.) *National Sovereignty and International Communication.* Norwood, NJ: Ablex.

WALLENSTEIN, G. D. (1977) "Development of Policy in the ITU." *Telecommunications Policy* 1 (March): 138-152.

3

INTERNATIONAL/INTERCULTURAL RELATIONS

Molefi Kete Asante

Our aim is to present a unified view of international relations which takes into consideration the Afrocentric view of the world. In this respect, this chapter introduces concepts which in their development suggest a much more harmonious potential for world relations. Intercultural communication, by virtue of the conceptual and research activity of communication scholars, has made leopard leaps forward in its theoretical and practical orientations. Much of the work in intercultural communication still relies on the formulations of the early period; new research has concentrated on the universals to be found in human nature; and perhaps the most promising work deals with how cultural centers relate to each other (Diop, 1978; Richards, 1979).

Cultural differences, not cultural similarities, are the base of the field of intercultural communication. If this were not the case, all of our discussions would be pointless. The modest intention of this chapter is to examine some existing notions regarding intercultural communication, present a rationale for an alternative view, and lay the foundations of a reexamination of intercultural and international relations. The field grew as an effort to capture the essential elements of difference between people

AUTHOR'S NOTE: Some of the ideas in this chapter were presented in a paper given to the Rockefeller Foundation's Conference on Black Communication, held in August 1979 at Bellagio, Italy. Further elaboration on the concepts of temporary communication estrangement and historical cultural cleavage will appear in the *International Communication Annual Yearbook*, to be published in 1980.

of diverse cultural backgrounds. Early works by Oliver (1971), Hall (1959), Pike (1966), Stewart (1973), Smith (1973), and Rich (1974) establish the idea of difference in intercultural communication by isolating cultural and value divergencies. Since the appearance of these early works the field has grown in two distinct ways (Asante et al., 1979). The two schools of thought are the cultural dialoguists and the cultural critics. In addition to the extended discussion of the schools of thought which appears in the *Handbook of Intercultural Communication* (Asante et al., 1979), several points can be made about cultural dialogue and cultural criticism as approaches to intercultural communication.

Cultural dialogue assumes that human beings can and should communicate with each other. One only has to compare the early works of Asante (1973), Rich (1974), Ogawa (1971), Blubaugh and Pennington (1976), and Condon and Yusef (1975) to see the tremendous humanism of their science. In effect, communication becomes for them a practical instrument for the bringing together of the world community. Perhaps the one primary fallacy in most of these works is that *the humanism itself is frequently nothing more than a eurocentric concept of what is good for the world.* It is this problem which still stands at the head of our inquiry into the nature of how human beings communicate across national and cultural boundaries. The cultural dialoguists dealt with the illusion of intercultural communication primarily defined through the notions of European philosophy of science and history. We cannot, of course, judge too harshly, but we must judge, because it is precisely in this respect that the field of intercultural communication has distorted world reality. Educated, for the most part, in American universities, these early dialoguists reacted intellectually to their encapsulated but could not bowl over the Eurocentric walls which trapped them.

On the other hand, the cultural critics have not sought to dispense with the trappings of a Eurocentric viewpoint. Pike, Hall, and Hoijer are strictly in line with the anthropological tradition, which, after all, is the most Eurocentric of the social sciences. Stewart, as a communicationist and psychologist, is concerned with perceptual realities. In *An Overview of the Field of Intercultural Communication* (1974) he assumes that all human beings perceive the world as a duality, or in binary terms. This assumption is based upon Stewart's Eurocentric notion of reality, even though in his attempt to define intercultural communication he is closer to a non-Eurocentric perspective than others of his colleagues in the cultural critic school of thought. What has been most overlooked by the cultural critics as well as by the cultural dialoguists is the importance of power relations in communication, a subject which stands out prominently in the arena of human interactions.

Acquisition, maintenance, and utilization of power represent cultural responses to environment and society. Therefore, how a group of people view the environment and their approach to nature and to their fellow human beings represent areas of fruitful discussion for intercultural communication, inasmuch as the particular cultural approach may constitute the substance of the communication. In every society there are acceptable and unacceptable ways of acquiring, maintaining, and using power; in a culturally interactive situation, these ways may be in conflict with each other. *Indeed, as propounded by Eurocentric social scientists, the idea of interaction may be the principal instrument of the transubstantiation of privilege and power into accepted reality.* It legitimizes the values of a Eurocentric theoretical perspective on human communication, and makes it possible for the strengthening of the established power relations by obscuring the power relations as power relations. In effect, this dynamic functions in much the same way as pedagogic action (Bourdieu and Passeron, 1977: 15). The dominated culture legitimizes its own domination by participating in the world view of the dominating culture. Thus, what Fanon (1968) demonstrated as a psychological and political truism for colonized people is also a communication and, by definition, interaction truism as well; the colonized people are often actors on a stage which they have not set. As long as the legitimizing concepts are acceptable to the "illegitimates," the dominated, then there is no need for the dominating culture to introduce brute reinforcement for the perpetuation and domination of its views, because to do so would be to disturb the accepted balance of power and create an awakening in the "illegitimates" toward the true nature of the communication interaction. Thus, when the white South Africans say that communication between the blacks and whites is good, they are speaking within the context of their domination in much the same way as white Americans who used to say that the blacks and whites in the South understood each other. In other words, not only is the language clear but power relations are also clear and are the basis for all communication.

RATIONALE

The founding interculturalists of the two schools argue from the same psychological or sociopsychological influence, although their objectives differ. That is, while one school may seek cultural criticism and the other cultural dialogue, they both are concerned with attitudes, perceptions, opinions, values, and cultural determinants. What is now necessary is a shift from the narrow sociopsychological perspectives with their concentration on how the individual is constituted within a culture, to the broad patterns found in cultural contexts. Such work will serve as the needed corrective to the founding interculturalists' emphasis on individual attitudes, values, and perceptions by refocusing attention toward the broad ideological questions which impinge upon our communication with persons from other cultures. This can be done without impairment of continuing sociopsychological work; indeed, it is impossible to separate these aspects of the field completely. Every intercultural interaction is a combination of cultural, ideological, and psychological factors. Our work in the broad cultural area with implications in ideology has been the weakest link in our theoretical chain; perhaps this is a result of the heavy American character of the early research.

Intercultural communication studies, for the most part, have sought to affirm human interdependence without negating human uniqueness. Human beings are not separated from their culture (Newmark and Asante, 1975) and cannot divest themselves of their culture (Hall, 1959); they are preeminently educated by their culture. Thus, how human beings interact, where they interact, how long, and in what expressive modes they interact are not independent and discrete functions but inherently culturally connected.

A successful and substantial bridgehead for intercultural communication is being erected by communicationists who understand the interconnectedness of all human societies. The works of Sanda (1979), Awa (1979), and Blake (1979) have opened new fields of inquiry to communication and development with respect to pluralistic societies. Appiah (1979) and Asante and Appiah (1979) have challenged the accepted Western-directed theories of communication. A whole new game has been suggested, in which the players will conform to a new set of theoretical rules not set by Western mores and values. This new game's rules must speak to the previously invisible realities of a complex world. In one sense, the earlier philosophical issues raised by The Centre Monchanin Fellowship are now beginning to be addressed. Their concerns, expressed in a series of fugitive papers, deal with the American base of intercultural communication as an academic enterprise. Developed in American circles, intercultural communication was thought to possess, in its initial conceptualization, the same traits of American social science imperialism which dictated how the world should respond to the great metropole, and how metropolitans should be taught to react to the world. It was thus seen by the Centre Monchaninists as an American undertaking for the benefit of American private and public agencies. The bridgehead which has now been set in place seeks to span the issues with the collective input of scholars from different cultures. It is only possible for communicationists interested in intercultural communication to examine theories which are based on Eurocentric foundations. Explorations by many contemporary thinkers in communication (Saral, 1979; Aboaba, 1979; Beltran S, 1975; and Vora, 1978) have begun to ask important questions regarding theoretical perspective. Their research and that of others in other areas of communication (Becker, 1977) continues to open new doors. The common perspective of these thinkers seems to be that there are different ways to formulate the cultural question. We do not have to view the world in Eurocentric or Americocentric eyes and claim that it is the only way to see. Undue emphasis upon how Americans should learn to understand and adjust to other cultures suggests that the field of intercultural communication has been chiefly oriented toward America. The research and theories of Asante and Barnes (1979), Newmark and Asante (1977), Saral (1979) and Howell (1979) are important in the new formulation of questions and researchable problems. Asante and Barnes (1979) establish the demystification process as applicable to any culture, regardless of host or sojourner. Earlier, Newmark and Asante (1975) showed the significance of the perception of self in intercultural encounters across cultures. Saral (1979) demonstrates that consciousness is a possible approach to understanding intercultural communication, particularly in its achievement in different cultures of the world.

Prior to a structural discussion of the three broad views of the world, it is necessary to place in focus the fundamental concepts which have served as basic organizing principles of Western, hence, American, social science. Only when the intercultural communicationist can truly distinguish the fundamental concepts of Western thought from the character of the world reality can we formulate a relatively free perspective on reality. Perhaps we shall discover that it is not possible; yet we will not know until we escape from the ethnocentric viewpoint which now constrains most of our work. The drama of Western social science is staged in the light of Hebraic-Graeco-Roman linearity. Such a presentation of reality turns on the assumption that all phenomena can be categorized and should be categorized. Phenomena remaining uncategorized are uncontrolled and uncontrollable. Thus, in Genesis, all the animals and plants were named by human beings. Differences manifest themselves in such categorizations, enabling the scientist to place each phenomenon according to some "fundamental" mode of existence, such as quality or quantity. However, categorization highlights differences and, as Richards (1979) observes when speaking of European Philosophy, "differences of kind imply differences of value."

Since no profound civilizations arose in Western Europe in ancient times (4500-1000 B.C., a period 3500 years), European entry into the common market of the ancient civilizations of Asia and Africa was spurred by the relinquishing of tribal religions and the acquisition of concepts from the Greeks and Jews. Early Greek civilization did not identify with the rest of Europe, preferring to recognize its African, specifically Tamarristic and Nubianistic, origins (Williams, 1976). The rise of Greek—more correctly, Athenian—culture occurred thousands of years after civilizing developments in African, mainly of Egypt and its older sister, Nubia, and, in Asia, mainly of India and China.

The rise of Christianity in Europe, borne as it was on the wings of Hebraic lore and spirituality, provided a stagnant Europe with a mission. Along with the mission, which now began to be interpreted by every European tribe as particularity of history dictated, came the concept of individual responsibility. A person possessed responsibility to God, family, and tribe. Each person had to find his or her place in the chain of nature. Human beings were also classified according to their ability to be responsible or to acquire responsibility. But like all such classifications, they were autobiographical. Europe was expansive in its outward thrusts, now that responsibility and hierarchy, corollaries of the individual worth hypothesis, were institutionalized.

Individual responsibility meant that each person was bound to achieve his or her own place in the panoply of human achievers. The command of the Christian Scriptures, "Go ye into all of the world" was the essential imperialistic mandate for a people who existed virtually on the fringes of history. Adventurism, military conquests, explorations, destruction of ancient peoples, ravishing of the forests, pollution of the seas, and the development of machines of warfare, were achieved in the name of progress. Honor and recognition were accorded those individuals who could rationalize the universe through classification. Consequently, the greatest European scholars were classifiers, while African scholars have been holistic. Morality gave way to progress; science introduced a new morality. Progress, as Richards (1979) correctly observes, is essentially expansionistic and arrogant. It could never be achieved, because it was essentially an endless pursuit. Molded to acquisitive instincts, imperial quests, and expansionism, it was an intellectual mode especially fitted to the European view of the world (Diop, 1978). Europeans sought to devise "universal laws of nature" in order to make the rest of the world intelligible to Europeans in European terms. It is out of this development that we get the emergence of the peculiarly Western concept of culture. A science, or universal science, of humanity became an instrument to impose Western cultural ideology, rather than the understanding of cultural experiences, on the diverse peoples of the world.

Classification of peoples allowed Europeans to speak of "progressive cultures," "backward cultures," "inferior and superior cultures," and "primitive and "advanced cultures." Europe was teacher and others were, by virtue of their lower places in this modern version of the Great Chain of Being, students. They were underdeveloped, culturally deprived, disadvantaged, and "culture-poor."

This conception of the world is demonstrably unsympathetic to alternative perspectives. Any paradigm may be employed to explain phenomena or events. Intercultural communicationists seek to establish that alternative paradigms are not only possible but necessary before we can fully appreciate and understand intercultural communication.

Research in the area of alternative paradigms is emerging. Nhiwatiwa's (1979) study on Afrocentric and Eurocentric communication is a remarkable endeavor. She demonstrates that the fundamental assumptions of the two views contain predictable points of communication tension. Indeed, she is certain that the philosophical bases of the two views of the world are in direct conflict. Analyzing the models of communication which emerged from the separate views, she establishes the rationale for a theory of communication growing from the appreciation of cultural differences. Previously, the work by Michael Appiah (1979) demonstrated the inability of communication models based on Western assumptions to say anything significant about African, particularly Ghanaian, culture in terms of communication. More recently, Aboaba (1979), in a brilliant analysis of freedom as it relates to press communication in societies, has demolished the notion of the "universality" of the Western-based concept of freedom of the press. In addition, Vandi (1980) has proposed an Afrocentric model of communication and development based on *The Mandingo Murruya*. A premier work in development support communications, *The Mandingo Murruya* is at once open, flexible, and circular; it is neither linear nor restrictive (Vandi, 1980). These are good signs, but not yet signs of the time. They have shown us that intercultural communication scholarship must stretch beyond adjusting the world to Western thinking or adjusting Western thinking to the world. We must seek to discover, reveal, 'and present alternative viewpoints for the explanation of intercultural phenomena. Only when this is done can we truly participate in a world of understanding; otherwise our research is condemned to a closed and inadequate conceptualization.

BROAD VIEWS OF REALITY

There exist in the world three broad views of cultural reality: Afrocentric, Eurocentric, and Asiocentric. These views of cultural reality have been fashioned by the histories, mythologies, motifs, and ethos of people

of geographically close gene pools. Communication between these population realities is the central international question of the contemporary era.
Indeed, neither of the realities can be considered absolute, without variations, or immune to individual modifications and growth patterns; nor can
they account for all of the combinations of cultural realities that we find
in various parts of the world.

In the three broad views of cultural reality we find the source of
communication conflict and harmony among most peoples. The Afrocentric viewpoint holds that all modalities and realities are united and
move in one grand manner. There can be no separation of material and
spiritual, profane and sacred, form and substance. Indeed, this view pre-
dates all contemporary systems thinking. The human being, acting with
personal power, can animate, activate, and galvanize the material or the
spiritual. The continuity from material to spiritual is the universal basis of
the Afrocentric viewpoint. Asiocentric viewpoints hold that the material is
an illusion—that the real only comes from the spiritual. Therefore, Asian
philosophical concepts are enamored with spirit-over-matter notions. In
contrast to this view is the Eurocentric perspective on reality. The Eurocentric viewpoint holds that the material, the experiential, is real and that
the spiritual is an illusion. Everything that is not within the realm of sense
experience becomes nonsense. Thus, scholars have written that Asians are
spiritualistic, Europeans materialistic, and Africans personalistic
(Anyanwu, 1979). Obviously the categories are much too restrictive, but,
based upon general philosophical orientations, they do establish a mental
picture, although possibly an oversimplification.

Each broad view of the world contains key constituents which may be
used in an analysis of intercultural communication between members of
the cultural groups. Therefore, communication between cultures is constrained by history, mythology, creative motif, and collective ethos. Apart
from the purely organic presentations of messages, our communication
with other cultures involves nearly immeasurable "noncommunicative"
factors. Of course, these factors in a general sense can be considered
primary communication elements. Every communication happens in
history, but it also involves the transmission of historical information. To
the degree that a discrete dyadic communicative setting reflects the history, personal or collective, of the participants, it is a historical event—that
is, an event occuring in history while conveying history.

History is the record of events, phenomena, and personalities which
govern a people's view of themselves. It is not so much what others say of
a people, but what that people knows or believes of itself that constitutes
historical data for communication. Only the perception of you by the
other person, as she sees through her own history, is important to the

communicative event. We accept the view of others when we believe that view to be reasonably close to our own.

Communication is impaired because we know a certain historical portrait is incorrect, but for the sake of achieving overall acceptance of a proposal or scheme we allow the incorrect view to persist. This we refer to as *temporary communication estrangement*. It is not effective toward mutual understanding and constitutes a nexus of confusion between two cultures. TCE exists when one allows an individual or a cultural view to "invade" one's cultural space with energy contrary to one's own. Noninterruption of such a dynamic in an intercultural encounter constitutes temporary communication estrangement. The receiver is the reason for the TCE, not the sender or initiator. Thus, although a TCE has occurred, the sender of a message may not know it has occurred. In fact, it is most likely that the sender is confident the receiver's actions or reactions indicate that effective communication has occurred. A receiver's refusal to challenge a view he or she finds unacceptable, in order to achieve some other purpose, may be the gravest communication error interculturally. What could be more important than an adequate presentation of all sides of an issue? How can communicators expect to achieve a holisitc flow of messages if TCE occurs?

Any historical perspective which encourages TCE is dysfunctional. Fanon understood the wretchedness of the political consciousness of colonized people. Sharpening the theoretical focus on interactions between colonizers and colonized, he was able to make political and social predictions (Fanon, 1968). We must understand, however, that the factors which give rise to the bifurcation between colonizer and colonized are much more culturally determined than Fanon expressed. It is, therefore, this view of history which stands as part of the substance of intercultural communication. On this historical content have been based numerous intercultural misunderstandings. We shall demonstrate, with clarity, we hope, the constituents of these intercultural communication misunderstandings when we examine the ramifications of an alternative view of intercultural communication.

In the constraining of intercultural communication, in much the same way that history is (Karenga, 1962). A cultural group's mythology provides the group with an understanding of its relationships, that is, the relationship of person to person, person to group, person to the environment, person to members of external groups, and person to supernatural forces. In one sense, the group's place in the scheme of the universe is recorded and established. The Zulu believe that they are the people of heaven; this places them in relationship to the rest of the world. The Jews have contended that they are the chosen people; the Chinese say that they are in the middle kingdom of the earth; the Yoruba were made a great people by the divine king Oduduwa; and the Asante say that the Golden Stool descended from the sky to firmly establish the Asante nation. Intercultural communication cannot effectively occur without regard for beliefs such as these. When conflicting mythologies encounter each other misunderstandings occur, unless the interactants are able to draw upon a common set of rules. For example, when the Europeans, primarily the Boers, penetrated South Africa in the nineteenth century, they met Africans, mainly the Xhosa, Kwoi-Kwoi, and Zulu. The Boers, with their mythology based upon acquisition of private property, encountered the Africans, who believed in the common use of the land; thus, the fencing-in and fencing-out behavior of the Europeans provoked the wrath of the Africans. A people accustomed to vast territories could not understand the white man's possessive and avaricious nature with regard to land. The two cultures met with different mythologies. Communication across cultures can only be effective if the communicators have empathy for each other's cultural perceptions. What is valuable in one mythology may not be valuable in another mythology. The Eurocentric perspective places a high value on individuality and salutes personal achievement. There is more community consciousness and a greater sense of group belonging among Africans. Mythology is significant because how we see ourselves (Newmark and Asante, 1975) and others dictates what responses we can expect; in fact, we get an idea of what responses ought to be made across cultures by understanding that mythology affects communication.

A third factor in intercultural communication which may constrain the interaction is creative motif. By creative motif we mean that guiding symbolic modality which is present in every cultural group. It is reflected in the customs, dress, art, music, and lifestyle of a people. Vygotsky (1962) and Sapir (1921) have expressed their views in terms of thought and language, indicating, as Whorf also did, that there is a clear relationship between language and thought. Indeed, the relationship between creation and thought is also clear. All motifs which are culturally based derive from the mythology and history of a people.

The final factor is ethos, the collective image of the cultural group; how it appears to other groups becomes the central question in determining ethos. Whatever a group's image may be in the minds of other people, that image is an element in the intercultural communication process because it is information, and all information at the disposal of a communicator is retrievable in given situations. Therefore, if the ethos of a group of people is one of thrift, then how the individual presents himself or herself will help in the communication assessment. It will be possible for the receiver of a message to have certain information which may be stereotypical in the encounter with the sender, and vice versa. Evaluation and reevaluation of this information is always necessary, but it is usually the place where people start. An ethos which is negative may bias communicators toward individuals and thereby becomes an obstacle to communication.

A cultural group bestows upon the individuals who comprise it and who participate in its perspective a status authority. Within the same cultural group this status authority is further distributed according to ranking within the society. Thus, in a communication situation involving a professor and a civil servant, a certain status authority would be distributed to each according to the established and accepted norms of the society. In encounters between cultures, that is, representatives of cultures, a similar process occurs based upon historical content, if no other external or situational authority is available. When a Japanese meets a Nigerian, the possibilities for status authority may reside either in the situation, who is positionally more powerful, (e.g., a laborer meeting a millionaire), or in historical content—i.e., in the knowledge, which may be incorrect, each has of the other's history, mythology, motif, and ethos. The truth of the matter is that no message is transmitted apart from some culturally imposed set of understandings, and no message is received apart from the same kind of constraints. Like ministerial or magisterial robes, a person's culture confers upon that person a particular legitimacy.

Few of us have ever looked at the cultural underpinnings of intercultural interactions. Historical experiences constitute abundant sources of information. For example, no appreciation of the African world view and its relationship to the European world view can take place without a firm understanding of the historical development of the peoples. Therein lies the continuing intercultural communication misunderstandings which plague the two views of reality. Diop (1978) correctly analyzes the situation when he posits a geographical determinism as responsible for the cultural adaptation of the African and European peoples. With their attitudes and predispositions developed in long-ago eras, the peoples of these two regions frequently meet with suspicion.

The continent of African is divided into three main geographical centers: the East, the cradle of human origin and civilization; the West, the area of wealth and international trade; and the South, the region of diamonds, gold, and prehistory. The East is comprised of countries like Kenya, Ethiopia, Egypt, Sudan, Tanzania, Uganda, Libya; the West is comprised of countries such as Chad, Morocco, Tunisia, Ivory Coast, Camroons; and the South is comprised of all countries below the Zaire River. This classification adequately deals with the historical development of the continent, particularly in regard to the life of the Sahara and the migration of the Arabs, with the religion of Islam, in the seventh century.

These latter two factors are important to a full understanding of the cultural and developmental processes of the continent of Africa. At one time the Sahara was fertile (Jackson, 1974). Furthermore, the overlay of the indigenous cultures of Africa with Arabic culture began in force during the religious invasion of Islamic Jihads from the Arabian peninsula. These circumstances added not only to the distortion of African history, but also to the distortion of the communication reality between Africans and non-Africans. The problem is so elephantine that it will take many years to remove. Nevertheless, it is necessary that we get our intellectual cranes working on the matter.

The continent of Europe is much smaller, of course, than Africa. Its geographical and topographical features are much harsher, allowing relatively less living space for the continent's inhabitants. Bitterly cold climates are found in the northern extremities of the continent, which have been shown to figure greatly in the development of European culture (Diop, 1978). In addition, it must be remembered that the White Plague decimated millions of Europeans before it was brought under control. Therefore, by the time the Europeans first came into contact with Africans on a large scale, say, in the fifteenth century, they had undergone some culturally shattering experiences. Africa, on the other hand, had been relatively free of such great catastrophies. Europe appeared to develop, as a result of its harsher environment, a patrilineal family structure; Africa was basically matrilineal. Europeans worshiped fire (universal flames); Africans did not hold fire in such veneration. Europeans kept their animals, particularly dogs and cats, in their homes; Africans kept their dogs and cats outside the homes. Europeans cremated their dead; Africans buried their dead. Europeans were principally hunters; Africans were principally agrarians. The White (Bubonic) Plague had caused Europeans to look elsewhere for livelihood; this produced the most fervent adventurism since the spread of Africans from Egypt by the Arab invasion.

When Europeans left Europe they went in search of gold and a place to live. Gold was the reason most of the forts were built on the Atlantic coast. Indeed, they named the area the Gold Coast and built a fort in Ghana called *El Mina, The Mine.* The White Plague had destroyed their economies and the Arab historians had left behind in Spain records of the rich kingdoms of West Africa. This tantalized the European mind at a time when Europe's fortunes had struck rock bottom. Slavery appears to have been an accident of history, in the sense that the chief commodity the Europeans sought was gold; they happened to find slaves. It is precisely in the African-European slave transactions that the cultural conflict in African-European communication finds its root.

African society had prepared a person to welcome strangers with open arms and to share food and shelter; Europeans had learned through their European experiences to guard houses, property, and food jealously. Thus, when the European was greeted by the African, he took graciousness and generosity to mean veneration and subservience. This became the principle by which the Europeans fostered their notion of white superiority. Intercultural communication between Africans and Europeans cannot proceed until this primordial error in perception is rightly placed. Unable to understand the European, the African participated in the illusion of understanding by saying that the European was different. On the other hand, the European's adventurism led him to say that the African would give property away in order to show friendliness. This message has been distorted for the last five hundred years and represents the *historical cultural cleavage. The historical cultural cleavage is the underlying symbolic misperception, which may have occurred several centuries ago, upon whose foundation rest persistent communication misunderstandings of people from the cultures involved.* One may consider the examples of the Arabs and Jews or the Zulu-Xhosa and the Boers. Among Europeans and Africans the historical cultural cleavage has involved a steady stream of misperceptions, suspicions, and misunderstandings.

An example from the English language will serve to demonstrate how the Europeans used their languages to conspire against the interests of African peoples. To indicate difficulty with living in a city or the entanglements one may find oneself in, the European may say, "This is like a jungle." We notice that the use of *jungle* here is meant to suggest something that is unfavorable or negative. This is because the use of the term is based upon the European's experiences in the forests (technically, there are no jungles in Africa) of Africa. The term establishes for the European that a certain place or situation is to be avoided. However, the African, or South American (in whose land jungles are found), may find the term jungle to have more favorable meanings.

Finally, the intercultural communication encounter involves more than words (Ramsey, 1979). Words may constitute a relatively small portion of the encounter in comparison to nonverbal factors (Cooke, 1972). Nevertheless, words have a far-reaching influence on the encounter because they contain all of the baggage of a culture. Depending upon the language of the encounter, the person whose cultural tongue is being used has the advantage in articulating meaning and relevance. In this respect language cannot be disassociated from the relation of cultural authority. *Boycott* remains the name of an Englishman, no matter who uses the word. To the degree that one uses the language one also participates in the culture. The full significance of intercultural communication as it is reformulated will be in the insistence of cultural pluralism. Therefore, the theoretical powers of the perspective are found in challenging the accepted ideas, reevaluating them in light of reality, and charting new roads for international cooperation and understanding. Thus, differing cultural systems can learn from each other and, in overcoming the misperceptions of historical cleavage, move to dispense with temporary communication estrangement and other forms of communication illusion.

REFERENCES

ABOABA, D. (1979) "The Nigerian press under military rule." Doctoral dissertation, State University of New York at Buffalo.

ANYANWU, S. (1979) "African philosophy and Western thought." University of Lagos. (unpublished)

APPIAH, M. (1979) "Okyeame: an integrative model of communication." Doctoral dissertation, State University of New York at Buffalo.

ASANTE, M. (1979) *Afrocentricity: A Philosophical Inquiry.* Buffalo, NY: Amulefi.

——— and M. APPIAH (1979) "The rhetoric of the Akan drum." *Western Journal of Black Studies.*

ASANTE, M. and A. BARNES (1979) "Demystification of the intercultural encounter," in M. Asante et al. (eds.) *Handbook of Intercultural Communication.* Beverly Hills, CA: Sage Publications.

ASANTE, M. [eds.] (1979) *Handbook of Intercultural Communication.* Beverly Hills, CA: Sage Publications.

BECKER, S. (1977) "Mass communication and political processes," in M. Cassata and M. Asante (eds.) *The Social Uses of Mass Communication.* Buffalo, NY: State University of New York at Buffalo.

BELTRAN S, L. (1975) "Research ideologies in conflict.' *Journal of Communication* 25: 187-193.

BEN-JOCHANNAN, Y. (1978) *Black Man of the Nile and His Family.* New York: Alkebu-lan.

BLAKE, C. (1979) "Rhetoric and intercultural communication," in M. Asante et al. (eds.) *Handbook of Intercultural Communication.* Beverly Hills, CA: Sage Publications.

BLUBAUGH, J. S. and D. I. PENNINGTON (1976) *Crossing Difference: Interracial Communication.* Columbus, OH: Charles E. Merrill.

BOURDIEU, P. and J. PASSERON (1977) *Reproduction.* Beverly Hills, CA: Sage.

CASMIR, F. (1978) *International & Intercultural Communication.* Washington, DC: UPA.

CONDON, J. and F. YUSEF (1975) *Introduction to Intercultural Communication.* Columbus, OH: Charles E. Merrill.

COOKE, B. (1972) "Nonverbal communication among Afro-Americans," in T. Kochman (ed.) *Rappin' and Stylin' Out.* Urbana: University of Illinois Press.

DIOP, C. A. (1978) *Cultural Unity of Black Africa.* Chicago: Third World Press.

FANON, F. (1968) *The Wretched of the Earth.* New York: Grove.

GOLDHABER, G. (1974) *Organizational Communication.* Dubuque, IA: William C. Brown.

HALL, E. (1959) *The Silent Language.* Garden City, NY: Doubleday.
Howell, W. (1979) "Theoretical directions for intercultural communication," in M. Asante et al. (eds.) *Handbook of Intercultural Communication.* Beverly Hills, CA: Sage Publications.
JACKSON, J. (1974) *Introduction to African Civilizations.* Secaucus, NJ: Citadel.
KARENGA, M. (1962) *Kawaida: Origin, Concepts, Practice.* SanDiego: Kawaida.
KUHN, T. (1962) *The Structure of Scientific Revolutions.* Chicago: University of Chicago Press.
McLUHAN, M. (1964) *Understanding Media.* New York: McGraw-Hill.
NEWMARK, E. and M. ASANTE (1975) "Perception of self and others: an approach to intercultural communication," in F. Casmir (ed.) *International and Intercultural Communication Annual.* Washington, DC: SCA.
NHIWATIWA, N. (1979) "International communication between the African and the European worldviews." Doctoral dissertation, State University of New York at Buffalo.
OLIVER, R. T. (1971) *Communication and Culture in Ancient India and China.* Syracuse, NY: Syracuse University Press.
OGAWA, D. (1971) "Small group stereotypes of Black Americans." *Journal of Black Studies.* Beverly Hills, CA: Sage Publications.
PIKE, K. L. (1966) "Etic and emic standpoints for the description of behavior," in *Language in Relation to a Unified Theory of the Structure of Human Behavior.* The Hague: Mouton.
POPPER, K. (1959) *The Logic of Scientific Discovery.* New York: Harper & Row.
RAMSEY, S. (1979) "Nonverbal behavior: an intercultural perspective," in M. Asante et al. (eds.) *Handbook of Intercultural Communication.* Beverly Hills, CA: Sage Publications.
RICH, A. (1974) *Interracial Communication.* New York: Harper & Row.
RICHARDS, D. (1979) "An Ideology of european domination." *The Black American* (1979) 18: 27-31.
SANDA, A. (1979) "Cultural self-comprehension in ethnically plural societies," in M. Asante et al. (eds.) *Handbook of Intercultural Communication.* Beverly Hills, CA: Sage Publications.
——— (1976) *Ethnic Relations in Nigeria.* Ibadan, Nigeria: Caxton.
SAPIR, E. (1921) *Language: An Introduction to the Study of Speech.* New York: Harcourt Brace Jovanovich.
SARAL, T. (1979) "The consciousness theory of intercultural communication," in M. Asante et al. (eds.) *Handbook of Intercultural Communication.* Beverly Hills, CA: Sage Publications.
SMITH, A. L. [Molefi K. Asante] (1973) *Transracial Communication.* Englewood Cliffs, NJ: Prentice-Hall.
STEWART, E. (1974) *An Overview of the Field of Intercultural Communication.* Pittsburgh: Society for Intercultural Education, Training, and Research.
——— (1973) *Outline of Intercultural Communication.* Washington, DC: BCIU.
VANDI, A. (1980) "The Murruya: an Afrocentric model of communications and development." Presented to the Thirtieth Annual Conference of the ICA, Acapulco, Mexico.
VAN SERTIMA, I. (1976) *They Came Before Columbus: African Presence in the New World.* New York: Random House.
VORA, E. (1978) "The development of concept diffusion models and their application to the diffusion of the social concept of race." Doctoral dissertation, State University of New York at Buffalo.

VYGOTSKY, L. (1962) *Thought and Language.* Cambridge, MA: MIT Press.
WHITNEY, F. (1975) *Mass Media and Mass Communications in Society.* Dubuque,
    IA: William C. Brown.
WILLIAMS, C. (1976) *The Destruction of Black Civilization.* Chicago: Third World
    Press.

4

EUROPEAN MYTHOLOGY: THE IDEOLOGY OF "PROGRESS"

Dona Richards

INTRODUCTION

We, as people of African descent, need to understand the nature of European culture, history, and behavior in order that we might be in a better position to deal with it, reject it, and to comprehend the dimension of its effect on us. Its effect has unfortunately usually been subtle, yet ideologically debilitating. For this reason I have devoted much of my energies to "White Studies," an endeavor which should be an important part of any Black Studies curriculum.

As a black anthropologist looking at white culture, I find the concepts of ethos, ideology, myth, and value to be especially useful in this study. My interest in this concept, the "idea of progress" as it is called, is more than academic; it is ideological. Its relevance to Pan-African self-determination may not appear obvious, and that is precisely the reason for my concern. The study of white culture is complicated by the fact that its ideological or "value" aspects are most often hidden beneath a facade of universalistic, scientistic, and "humanistic" rhetoric. We begin to adopt the values of our oppressors as we assimilate the language of academia from within their institutions of learning. European conceptions must be philosophically and critically analyzed so as to lay bare their value-content. The "idea of progress" in Western thought is just such a phenomenon. It is an essential dynamic of European ideology, misunderstood by us to be a

universal statement of human value and motivation. This idea, along with
our acceptance of it, has helped tremendously in the destruction of the
black self-image.

In order to reveal this ideological theme effectively, I will, in this
chapter, first attempt to expose the way in which it operates *within*
European society—to look at how the idea works, and the way in which it
gains not only philosophical acceptance but ideological force. I will then
explore the means by which it helps to determine and to rationalize
European behavior *externally*. I hope to demonstrate how the "idea of
progress" becomes an ideology of imperialism toward others and of the
oppressive technical ordering of the society internally. Perhaps, if these
things become clear, we will be able to raise critical ideological questions
for ourselves: "Is what we want to achieve simply an uncritical imitation
of what the white man has created?" (Edward Wilmot Blyden asked this
question in 1881; see Blyden, 1967: 91-92.) In discussing these issues we
can create an intellectual atmosphere which demands answers to such
ideological questions.

I. FROM "IDEA" TO IDEOLOGY:
THE SHAPING OF EUROPEAN SOCIETY

EXPOSING THE CULTURE-BOUND

The "idea of progress" is a fundamental aspect of the Western philosophy of life, providing moral justification for the technical order and giving
direction to the strivings of individuals within the society. It has contributed to the formation of Western-European social organization by
helping to provide the ideological substratum out of which the oppressive
technical order was created. The concept has profound implications. Its
effects have been powerful and have spread to other cultures. It has been a
potent tool in white hands.

Within the setting of Western culture, however, the relativity and
ideological significance of the idea is difficult to discuss. More than a
conceptual tool, it has become part of the meaning of existence for white
people. In the classroom the attempt to present the idea as being culturally
bound is met with blank stares. "What do you mean? *Everyone* wants to
make *progress!*" Moreover, because the idea combines Western-European
metaphysical assumptions, world view, and values so intricately and is so
deeply embedded in them, finding the right way to present it, so that its
cultural implications for white behavior, attitudes, and world posture
become evident, is not an easy task.

The critical conceptual step is that by which action directed toward a concrete objective becomes confused with change which is merely reflexive—that is, in which the object is "change" itself. The "progress" toward which Western people perceive themselves to be "moving" is neither concrete nor "reachable"—a spurious goal indeed. Then why does the idea have such attraction for the Western mind—a mind which is at once rationalistic and empirical ("Show me!")? The answer lies in the fact that this ingenious invention, "progress," born out of the white ethos, is ideally fashioned to encourage the growth of the technical order while at the same time justifying European cultural and political imperialism. Let us see how this is achieved.

The Western-European ethos is expansionistic. To white people, the universe represents actual physical space into which they can impose themselves. Their movement in this respect is never *from* place *to* place (they are no nomads). It is not displacement, but *increase*. White people expand and extend their possessions, never relinquishing territory they have claimed. They never migrate, but always conquer and consume. By this process white people themselves becomes "bigger." The European idea of progress allows for this same kind of "movement" and "increase." Conceptually, "progressive" motion consumes all of the past within it, and "progress" is not merely "different from," it is "more than." The idea is, in this way, essentially expansionistic. "It contains within itself the germs of indefinite expansion (Beard, 1955: xxviii). What it implies is that there is no fixed limit to change, no boundary limiting the expansionist thrust. Instead, Europeans see themselves as being morally obligated to ceaselessly move/change/expand themselves; *that* is the nature of "progress."

For the Western-European it is the abstractness of the idea which makes it "ideal." Interestingly, this is precisely the nature of Plato's ideal state; it can only be *approximated* by humanity. The commitment to imitate it necessarily entails endless and infinite effort, and therefore assures a certain style of behavior. In opposition, Arthur Lovejoy and J. B. Bury contend that Plato's conception is antithetical to the "idea of progress" in that it involves a commitment to an absolute order already conceived. But what they fail to understand is that it is the absolute order (the "establishment") which itself becomes the *agent* of change (as Theodore Roszak points out in his introduction to *Sources*; see Roszak, 1972). The "establishment" changes in order to remain the same. (One becomes more at home with this seeming paradox the more one studies cultural phenomena. Culture is tenacious, ingeniously using varied techniques to ensure its own survival.)

Admittedly, change is much more the order of the contemporary West than it is of ancient Greece, but Plato's Absolute can still be interpreted to ideologically support *a certain kind of change, in a particular direction,* within a determined and well-defined form. The "idea of progress" does precisely the same thing. What it limits is the *kind* of change which can take place. Ecological sanity, for instance, is not "progress." Prohibiting the building of nuclear reactors is "unprogressive."

It has mistakenly been regarded as a "theory of history." It is not. It does not necessarily imply optimism. It has been misunderstood to refer to a way of interpreting the future. It does not. The "infinite future," once it has been postulated, becomes irrelevant. It is the subtlety of this phenomenon ("idea") which contributes to its distinctiveness. It is a mood—not one of optimism, but of arrogance, superiority, power, and exploitation. These need not be synonymous with optimism. It is common for persons committed to the "Western way" to express concern over where "it" is all leading, and yet to be convinced of their obligation to "take it there" and, what is more, to be convinced of their obligation to bestow the leadership of their culture upon those, less fortunate, who do not know the way.

The idea of progress is a directive of Western behavior, a determinant of attitude, a device whereby Western-Europeans judge and impose their judgments on others. Europeans who "ennoble" the "native" do so from the pinnacle of a state of "progress" which they believe it is incumbent upon "Man" to achieve. It is the Western counterpart of what is meant by tradition when it is said that tradition functions normatively in "traditional" societies. It is the idea of progress which helps to guarantee that Western commitments and values will *not change,* but will always remain *within the same modality.*

The "idea" is more a methodological commitment than a theory of history. It is a process, an operational mode. Its referent is rationalism— not a euphoric or glorious state of perfection in the future (only for Marx does it seem to have this connotation). In fact, its viability contradicts the possibility of such a state. Its mood is much closer to a "survival of the fittest" aura. It is concerned with the evolving, not with the end, product. Progress is always there to be made, because its index is wherever one is at a given time. There is always a "proper" way to attack a problem rationally. Rather than presuming there is perfect state ultimately to be reached, it rests on the presumption of cease-less "problems," constant tension. It presupposes disharmony, disequilibrium, imbalance.

The Republic can be interpreted in this way, as a paramount guide to activity, in an endless approach to unattainable perfection—an ideal which, like Xeno's paradox, allows for an infinite degree of approximation without the possibility of duplication. It is the solving of the problem in the most "rational" way which *is progress.* That is the thrust of the idea within European culture. Its outward thrust, i.e., in relation to other cultures, is to make the "rational" way (the white, European way) best.

E. O. Bassett says that, in Plato's view, "society executes an infinite progression." Furthermore, the end of progress is progress; "the aim is but a directing principle. . . . Since the social as well as the universal aim is maximum orderliness, progress must be perpetual" (Bassett, 1927-1928: 476). But Lovejoy and Boas argue that "the Romantic idea of endless progress for progress' sake is alien to Plato's thought" (Lovejoy and Boas, 1965: 168). Popper (1966: 4-5) agrees:

> Plato's sense of drift had expressed itself in his theory that all change, at least in certain cosmic periods, must be for the worse; all change is degeneration. Aristotle's theory admits of changes which are improvements; this change may be progress. Plato had taught that all development starts from the original, the perfect Form or Idea, so that the developing thing must lose its perfection in the degree in which it changes and in which its similarity to the original decreases.

But the trick is that the perfect Form exists only as Idea. If one's interpretation of Plato emphasizes the concrete political, sociocultural implications of his theories for human organization, then it becomes clear that all actual development in the sensate "world of becoming" may properly start from a conceptualized perfection, but certainly not with the "Perfect State." Actual movement is, therefore, not *away from* but *toward* the Ideal. If the Ideal could be actualized, then once this had occurred, all change would, indeed, be for the worse. But such, for Plato, was a contradiction in terms.

Joel Kovel says that the "practical genius" of Protestantism and of the West in general "was to discover that the more remote a desired goal, the more passionately a man would seek it." I would insert "European" before the generic term "man"; and in my view, this is one of the normative functions of the Christ image, insofar as he is a deity conceived as "pure spirit." He is the "human" who is not human, the "more than" human being who only incidentally, and *very* briefly, took "human" form. This image calls for the emulation of that which is superhuman and therefore unrealizable by human beings. (African deities are criticized as being "too human" in conceptualization; they are therefore "primitive" in European judgment.) As Kovel says of European value, "all that 'counted' was Movement, striving for an endless goal that became ever more remote precisely through the process of striving" (see Kovel, 1971: 125, 128). One never reaches "progress"; one *makes* progress," and, in the Western view, there is always more of it to be made. This supports the ego which must extend its domain indefinitely, the ethos which manifests an insatiable will-to-power.

The white self-image requires an "inferior" to which it relates as "superior." The idea of progress helps to explain to Western-Europeans in what way they are "superior." They believe, and are able to make others believe, that since they represent the most "progressive" force at any given moment, they are most human and therefore "best." Others in the world represent varying degrees of inferiority. This characteristic of the European ethos is already observable in the archaic West. In comparing the Romans with other peoples, Aristides (1958: 40) claims not only that they are greater than their contemporaries, but that they are greater than anything which preceded them.

> Hence the inferiority of those who lived in former times appears because the past is so much surpassed, not only in the element at the head of the empire, but also in cases where identical groups have been ruled by others and by you.

While a particular kind of "improvement" may be essential to the idea of progress—ethnologically, in terms of the European ethos—an equally significant aspect of the idea is the assumption that the present is probably better than and superior to the past. The way the idea is put firmly into the service of European cultural imperialism is that the superior present becomes something more than merely what is occurring (or exists) now. What is "progressive" or "modern" is the proper form or model for what *ought to* exist in the present. Therefore, existent forms which do not conform to the progressive (modern or Western) model are not really part of the present—they are "outdated" or "backward." In this way, European culture, in the vernacular of European cultural chauvinism, is made to be superior not only to what precedes it—as does its own past—but also to coexistent "unprogressive" cultures. In other words, the idea of progress provides a scale on which to weigh and by which to compare people via their cultures (their group creations). The Western-European ethos requires a self-image not merely of superiority but of *supremacy,* and the idea of progress makes white people supreme among human beings. It is superiority placed into the dimension of lineal time, and then the logic of lineal time placed into a timeless dimension. Without the idea and this conceptual sleight of hand, cultures would merely be different; Western culture would merely be intensely and obsessively rational. *With* the assumption of the idea of progress, the West becomes "better." In the ways indicated above, then, the idea of progress supports the expansionism and supremism inherent in the Western-European ethos.

THE INEVITABILITY OF "PROGRESS"

The idea of progress is a "philosophy of change" and, as such, tends to support any innovation, anything "new." Wherever this force leads is by definition "good"—whereas in the context of other world views what could be defined as "progressive," activity depends on concretized goals. The idea of progress transforms what is merely "change" into "directed movement." Participants in Western culture *perceive* change in this way. Continually influenced by the images of technology, they are provided with directive signposts and the standard which gives order to otherwise directionless motion. Technology provides the model of "efficiency," a model which more perfectly than anything imaginable concurs with the philosophy of change—for, in the European view, there is no end to efficiency either. No matter how effectively a machine may perform its function, it can always be made more effective and thereby a "new" and "better" machine. Progress is, in this way, "proven," and Western-Europeans can be said to "advance" as technology" advances." It does not matter that there is nothing toward which they advance. Their innovations all seem to contribute to greater order in their society— at least, to a certain *kind* of order. The rationalization (in the Weberian sense) of their culture gives them the impression that they have organized their lives more efficiently. This kind of organization is proof of progress, just as their machines are. All of this taken together means that they are "smart" and getting "smarter," the "best" and getting "better." To the Western self, progress is obviously *more* than an idea. When technology dominates in this way, it is the inexorable drive for power and control characterizing the European ethos that is ideally complemented; but Europeans understand their nature to be the nature of all people, and they project this attitude onto the world, dominating it.

The idea of progress had an irresistible attraction for Europeans; it was, after all, created out of their own sentiment, their ethos. It corresponded to their world view and comprised part of the conquering mood. But it was technological efficiency which "clinched it"—which provided tangible evidence of material gain and accomplishment. Technological success gave Western-Europeans the illusion of an objectively ("universally") valid criterion by which to judge their progress. If power over others is the ultimate and ever-present goal—and clearly technological superiority brings power—then progressive ideology, a philosophy of change, is most certainly "right"; obviously a cyclical (African) as opposed to lineal, view, or, in Charles Beard's (1955) Eurocentric characterization, "the belief in the vicious circle," has certainly led to "powerlessness" (or so the argument goes).

The themes of Western-European culture and ideology complement one another and converge in this way until progress becomes a cultural fact. The more particularized and hardened it becomes in the Western experience, the more housed this fact must be in the language of universalism. White persons are not like other people—their goals and ideals do not seem to work for them unless they can conceive of them as universal goals. The idea of progress is nothing if it is not projected as having universal significance; otherwise it does not work. It must be an implicit statement of value, explicitly stated as a "neutral" fact. As with other aspects of the Western ideological matrix, progress cannot be acknowledged as value-based, because the "scientific" (which to the European connotes the highest value) must be valueless. Statements, dogmas, positions, European "choices" can then be imposed upon the tastes of others. European predilections, tendencies, perspectives become that which is "proper" for all. The idea of progress pervades the European intellect—the European consciousness as well as the European moral sense—and *all* who succumb to it are duped by the sleight of hand by which a chosen way simultaneously becomes "inevitable change" and a Western goal becomes "the human goal."

The idea of progress accomplishes all this, so that when someone who describes himself or herself as a "racialist" or talks about the "importance of race in civilization" (Wayne MacLeod [1968], for instance), he or she is merely making sense of the "facts." Once progress becomes ideology—once it becomes incorporated into the presupposed matter of culture—there is no way out. It is inextricably bound to Western technology, and the technical obsession is the white person's creed, just as is the idea of power over nonwhites. MacLeod is quite right when he points to the weaknesses in Ashley Montagu's arguments. Montagu (1968: 3-4) representing the "enlightened" liberal position, argues that technical advances are due to "accidental factors." He misses the point. They occur in greater numbers where they are encouraged, even mandated, by a culture which lives for them and by them. The possibility that European-style progress could be rejected does not occur to Montagu any more than it does to MacLeod. To the European mind there is no such possibility. "Enlightened," "liberal" and "racialist" alike, *both* have unconsciously universalized the particular. Both are progressive. For both, progress is a given in experience and assumed to be everywhere. I am saying here that the European idea of progress is inherently racialist ideology. Once it is accepted, the progressive person must always be identified as a white person.

METAPHYSIC AND ETHOS

Via the Western-European idea of progress it is possible to see how the metaphysical (ontological and epistemological) definitions of a culture translate into its ideological (value and behavioral) aspects. The assumptions of cause (especially Aristotle's final cause), of lineality, and the sense of telos or "purpose" in the Western metaphysic, as well as a dependence on abstraction, are all necessary conceptual ingredients of progress ideology. Its assimilation depends on the mental habits encouraged by these forms of thought. Its acceptance as a predominant molder of group activity is dependent on a frame of mind already or simultaneously conditioned by "lineal codification" (Dorothy Lee's term) and causalist epistemology. Phenomena must relate to one another within a lineally defined whole, where "causes" precede "effects," and growth implies the incorporation and surpassing of that which has come before in a way that precludes repetition. Progress does not recur; it is triumph over the past. The need for and feeling of triumph is an essential ingredient of the idea of progress. In the European view, life is a continuous struggle, based on competition, and meaning is derived from "winning." Hidden behind the so-called universalism and humanism of the concept are the exigencies of an ethos that feeds on subjugation—surpassing, conquering, winning. Progress means "we are winning; we have triumphed over!" The enemy is vaguely felt, not conceived, to be "everything else out there"—not only nature, but other people, other ways, ideas, forces, beings. The enemy against which the white person competes is everything that he or she is not. The idea involves continual movement, because the enemy is never totally subdued. "He" seeks to close the gap, and we must stay ahead of "him." Progress is *staying ahead*—it is "defeating" the present.

The way in which "history" and "time" are perceived is critical to the European understanding of the meaning of human experience. The idea of progress both creates Western history and simultaneously stands outside that history, becoming an absolute in Western thought. It achieves a unique combination, the illusion of "unchanging change," thereby providing a dynamic principle while at the same time satisfying what Lovejoy (1966: 12) calls the "eternalistic" pathos.

The assumption of lineal time is an ontological prerequisite to the idea of progress. Evolutionary development, an ingredient of the idea, necessitates that points be connected; this is the conceptual function of the line. The written word is the medium of the line, and it provides evidence to the Western mind of progress, because words accumulate. In this way, "more" becomes "better."

Progress is an argument for the discarding of the past. Yet evolutionism, its sibling idea, involves a strange kind of incorporation. Evolution requires the perception of reality as the continual development of a single entity—a single being. Yet, while the form is evolving, its prior essence is being denied. Progress makes "garbage" of the past. The concept of newness (value, in progress ideology) does not mean *new* in the sense that a baby is new. It means *different* from that which has been seen before, whereas even a newborn baby, in the African conception, is the timeless *re*creation of man. In progress ideology, what precedes on the line is always destroyed and denied.

The European "represent[s] the sequence of time as a line going to the infinite." That is a description of the idea of progress. Uniform and undisturbed flow of time can only be imagined as a line (see Juenger, 1956: 39-40). If other concepts of time are admitted as plausible or operative, the idea of progress does not work. In order for it to work, what must be assumed is a single, infinite, and infinitely divisible time.

In Dorothy Lee's (1959: 110) words, the line "underlies our (western) aesthetic apprehension of the given," and progress is the "meaningful sequence" for Westerners. A people that is not progressive "goes no-where." The idea of progress "makes sense" because Western-Europeans think in terms of "climatic historical sequence" (Lee, 1959: 91). They are concerned not with events but with their own place within a related series of events (Lee, 1959: 94). As the idea of purpose permeates Western life, so the idea of progress gives the impression of purpose in change.

PROGRESS: "SCIENCE" AND EUROPEAN DEVELOPMENT

A compelling question in this discussion is, "How does the idea of progress relate to European history and development, and what is its relationship to science as it is known in the West?" According to Bury (author of the one major noncritical work devoted to this concept), "it is not till the sixteenth century that the obstacles to its [the idea of progress's] appearance definitely began to be transcended and a favorable atmosphere to be gradually prepared" (Bury, 1955: 7). I would put it differently. In the archaic West, the proper metaphysical atmosphere was already being created in which a subsequent ideological synthesis could take place. The germs of the idea had been planted and some of its ideological functions were already in operation. Sixteenth-century Europe embraced the idea as a fully matured concept because it was also in the process of assimilating an individualistic, accumulative, technocratic ethic in the form of materialistic capitalism. Protestantism supported this tendency and so did the ideology of progress. These aspects of European culture reinforced one another, became identified with one another, and grew together. Their combined momentum in the sixteenth century merely represented the final unbridled commitment to rational forms. The seeds of all of them are to be found at whichever point there are enough uniquely combined traits to be identified as "European culture." The distinguishable periods in Western-European history are ethnologically a matter of difference in emphasis, intensity, and stage of development only. At one point, metaphysical possibilities and tendencies existed; at another, hardened and definitive cultural facts were present, which inescapably began to shape the forms within which people lived.

It was not until the appearance of Francis Bacon and others in the late sixteenth and early seventeenth centuries that "science" triumphed and the idea of progress concomitantly became the unchallenged cultural philosophy of the West. The significance of the Baconian attitude was the formal demise of the tension (albeit ineffective) between Western arrogance and the Western sense of the supernatural. The scientific pursuit became a religion, and Western-Europeans were no longer embarrassed by their own lack of humility.

It is of value to bring attention to the critical relationship between Christian thought in its Western form and the pattern of European ecological behavior. Few are willing to admit or discuss the extent to which European Christianity is predicated on a world view which supports the exploitation of nature. The image with which we are usually presented is that of the life-and-death struggle between religion and science as representing two antithetical frames of mind. Actually, Christian thought provides a view of man, nature, and the universe which supports not only the ascendancy of science, but of the technical order, individualism, and relentless progress. Emphasis within this world view is placed on humanity's dominance over *all* other beings, which become "objects" in an "objectified" universe. There is no emphasis on an awe-inspiring God or cosmos. Being "made in God's image," given the European ethos, translates into "acting *as* God," recreating the universe. Humanity is separated from nature, which becomes "fodder" to be used in whatever way humanity sees fit. It is a concept of control and dominance, not of harmony, equilibrium, and respect. World views such as that of traditional Africa, in which spirit is recognized in all natural beings, are considered to be "superstitious," "ignorant," and are derogatorily labeled "animistic." European-Christian thought sets the tone for a rampant exploitation of nature as well as of people and their cultures.

Lynn White, Jr. (1969: 350), in an impressively perceptive article, remarks:

> The present disruption of the global environment is the product of a dynamic technology and science. . . . Their growth cannot be understood historically apart from distinctive attitudes toward nature which are deeply grounded in Christian dogma.

But this should not surprise us, for ethnologically the relationship between European Christianity and the idea of progress makes sense, since religion in any culture is to be understood as the sacralization of ideology. Hence, Christian thought facilitated the acceptance of a scientific world view, and in the centuries which followed the Baconian era's rationalistic epistemology was totally identified with rationalistic culture. The marriage argued for in Platonism was finally consummated.

By the late nineteenth century, the concept (of progress) had been largely assimilated to the values of a complex and expanding industrial order. Progress could now become a slogan to defend the course of technological innovation and economic rationalization and concentration [Williams, 1970: 469].

As we Africans became more "sold on" (and "sold into") white culture, another sacred cow joined forces with "civilization," "progress," and "Christianity" to convince us of the superiority of the Western-European way: "science." In the contemporary battlefield, in which minds and souls are the objectives and victims, this is still the term which holds us most in awe—*science*. The very word resounds with majesty, like *truth* and *knowledge*. For if nothing else is "neutral," certainly this must be. Like some great almighty and "objective" force, it carries us small humans along, into ever more progressive stages; it is not to be judged or questioned, just worshipped. But again, what is called science in the West has been determined, weighted, and directed by Western value, implicitly stating that value; and we, indeed, have accepted it as "pure." The ideology of progress has helped to make this possible.

Progress determined what was meaningful to the European and what lacked value—what was ethical and what was not. It became a frame of reference, and ideological base out of which other concepts were created and by which they were judged. It was a paramount criterion of suitability. It became linked totally with the scientific-technical and with the power relationships their development suggested. Progress became identified with scientific knowledge. Europeans had to control and use nature to their advantage.

After Bacon, the pursuit of science became morally self-justifying. It became morality itself. The mad scientist of the Western nightmare fantasy is simply acting out zealous loyalty to the Baconian-Western creed. Descartes, becoming fanatically committed to this creed, took on the task of contributing an "invulnerable method" to the edifice which was being constructed. Notice the intensity with which he worked at severing "mind" from "body" in the *Meditations*. All such metaphysical manipulations contributed to the success of the progress ideology and the scientific world view. Both the Baconian attitude and Cartesian epistemology were intensifications and developments of possibilities already present in the matrix of the culture.

I have said that the idea of progress was created out of the Western ethos, encourages it, and is, therefore, ideally suited to the Western world view. Henryk Skolimowski (1974: 56-57) supports this point and says that "forces which significantly contributed to the formation of our concept of progress" are "the crusading spirit of medieval Christianity," "the white man's mission," "the expansive restlessness of the white man," and his "acquisitive instinct."

All ideologies must state choice in terms of necessity—what has been ideologically created in terms of what is given. The functioning of culture as a synthetic whole requires the commitment of people, and that commitment requires the conviction that one way of life is right for them, as opposed to having been chosen by them—even though they *mean* precisely the same thing. But only in the context of the Western-European ethos does it become necessary to create a category of thought and action ("scientific progress") which is said to be void of ideology and belief. Because only the European ethos makes the *imposition* of that belief on others paramount. By dehumanizing science, the Europeans seek to place themselves above other people who are not "scientific." They have convinced themselves that the character of their life and culture is not a result of ideological choice, but rather of universal human needs met by the principles of "science." In Western culture the phrase, "need for invention," is used normatively to impress others with the inevitability of Western-style development. The fact that *"Different Ideologies define the need for invention in different ways"* (Skolimowski, 1974: 70-71) is ignored. But the ideology of progress is inherently imperialistic and cannot admit of these other possibilities.

How is the concept of "modernity" itself related to the ruling ideology of the West? Progress, in combination with scientism, acts to encourage the use of the term *modern*. *Modern* is, indeed, so much identified with *Western* that it is difficult to see how it can be useful as a tool of analysis or description. Insofar as it means anything other than "that which presently exists," it has been tied to Western technology and the way of life which accompanies it. Even the term *contemporary* connotes for Western people a quality possessed by the most "advanced" evolutionary stage and level of progress. It is the particular kind of tyranny of the ideology of progress (its universalization and unidirectional character) in combination with the overwhelming success of the white man, "the conqueror," which makes the argument that Western forms are universal seem all the more plausible—in spite of that argument's inaccuracy.

In European history, the process of "the mechanization of the cosmos" (Skolimowski, 1974: 75) displayed development along a consistent theme. The Platonic emphasis, while not on the mechanical tool, mandated the use of "objectification" (separation of the "knowing self" from the "known object" as the essential "tool" of conceptual rationalism. The etiological and metaphysical relationship between objectification and "mechanization" is important. Intense objectification is a prerequisite for the despiritualization of the universe, and through it the Western cosmos was made ready for ever-increasing materialization until, indeed, there was no cosmos, no perception of cosmic order. Plato prepared the West for excessive development in a particular direction, paved the way for Bacon's influence and for an obsessive commitment to the idea of progress in its materialistic emphasis. The Western idea of progress is indeed a part of its "rational" heritage.

As Pan-Africanists, one of our consistent and pressing concerns must be with the nature of Western culture and with its cultural imperialistic expression. The idea of progress is part of that expression. We must devote our energies to a critical discussion of such concepts from an African perspective. The idea of progress must be understood by us to be part of a mythological system used to create and sustain the symbols of whiteness and Westernness as valuable characteristics, and of blackness and Africanness as demeaning ones.

The critique from *within* Western culture is most often tenuous and weak, suffering from the same Eurocentrism it criticizes. Conventionally, the failings to Western-Europeans are universalized and made to be simply the ills of modern humanity. Acceptance of this interpretation is costly for us, for it leads away from, rather than toward, an *African* alternative.[1]

II. AN IDEOLOGY OF IMPERIALISM: CHRISTIANITY, PROGRESS, AND AFRICA

As concerns people of African descent, the ideology of progress has explained to white people why it was their duty to exploit, conquer, and control us and others different from them. It became an ideology of supremacy, a well-constructed mythology of superiority. The point is that the rationale for an oppressive technical order, the rational ordering of the universe, and the endeavor to destroy, dominate, and exploit people of African descent unite in a single ideological concept, the European ideology of progress.

The trappings of religious ideology were used very successfully against a genuinely spiritual people to convince them of their own inferiority,[2] and to rationalize their victimization. These, of course, were related endeavors. From the beginnings of the institutionalization of European Christianity ("Christianism"), the intimate connections between "Christianity", "Progress" and imperialistic behavior becomes visible. Christianity and progress meshed in a consistent ideological statement—"It behooves the 'civilized' to 'Christianize' the world"—one which becomes imperialistic when stated politically. It was Constantine's achievement to fully realize these implications. In 312 "A.D." he needed a new weapon in his struggle for the rule of the Roman Empire. He decided to use a cross, as it had appeared to him in a dream, inscribed "conquer by this":

> He looked upon himself as designated by God to rule the Roman world. And in return for this divine recognition he felt the obligation to promote the cause of Christianity in all possible ways. . . . Constantine saw in Christianity the religion which could and should provide a spiritual bond among his subjects as well as a moral basis for political loyalty to himself as the elect of God [Boak, 1955: 433].

No matter how good they make it sound, we should be able to see through such rationalization. It is an old story for us. The Christians divided the world into "Christians" and "heathens," "Christians" and "pagans." Heathens were (are) godless, irreligious people. By implication, then, Christians had a cornerstone on religion. Pagans were people of the countryside and backward. Christians were associated with the cities, and therefore with progress. In Western value terms, "country" is inferior and "city" is superior. Christianity brought with it the Western-European idea of progress, while at the same time reinforcing the archaic or nascent European self-image.

Christian ideology is teleological, providing a conceptual model peculiar to Western perception, based on a particular image of humanity (that of the white person). The Christian-Western interprets humans as beings who derive meaning from their ability to move toward a universal goal—at once "progressive" and "rational." Reinhold Niebuhr (1946: 24) proudly declares that "the idea of progress is possible only upon the ground of a Christian culture." And in Mbiti's view (1970: 128), African religion is "defeated" because it does not offer a conception of an abstract future and "glorious hope" of redemption and immortality, as is offered by Christianity. Being African, Mbiti should understand that for the African, immortality is achieved through association with the vitality of life.

European Christianity participates in European chauvinism. It emphasizes the "we/they" dichotomy on which Western-European nationalism (culturalism, racialism) depends. It provides images of Westerners and non-Westerners which mandate unlimited expansion of white, Western political control. The essence of the Judeo-Christian tradition is its assumption of theological and moral evolution leading to the superior and humanly proper conception of one God as the ultimate abstraction. The Christian mandate to impose this conception on other peoples represents the epitome of the Western ethos. Essential to this proselytizing mission is an invidious comparison in which non-Westerner in general and Africans in particular not only come out losers but are victimized as well. The "pagan," "heathen," "idolater," "polytheist" *has* no religion in terms of Western value, but is morally inferior, less than human. Whatever is done with the objective of making pagans "more human" (e.g., imposing religion on them) is justifiable.

Christian ideology provides moralistic and universalistic terms of disparagement for the peoples who are objects of Western imperialism, as well as moral justification for their subjugation and exploitation. Progressivism cannot easily be distinguished from Christian ideology. The pagan becomes not only nonreligious, but *pre*religious—backward, ignorant, lacking in the intellectual acumen to develop, reach, attain civilization (white, Western-European culture)—"primitive," "retrogressive," "retarded." The white, Western-European at any point in history represents the "highest," "most superior" form of "man."

Here are exposed the mythological conceptions which provide ideological support for European dominance. They rest on a belief system which makes possible and supports imperialistic behavior. The ideology of progress helps to form these conceptions. The imperialistic drive becomes "moral" in the context of this mythological system. The concept of the "cultural other" sanctions behavior toward those of us who become symbols of "nonhumanness." The concept of the cultural other is created to satisfy the Western-European ethos and is dialectically related to the white self-concept. The cultural other is black, bad, and nonhuman, the dialectical opposite of the Western self. That self is conceived of as superior—an image "explained" by the idea of progress mythology. This mythology provides a scale by which to judge superiority or inferiority, a criterion for superiority. The superior are the more rational, the smarter ones, the more moral, the ones who invent and discover everything of value. They "own" developed society. They are white. After using the ideology of progress to transform people of other cultures into savages, whites can make themselves responsible for the "welfare" of those savages—e.g. imperial control, dominance.

The ideology of progress allowed white people to speak with impunity of "civilized" and "superior" races in the nineteenth century, and later allowed them to speak of "developed," "advanced," "modern" nations. This part of the mythology helps to explain the "settler syndrome." White people are always justified in taking land from blacks and others who are not white. They, the whites, have the "expertise," the "drive," which allows them to make proper use of it; whereas these cultural others "waste" land, whites "develop" it. Colonialism in Africa, South-African apartheid, white dominance in Zimbabwe, European treatment of native Americans, Jewish settlers on the Gaza strip (to name only a few instances) are all part of *one* culture, *one* movement, *one* ideology exhibiting the attitude, "This place was nothing before *we* came here." Acceptance of the ideology of progress makes this argument plausible. "Put the nonhumans in reserved, inarable areas, since they do not value the land anyway." This is indeed why white people the world over, no matter how "enlightened," find it difficult to totally condemn the white South-African regime. Clearly and simply, their presence in Africa ensures "progress" (or so says European mythology).

The Western self-image is unique. It requires a negative image of other people in order to be positively reinforced. It is, therefore, we might say, *dependent* on these negative images of others. The thought forms, institutions, ideological constructs which exist within the matrix of the culture must perform the task of creating positive images of the European self, and conversely, negative images of others. The European ethos derives pleasure from and seeks satisfaction in the superior/inferior relationship which translates into "justifiable" European dominance. Both Christian ideology and the ideology of progress perform this function for European culture. The African has long been a whipping boy, fulfilling the negative, devalued, and inferior part of this dichotomy. Africans were "heathens" and therefore fair game for proselytization. For godlike, white superiors to control them was to save them from the sin of "ignorance" and "blackness." It also meant bringing "civilization" to them, and therefore "progress." This was all that was needed to ideologically support a pattern of behavior so consistent, so terrifying, and so successful that it all but destroyed the positive African self-image.

Most Pan-Africanists and African ideologues have failed to effectively reconstruct a positive African self-image because they have either accepted European "Christianism" or the European mythology, and therefore definition of, progress (or, as is usually the case, a combination of both). Quite simply, if civilization represents progress, and civilization is defined by whites in terms of their values and self-image, then to want to progress is to want to be white. Conversely, in white terms, the opposite of civilization is "the primitive," or "that which we want to move away from." It is black, "that which we do not want to be." Any amount of praise bestowed on Africa *within* the conceptual framework stated above, will *only succeed in enhancing the white Western-European self-image, at the expense of a positive African self-image.* That is why it is a mistake to isolate certain aspects of African culture and history as representing the heights of civilization, *using the European definition of that term.* What are we really saying about ourselves when we do that?[3]

To progress, does one have to be white, Western, and European? Does being civilized mean acting like white people? Does being religious mean being Christian? Did the idea of brotherly love originate in the European tradition? Was it nurtured therein? If we reject aspects of our African heritage, let us be very clear about our reasons for doing so. These actions should not be based on our internalization of some abstract concept or mythological structure created by our enemies. Our myths must work for *us.* If we want to *progress,* let us be very specific about what we are progressing toward and why. Let us concretize our goals and not leave them vaguely defined in terms of the rhetoric of Western-European values. If you choose to be a "Christian" you will most certainly have to reject the European conceptualization of what that means (that is, if you want to embrace your African heritage as well). Our ideals cannot be defined by what whites are. They must be defined in terms of African self-determination and a positive African self-image.

But if we are neither to emulate white behavior nor to adopt European conceptions, what theoretical models shall we use? (Are there any others?) *All cultures* are based on and create ideological constructs and mythological systems which provide the symbols which make them work. African metaphysical conceptions and the African world view are among the most profound. We should be about the business of rediscovery and reevaluation—*not* merely on a rhetorical level, but fundamentally and in relation to concrete and practical political goals. More and more, Europeans are becoming convinced of the limitations of their traditional conceptions. Sadly, we Africans, so anxious to imitate a dying culture, rush to give up breast-feeding because we want to be "civilized" and "sophisticated," while many European physicians are trying to convince mothers that breast-feeding is best for their babies and themselves. What irony! Must we wait until the white tells us that our culture has value in order to appreciate it?

The traditional African view of the universe is as a spiritual whole in which all beings are organically interrelated and interdependent. The cosmos is sacred and cannot be objectified. Nature is spirit, not to be exploited, and there is no obsession with changing the natural order for the sake of change. Use without replenishment is sacrilegious because all beings exist in reciprocal relationship to one another; we cannot take

TABLE 4.1   European Mythology (implications for the African heritage)

Ideology	The Cultural Other		Behavior Dictated		White Self-image
Christianism	heathen: nonreligious, immoral	M U S T	saved		Christian Saviour
Idea of Progress	backward	B E	developed, advanced	B Y	"modern" man
Evolutionism	primitive		civilized		"civilized" man

without giving, and that is what the ritual of sacrifice symbolizes. Only profane or ordinary time is viewed in terms of simplistic lineal relationships, but within sacred, cyclical time the past, present, and future become one. This conception allows us to draw strength from our origins (and ancestors) in order to build, survive, and create. The mode of harmony (rather than control) which prevails does not preclude the ability to struggle when necessary. Spirit is primary, yet manifested in material being. This world view allows for depth of spirituality, belief, and humanism.

If we are to be developed, let *us* do the developing. And first we must decide what *development* means. Change and technology are necessary, but the *extent* to which they are needed must be determined in relation to the happiness, well-being, and self-determination of our people, not merely by imitation of the West. We cannot allow an obsessive, technical order to destroy our humanity—our Africanness.

CONCLUSION

Insofar as we continue to accept the rationalization of our victimization by assimilating European chauvinistic ideology and mythology, we have ourselves to blame. The rhetoric and semantics of "science" help to disguise the thrust of that mythology and make it more difficult to reject. It is critical, therefore, that we in Africana Studies devote more of our energies to revealing the mythological, ideological, and value aspects of concepts like the idea of progress, so that they can no longer be used to enslave African people psychologically and ideologically.

Science and technology as used in Europe an culture have been defined in the context of an "acquisitive, conquering, materialistic" (Skolimowski, 1974: 82) ideology, of which the ideology of white supremacy is a crucial ingredient. Neither science nor technology need be used in this way, so that the rejection of the European idea of progress by no means implies some sort of mystical escapism or retreat from the real problems and contingencies of nation-building which we face.

Progression toward an abstract goal should not become an ideology. It should *not* be an end in itself. *Progress* must be defined in terms of other objectives and goals which are more meaningful in a human and African context. Any commitment to reject European value and to repudiate European historical behavior must necessarily reject the ideology of progress, for its triumph has succeeded in dehumanizing the culture in which it was born. It inherently implies the inferiority of black being, and justifies Pan-African exploitation. When black people uncritically adopt the ideology of progress as it is here defined, they can become overseers on the plantation, tools of the white person used to control other Africans. Let us clearly understand that the syntax of the European idea of progress is the language of white nationalism and Western chauvinism. We have been successfully victimized in part because we have internalized alien concepts which define us negatively. If Black Studies is to be a viable and worthy endeavor, it must be devoted to the task of demystification. Unfortunately this is a long and difficult endeavor, and we have only scratched the surface.

NOTES

1. For further theoretical and critical discussions of the progress ideology, see Juenger (1956), Aron (1968), Mumford (1963: especially 182-185), Diamond (1974: Introduction), Roszak (1973, an especially fine work, and 1972: Introduction), and Skolimowski (1974).

2. See Kofi Awoonor's (1975: ch. 2) sensitive discussion of the effects of missionary Christianism on the African self-image.

3. See Cook (1970: 155) for support of this point. Her entire article is relevant to the issues being raised here.

REFERENCES

ARISTIDES (1958) "To Rome," p. 40 in *History of Western Civilization: Selected Readings, Supplement.* Chicago: University of Chicago Press.

ARON, R. (1968) *Progress and Disillusion.* New York: Praeger.

AWOONOR, K. (1975) *The Breast of the Earth.* Garden City, NY: Doubleday.

BASSETT, E. O. (1927-1928) "Plato's theory of social progress." *International Journal of Ethics* 28: 476.

BEARD, C. A. (1955) "Introduction," p. xxviii in J. B. Bury, *The Idea of Progress.* New York: Dover.

BLYDEN, E. W. (1967) *Christianity, Islam, and the Negro Race.* Edinburgh: Edinburgh University Press.

BOAK, A.E.R. (1955) *A History of Rome to 565 A.D.* New York: Macmillan.

BURY, J. B. (1955) *The Idea of Progress.* New York: Dover.

COOK, A. (1970) "Black pride? some contradictions," in T. Cade (ed.) *The Black Woman.* New York: Signet.

DIAMOND, S. (1974) *In Search of the Primitive: A Critique of Civilization.* New Brunswick: Transaction Books.

JUENGER, F. (1956) *The Failure of Technology.* Chicago: Henry Regnery.

KOVEL, J. (1971) *White Racism: A Psychohistory.* New York: Vintage.

LEE, D. (1959) *Freedom and Culture.* Englewood Cliffs, NJ: Prentice-Hall.

LOVEJOY, A. O. (1966) *The Great Chain of Being.* Cambridge, MA: Harvard University Press.

LOVEJOY, A. O. and BOAS, G. (1965) *Primitivism and Related Ideas in Antiquity.* New York: Octagon.

MacLEOD, W. (1968) *The Importance of Race in Civilization.* Los Angeles: Noontide Press.

MBITI, J. S. (1970) *African Religions and Philosophies.* Garden City, NY: Doubleday.

MONTAGU, A. (1968) "The fallacy of the primitive," pp. 3-4 in *The Concept of the Primitive.* New York: Free Press.

MUMFORD, L. (1963) *Technics and Civilization.* New York: Harcourt Brace Jovanovich.

NEIBUHR, R. (1946) *The Nature and Destiny of Man, Volume I.* New York: Scribner.

POPPER, K. (1966) *The Open Society and Its Enemies, Volume I.* Princeton: Princeton University Press.

ROSZAK, T. [ed.] (1972) *Sources.* New York: Harper & Row.

ROSZAK, T. (1973) *Where the Wasteland Ends.* Garden City, NY: Doubleday.

SKOLIMOWSKI, H. (1974) "The scientific world view and the illusions of progress." *Social Research* 41, 1: 56-57.

WHITE, L., Jr. (1969) "The historical roots of our ecological crisis," in P. Shepard and D. McKinley (eds.) *The Subversive Science.* Boston: Houghton Mifflin.

WILLIAMS, R. (1970) *American Society: A Sociological Interpretation.* New York: Knopf.

5

THE CULTURAL DIMENSIONS
OF "THE RIGHT TO COMMUNICATE"

Njoku E. Awa

CONTEXT

The right to communicate, viewed as a separate and overarching human right, was first formulated by Jean d'Arcy in an article for the *EBU Review*, in 1969 (see Harms et al., 1977). In the past dozen years, the idea has received enthusiastic support from many scholars, while provoking harsh rejoinders from those who view it as yet another attempt to consolidate Western influence over the communication systems of low-technology nations. A topic of considerable interest within the development work of UNESCO, the right to communicate is still evolving—some would claim, in no particularly useful direction. The extravagant claims that greeted its first appearance have, however, been tempered by a more considered, growing body of theory.

Investigation has focused more recently on the cultural and intercultural implications of adopting, in an international forum such as UNESCO, a statutory right to communicate. Low-technology nations have been vigilant in resisting attempts to reintroduce the discredited idea of "the free flow of information," which would in their view have legitimized domination of world communication by a few high-technology nations. Some Third World leaders, however, have cautiously welcomed the right to communicate.

For the right to communicate concentrates attention on the participatory and the interactive aspects of communication. The frantic activity that it has provoked in academic circles speaks eloquently of a reconsideration of the entire process of communication. The limitations of Lasswell's generally accepted model, "Who says what? In which channel? To whom? With what effect?" have been revealed more starkly during this debate. The right to communicate is, then, important both in the theory of communication and in the international political forum. In both cases, it appears to offer opportunities to sidestep authoritarian assumptions about communication, and to replace them with more democratic, participatory concepts.

UNESCO has convened a number of conferences to examine this emerging right. An earlier version of this chapter was presented as an invited contribution at the Meeting of Experts on the International Issues of the Right to Communicate, held in Manila, the Philippines, 15-19 October 1979 (see UNESCO, 1979).

INTRODUCTION

The debate about the "right to communicate" has for a decade concerned scholars and national representatives. The definition of the right is still evolving. It is in some ways still amorphous, not yet susceptible to rigorous analysis; and it is subject to widely differing interpretations. One reason for this is that the concept refers to different rights at different levels of social complexity.

The ability to communicate is a defining ability of human beings, and the development of communication is indistinguishable from the development of the individual. From the time it is born, the infant demonstrates this proposition by crying, which is itself a basic form of communication. As the infant develops, it learns to interact with its environment by means of speech communication, in ways that are expressive of its human attribute as a symbol manipulator and of its desire to integrate itself with its milieu.[1] Indeed, the inability to communicate is viewed in all societies as sufficient cause for medical intervention, whether to counter physiological trauma such as paralytic aphasia, or psychological trauma such as the catatonic forms of schizophrenia.

While self-expression, the *ability* to communicate, is a fundamental human attribute, however, statements of the *right* to communicate have developed differently in different national cultures. The right is usually constrained by social and legal obligations. Other citizens are protected from certain forms of expression, such as slander and libel, and citizens' property interests are maintained as copyrighted material. Societies have also attempted to limit communication through censorship and control of the means of communication, especially control of the mass media. Furthermore, the correlative rights of privacy, not to communicate and not to be communicated with, have provoked radically different legal instruments.

The fact that each society has developed its own version of the right to communicate, and has framed in it a different legal and political context, has resulted in conflict at the transnational level. In some Western cultures, the variants of free self-expression, such as freedom of the press, have achieved legal status. These variants have occasionally been invoked as morally desirable truths in international communication, assumed to operate even in those countries where their legality has not been acknowledged. Most recently, this process can be observed in the international debate over "the free flow of information." Demands for such freedoms have triggered fierce counterdemands for regulatory policies in international communication, especially in low-technology nations where cultural and political imperatives have tended to dictate a modified interpretation and implementation of self-expression. For Western journalists, meanwhile, the denial or curtailment of their freedom to write or publish on any topic in any nation is an infringement of a natural and automatic right, constitutionally guaranteed in their countries of origin.

Each position is defensible. Western journalists have fought hard and long to establish and protect the right to free self-expression, and their determination to preserve it in other countries is compounded by the relative weakness of the low-technology nations that attempt to control the gathering and dissemination of "news." Many nations, meanwhile, are fighting to stem the rapid erosion of their cultures by the content of and the general messages purveyed by the international media, which are largely controlled by alien entrepreneurs with aims inconsistent with those of the governments of low-technology nations.

At the heart of the conflict that has developed over the last several years about the right to communicate, is the meaning assigned to the word *communication*. The question at issue is whether the process is to be seen as one-way or two-way. The *Oxford Dictionary of English Etymology* indicates that *communication* and *community* are drawn from the same Latin root: the *communis*, which means the shared, the common, and the public. In this initial sense, communication must be viewed as a transactional process, involving a mutuality or equivalence of influence between sender and receiver. To think of it as a one-way process is to deny the significance of one of the key elements of transactional communication, feedback, and subsequent use of feedback. Yet the discipline of communication has tended until recently to concentrate on the one-way flow of information; the authoritarian aspects of Lasswell's famous formulation of what happens in communication are obvious. As communication science has moved toward a more consistent examination of the transactional model, international policy has shifted from a consideration of the right to a "free flow of information" to a "right to communicate."

The right to communicate is, however, limited by the control of the means of communication at the transnational level. This chapter analyzes the unidirectional flow of international communications within the ideological framework of the right to communicate. It pays special attention to the concept as it is defined by its major proponents—generally, experts from the Western, high-technology nations—and to the cultural impact of its exercise on the nations of the Third World.

TOWARD A DEFINITION OF THE RIGHT TO COMMUNICATE

Terms such as *free flow* and *right to communicate* pose problems when one attempts to define them. Often their actual operation stems from the dialectic generated by contradictory definitions or understandings. They result in smokescreens that conceal and mystify the activities of raw power.

The right to communicate may prove an exception to this general tendency. The concept of free self-expression, which is related, was not originally designed to operate extraterritorially. According to Frank Thayer (1962: 82),

> liberty may be defined as the right to use one's faculties; this liberty includes the natural right to self-expression, which we may take as the *liberty to communicate* (speak and write). The right of self-expression, originally what may be termed a natural right, has become a civil right, or a *right guaranteed or established by* government [my emphasis].

The right to communicate and its attendant rights, however, have been greeted skeptically and occasionally with open derision by the nations of the Third World. Journalists' claims to a right to communicate demonstrate an attempt to globalize a predilection shaped by historical event in one particular culture; and that predeliction is indissolubly linked with that culture's dominant stance in world politics. Were the right to communicate based on historical struggle in Gabon or Nicaragua, it is extremely unlikely that it would ever have achieved international attention.

Where does the current formulation of the right to communicate come from? The First Amendment to the Constitution of the United States

states, inter alia, that "Congress shall make no law . . . abridging the freedom of speech of the press; or the right . . . to petition the government for a redress of grievances." Despite the national character and weight of this provision, each of the various states of the Union has taken steps to reaffirm the inviolable, sacred nature of freedom of speech. For example, Article 1, Section 5, of the Constitution of Alaska states that "every person may freely speak, write, and publish on all subjects, being responsible for the abuse of that right." West Virginia spells it out even more clearly: "No laws abridging the freedom of speech, or of the press, shall be passed; but the Legislature may be suitable penalties, restrain the publication or sale of obscene books, papers, or pictures, and provide for the punishment of libel, and defamation of character, and for the recovery, in civil actions by the aggrieved party, of suitable damages for such libel, or defamation" (see Thayer, 1962: 92, 101).

These are both the constitutional roots and the basis of current definitions of the right to communicate. The adoption of the First Amendment and its affirmation and reiteration in state constitutions were the culmination of a long, bitter struggle by the American people against censorship by British colonial governors and authorities, and their attempts to stifle, free thought and free expression.[2]

Such legal instruments may be a legitimate source of pride at the national level, as they enshrine the successes of independence. The assumption, however, that the concept of the right to communicate is a *general* right, rather than a culturally shaped and culturally specific concept, is invalid. Current problems in transnational communications stem largely from the manipulation of the concept in countries that did not participate in the struggle leading to its enactment as a legal instrument.

Thus, the right to communicate has entered the arena of international debate bearing two main problems. The first is that the right appears value-free, but is in fact value-laden. Without an acknowledgment of this, the use of the concept is seen to result, by those that do not share the implied values it bears, in another Western mystification of power and its effects.

The second is that, in its national context, the right carries correlation responsibilities. Thus, both the First Amendment and derivative state laws on the right to communicate stipulate that the violation of this right is punishable in judicial proceedings. Third World nations, however, do not have, nor can they exercise, jurisdiction over those violations that transcend national boundaries. For example, former Prime Minister Indira Gandhi charged the media of the powerful countries with denigrating the leaders of the Third World and falsifying their images (see Sussman, 1979: 130). Yet she had no recourse, and no way of countering the effects of public ridicule and contempt, within the context of the right to communicate. This is a vivid illustration of the problems created in the international arena by rights that were originally formulated in purely national terms, but which are now being promulgated shorn of their correlative duties.

This is a major source of frustration with the Western media for leaders of the Third World. Scurrilous remarks made about such leaders may be printed and aired in the media of the West as if they were truths, and nothing but the truth. The leaders thus denigrated have no recourse in the West—there is no "equal time" provision. Because of the transnational effects of Western media, meanwhile, these comments, whether true or false, can rouse intense feelings of distrust for a leader in his or her own country, reduce his or her credibility, and cripple the foundation of his or her political support.

The impotence of the leaders of low-technology countries, faced with the overwhelming dissemination capabilities of the Western media, and its consequent effects, should not be underestimated in the international arena. Mutual misunderstanding of peoples and leaders is rife, and the reasons, while plain enough, are difficult to counter.

MEDIA OWNERSHIP AND THE ONE-WAY FLOW OF INTERNATIONAL COMMUNICATIONS[3]

The right to communicate concentrates attention on the participatory aspects of communication, that is, on the interchange of messages transacted on the basis of mutual ability and mutual respect. Yet at the international level, the infrastructure of communications contradicts the central proposition of participation. The print media provide an excellent illustration of this.

Consider how Europeans and Americans become informed about events in other countries, especially in low-technology countries. Very few Western newspapers could even think of supporting their own staff correspondents in Senegal or Costa Rica. Fewer still have the kind of bilateral arrangements with Third World newspapers that, for example, sees the London *Sunday Times* and the Boston *Globe* regularly exchanging reporters for six-month assignments.

Information about the Third World comes almost exclusively through the wire services. The five major services are summarized in Table 5.1. This examination is concerned with the practical impact, rather than the lofty ideals and intentions, of the wire services. Information about Africa has been disseminated in the West almost exclusively through Reuters and

TABLE 5.1   The Wire Services

Name	Nationality	Ownership	Location
Reuters	British	Private ownership	London
TASS	Russian	State	Moscow
AP	American	Newspaper members	New York
UPI	American	Private for profit	New York
AFP	French	State/private	Paris

AFP; Latin America has become known mainly through AP and UPI; Asia, through AP, UPI, and Reuters; and socialist countries through TASS. The hegemony of Reuters and AFP in Africa has only begun to be challenged by the other three wire services. This is true to an even lesser extent of the dominant market position of AP and UPI in Latin America. Americans' knowledge of events in Africa presently depends very largely on the fledgling organizations of "stringers" being developed there by AP and UPI. But this recent quantitative improvement in the coverage of African events for American newspaper and magazine readers does not necessarily imply any qualitative gain.

All wire services perform three main functions: They gather information; they process it; and they disseminate it. Each of these functions implies a technological capability and an editorial process; both have important effects on information that can alter the economic and sociopolitical well-being of the nations of the Third World.

The wire services transmit "news" in both directions. For low-technology countries, there is little chance of establishing and operation expensive and technologically sophisticated information systems to match those of the West. They are largely excluded from editorial control of the international flow of news. Such countries are therefore dependent on the wire services both for their received images of the outside world, and for the images that the rest of the world receives of them. The communication system is sealed: The wire services are owned by and operated from technologically sophisticated countries, and Third World countries, neither owning nor directly participating in the technology, are forced to remain passive consumers of "Westernized information."

The system offers the countries of the Third World no opportunity for feedback and participation. Furthermore, news of Western countries takes on an inordinate significance in the print media of the low-technology nations. As Wilbur Schramm (1967: 65) says,

> we must conclude that the flow of news among nations is thin, that
> it is unbalanced, with heavy coverage of a few highly developed

countries and light coverage of many less developed ones, and that, in some cases at least, it tends to ignore important events and to distort the reality it presents.

This conclusion, though more than a dozen years old, is still valid. More recently, Herbert Schiller (1974), summarizing research of the 1960s and the early 1970s, notes one of the political results of this kind of imbalance. Countries of the Third World have increasingly refused to countenance the free flow of information as a desirable international goal, having had firsthand experience of the occidental political dominion that the phrase masks.

It is in this context that international debate has switched to a "right to communicate." Yet, that right can have no more meaning than free flow until low-technology nations are enabled to participate in the international exchange of news *as equals.*

THE CULTURAL DIMENSIONS OF
THE RIGHT TO COMMUNICATE

The Western nations' position in the gathering and transmission of hard news parallels the export of "software" to Third World nations. With reference to films and movies, Guback (1977: 35) notes that

in the early 1970s the nations of the world were annually producing about 3500 feature motion pictures. Although only about 5 percent were of American origin, American films occupied about 50 percent of theatrical screen time in what is called the Free World. . . . Pictures made in the United States dominate their own home market, and are shown in 100 other countries.

Guback also notes that 50 percent of the "theatrical revenues" of American film companies come from other countries.

African countries are more dependent upon, and thus more susceptible to the influence of, Western film industries because, of all the regions of the Third World, Africa has the least potential for the development of an indigenous film production capability. The impact of this on African cultures has been portrayed eloquently by Buback (1977: 35): a large number of "African nations are faced with films produced by an alliance of European colonialism and American imperialism—films whose values will probably submerge, if not pulverize, distinct African cultures and heritages, or menace them with extermination by a global commercial culture flowing from a few centers in the industrialized world."

In the case of television programming, Tapio Varis' (1974) survey of program imports throughout the world shows dramtically the heavy reliance of many Third World countries on imported materials. Among the most notable figures in his study are these:

- Guatemala imports 84 percent of its TV programs.
- Malaysia imports 71 percent.
- Singapore imports 78 percent.
- Zambia imports 64 percent.

By contrast, Varis found that sample commercial stations in the United States import 1 percent of all programming. Thus, Zambians, Guatemalans, and other Third World viewers are constantly exposed to popular culture of the West, in reruns of *I Love Lucy, Bonanza,* and *Police Woman.* Not only does the content of this programming help to encourage consumerism, but the programs concerned are specifically designed to accommodate direct advertising.

It is often claimed that mass communication systems reflect and support cultural values, rather than direct them. But it is evident that when the cultural values subsumed in the message are not those of the recipients, and apparently neutral and innocuous message may have important political and social effects. Television entertainments do not simply entertain; they teach the cultural and material values that they assume, values which may well be contrary to the social or the political aims of the government of the importing country. Viewed in this light, the significance of both the wire services and the multinational media corporations becomes more readily apparent: Their effects exemplify the imperialistic tendencies of dominant values when applied to and forced on other, and in this case technologically weaker, nations.

Tapio Varis (1974) has examined the cultural content of programming in Western television in the study already mentioned. He notes that exporting countries generally aim to enhance their own image; that program exchange is commercially based rather than in any real sense "international"; that Third World nations import a disproportionate amount of software; and, furthermore, that foreign materials dominate prime-time viewing in weaker nations.

RESPONSIBILITY OF ELITES OF THE THIRD WORLD

Varis also notes that viewing is frequently limited to the rich and the elites of the countries of the Third World. It is this group that bears the greatest weight of responsibility in the development efforts of their nations.

Those charged with countering the effects of the industrialized world's domination of the international media are the only members of their low-technology societies who can afford television sets, and thus form the audience most regularly saturated by the cultural messages that accompany imported programming. This exemplary case of *quis custodiet ipsos custodes* is, however undesirable, hardly surprising.

Individuals defined as the elite of low-technology countries are those who have already been chosen by the criteria of the "developers" as the best representatives of their changing societies. Generally educated in schools patterned along Western lines, and later immersed in the foreign culture for several years, in universities and colleges abroad, they become administrators and political leaders with a view of desirable change largely shaped by Sandhurst or Harvard, Stanford or the Sorbonne. Heavily dependent on foreign and international funds, their development projects are, moreover, likely to be evaluated not according to local conditions but by more general, Western-based standards.

To this elite, then, the superficiality of Western cultural imports is unexceptionable, as the elite's members have been exposed to that culture previously, and unimportant, in comparison with the task of national development. Rather than antagonize Western importers, national elites frequently allow Western popular culture unlimited access to local markets. While understandable, this can have serious effects, especially when the priorities of national development conflict with imported cultural values: when, for example, calls for national cooperation founder on the reefs of an imported individualism, or budget allocations are forced to ignore the rising tides of consumerism.

Multinational media companies thus share the blame for cultural erosion with the national elites of low-technology countries. The impact on music, education, clothing, dance, and the material cultures of the nations of the Third World has been, and continues to be, enormous. Internationally, the trend has been to adopt the Western model of the nation-state, partly, at least, because it is the only model available. As low-technology countries are largely dependent on Westernized information, alternative models of development based on self-reliance, partial decentralization of the nation-state, and the *selective* adoption of alien technology and ideas, receive little publicity. The very different examples of Tanzania and China, though in some respects worthy of emulation, have been ignored by Western media because they are perceived to pose threats to the (Western) status quo in the independent paths that they are creating toward national development.

National elites that espouse the ideals of the right to communicate are obliged, for reasons of national self-interest, to insist on the accompanying rights not to communicate and not to be communicated with. Yet the weight of the international media is such that when these rights come into conflict, as they inevitably do, attention is only paid to the breaches of the right to communicate. The underreporting of alternatives continues to bedevil the development attempts of Third World nations.

There is in these conflicts a mission of immense importance for UNESCO and similar transnational organizations. The right to communicate, as I have noted earlier, is constrained on the national level by legal statute; and when that right clashes with other rights, such as the right to privacy, a court system exists to adjudicate problems. Such a system already exists for the international allocation of wavelengths for broadcasting purposes. The debate about the right to communicate, and its concentration on the *mutuality* of effect in communication, has indicated clearly the need for international adjudication of conflicts of interest in other, more substantive areas. International arbitration should be made available where the media's editorial privileges, and cultural and overt message content, are felt to be obtrusive and even destructive by nations unable to participate directly and as equals in the ownership and operation of international communications.

Should such a system of cooperative, international regulation of messages and their implications grow from the current debate on the right to communicate, then the right may be viewed as a banner of hope in the currently troubled international political situation; for to move toward international agreement on this front is to raise realistic hopes of an eventual world community that espouses differences as fruitful and is based on respect and tolerance.

CONCLUSIONS

1. Communication between nations is presently unidirectional, flowing from high-technology nations to low-technology ones. Furthermore, the information received in the low-technology nations is largely "treated" to aid the goals of the sender. In this sense, international communication is anything but international. This makes the right to communicate at the international level the prerogative of those with the technology for gathering, processing, and disseminating information. Edgar Dale (1967) writes, "We communicate best when we participate as equals." For true communication between nations, mutual respect is more important than a mutual perception of equality.

2. As originally conceived by the architects of the U.S. Constitution, the concept of the right to communicate was an internal matter, and was not intended to have extraterritorial effect—for example, on the media policies of the Third World. To achieve international recognition of such a right, the United States and other Western countries must submit to a reappraisal of the right as it affects the countries of the rest of the world. The reactions of Third World countries to attempts to implement this "right" in their territories have ranged from verbal aggression to physical harrassment to the explusion of Western journalists. Clearly, some of these reactions are not defensible, but they manifest the disgust of Third World leaders and peoples with journalists who attempt to exercise rights in a context where they are shorn of their attendant responsibilities.

3. The right to communicate, as presently exercised by powerful nations, means, on the one hand, giving home audiences what they want to view, read, and hear about low-technology nations—namely, disaster stories based on audiences' stereotypes of these nations—and, on the other hand, selling all kinds of software to Third World nations, including publications with prurient and unsuitable content. This has resulted in a cultural disorientation of vast segments of the youth of Third World countries, and in places the virtual extermination of values that for centuries have served as rallying forces for cultural integration. Taken together, these problems indicate that low-technology nations are paying a price out of proportion to the benefits they have derived and can expect to derive from the preservation and internationalization of an instrument that stems from outside their territories.

Since little can be gained from the defensive interpretations of the right to communicate of both the media-rich and the media-deficient countries of the world, reexamination of the right must necessarily involve bilateral actions, with UNESCO acting as arbitrator.

4. Finally, some ideas at a more immediate and practical level should be considered for adoption by UNESCO. The news agencies of member nations should be helped to develop press rooms in major centers, telex transmission services, news tickers for domestic news agencies, and so on. More extensive assistance should be provided to assist national news agencies in pooling resources in order to form regional agencies of a size and economic strength comparable to the major wire services. These moves might help to offset the current competitive advantages of the "Big Five," and widen the avenues of international communication.

UNESCO should also consider the establishment of regional training and production consortiums in the countries of the Third World for the development of materials (the software) that are sensitive to and rooted in local cultural values.

NOTES

1. For a detailed discussion of the functions of speech communication, see Dance and Larson (1972).
2. For a study of this struggle in one state, see Duriway (1906).
3. This section is based on Awa (forthcoming).

REFERENCES

AWA, N. E. (forthcoming) "World order and world community: a communications perspective," in R. Beggs (ed.) *Beyond Tomorrow: Ways Towards World Community.*
DALE, E. (1967) *Can You Give the Public What It Wants?* New York: Cowles Education Corporation.
DANCE, F.E.X. and C. E. LARSON (1972) *Speech Communication: Concepts and Behavior.* New York: Holt, Rinehart & Winston.
d'ARCY, J. (n.d.) "The right to communicate," Discussion paper 36, International Commission for the Study of Communication Problems, UNESCO.
DURIWAY, C. A. (1906) *The Development of Freedom of the Press in Massachusetts.* New York: Longman.
GUBACK, T. H. (1977) "The international film industry," in G. Gerbner (ed.) *Mass Media Policies in Changing Cultures.* New York: John Wiley.
HARMS, L. S. and J. RICHSTAD [eds.] (1977) *Evolving Perspectives on the Right To Communicate.* Honolulu: East-West Communication Institute.
HARMS, L. S., J. RICHSTAD, and K. A. KIE [eds.] (1977) *Right to Communicate: Collected Papers.* Honolulu: University of Hawaii at Manoa, Social Sciences and Linguistics Institute.
SCHILLER, H. I. (1974) "Freedom from the 'free-flow.' " *Journal of Communication* 24 (Winter): 110-117.
SCHRAMM, W. (1967) *Mass Media and National Development.* Stanford, CA: Stanford University Press.
SUSSMAN, L. R. (1979) "Mass news media and the Third World challenge," in D. B. Fascell (ed.) *International News: Freedom Under Attack.* Beverly Hills, CA: Sage Publications.
THAYER, R. (1962) *Legal Control of the Press.* New York: Foundation.
UNESCO (1979) *Meeting of Experts on the Right to Communicate, Draft Report.* Manila: Ministry of Public Information, Republic of the Philippines.
VARIS, T. (1974) "Global traffic in television." *Journal of Communication* 24 (Winter): 102-109.

PART II
PSYCHOLOGICAL EXPLORATIONS

To disentangle the knots of the relationship between psychology and its users requires patient inquiry into the nature of how we are affected by the discipline. It is necessary for us to give special attention to the development of the complexities surrounding the knotted threads of our study. Our authors take a holistic view of the problems of society as they relate to psychology. Consequently, they are interested in discussing how we form our opinions, make our decisions, and maintain our psychological health. They do so in subversive ways, questioning the pathological models and setting up more culturally specific norms for evaluation.

An important task of the new social scientists is to challenge the traditional views which have seen a multiethnic society through mono-ethnic eyes. Baldwin's article is penetrating in its discussion of the psychology of oppression. He demonstrates what happens to victims and the resultant behavior of victimage. Pennington demonstrates how guilt provocation has been used as an instrument of change in African-American communication. Spratlen deals with new research on marketing for the African-American consumer. Burgest studies the relationship of Blacks to Blacks. All of these studies seek to weave new fabrics in social science. They are innovative and challenging.

6

THE PSYCHOLOGY OF OPPRESSION

Joseph A. Baldwin

AFRICAN AND EUROPEAN COSMOLOGY

A number of black social analysts have convincingly maintained that fundamental lines of distinction can be drawn between the historical characters of the approaches of African and European world to the maintenance of their survival. On the one hand, it is argued that the European approach exemplifies a "humanity *versus* nature," or antagonistic, style of operation, while the African approach, on the other hand, exemplifies a "humanity-nature unity" or "oneness with nature" style of operation (Akbar, 1973, 1976; Botchway, 1971; Carruthers, 1972, 1977; X(Clark), 1972; X(Clark) et al., 1975; Dixon, 1976; Erny, 1973; Mbiti, 1970; Nobles, 1972, 1976a, 1976b, 1976c). Consistent with these notions, it has been shown that the Africans seek to achieve a comprehensive understanding of nature to facilitate a more complementary coexistence with it. On the contrary, it has also been shown that the European style of operation represents a relentless propensity toward achieving ultimate mastery and control over the universe. The European thrust, according to this view, is operationally manifested within the contexts of oppression, supression, repression, and the unnatural alteration or reordering of all objects having existence outside of the European world (Carruthers, 1972). Needless to say, the historical and contemporary data supporting these conceptions are strikingly consistent (X[Clark], 1972; X[Clark] et al., 1975; Dixon, 1976; Nobles, 1972, 1976b, 1976c; Williams, 1971; Wright, 1974; Asante, 1980).

For our present purposes, the important point in all of this is that this analysis clearly suggests a fundamental distinction between the philosophical styles and/or ethos of the African and European worlds in terms of their approaches to survival. In other words, this distinction suggests that different psychosocial patterns of operation tend to characterize the respective cultures of the African and European worlds. From such an analysis, then, it becomes readily apparent that Africans and Europeans *define* the world, reality, and so forth, quite differently. It is therefore assumed that their respective intellectual, emotional, and physical approaches to the world naturally follow these lines of distinction. Some of the authorities cited earlier (e.g., Carruthers, 1972; Nobles, 1976c; Williams, 1971; Wright, 1974) have even suggested that this type of perspective may very well explain how the African and European worlds arrived at their present sociopolitical positions—that is, how the European world came to achieve its oppressive control and domination over the African world. Again, however, the point of note here is that this perspective clearly indicates that the African ethos and the European ethos constitute quite distinct and racially specific cosmologies. Hence, the two cultures' respective *definitional orientations* to their survival, to the world, no doubt correspond to their distinctly different racial-cultural realities. Africans and Europeans define the world from distinctly different perspectives and in distinctly different terms, and their racially specific definitions tend to characterize their distinctly different social realities.

THE NATURE OF DEFINITIONAL SYSTEMS

The significance of definitions, of course, resides in the fact that they determine or dictate the *meanings* that we attach to events that we experience in our day-to-day existence. That is, our definitions determine whether we consider these events as important or unimportant, as good or bad, as true and factual or as untrue and fictitious; or whether we in fact attend to them at all. Thus, we make assumptions about the events that we experience based on our "predisposed" beliefs about and attitudes toward the nature of things. These beliefs and attitudes comprise a set of ideas which define for us the nature and/or meaning of events that we experience. They constitute our definitions and ultimately determine how we experience (perceive and respond to) the various phenomena that characterize the ongoing process of everyday existence (Amini, 1972; Kungufu, 1976).

Our definitions therefore dictate how we, as individuals, will perceive and respond to our "experiential reality." In fact, our definitions actually determine what our reality is or will be by *predetermining* how we will ultimately experience it. We acquire our definitions primarily through our sociocultural indoctrination, that is, from our socialization into our culture or social system. Consequently, one's definitions actually constitute a collective or shared phenomenon. In other words, definitions comprise an institutionalized process, because they represent the modal or normative beliefs and attitudes (i.e., the conceptual frame of reference) of a social system. These shared definitions thus represent a *definitional system,* and it, in turn, represents the ideological or philosophical base of the social system to which it is indigenous. The definitional system forms the basis for the cohesiveness and continuity of the social system because it derives from and subsequently reinforces the social reality (collective experience) in which the social system itself is anchored. It gives the social system its identity, its distinctness. A definitional system, in the broadest sense, is therefore essentially the same as the "world view" of a social system—its peculiar philosophical orientation to the world.

In short, I am proposing here that definitions ultimately determine: (1) the meanings or values that people attach to their experiences (including their experience of themselves), and (2) how they subsequently react to them. In its most basic function, a definitional system *prelimits the conceptual range of the meanings that members of a social system will ultimately attribute to their experiences.* This occurs primarily because definitions create in the individual a type of "perceptual set" or cognitive-emotional predisposition to experience events in a characteristic (thus predictable) manner. Being an institutionalized process means that the influence of a definitional system is so thoroughly pervasive and subtle that one hardly attends to it in any overt or highly conscious sense. The prescriptions of the definitional system are simply experiences that members of the social system take for granted through their habitual or customary operation in accordance with them. The definitional system then dictates the normative way of thinking, feeling, and acting for those indigenous members of the social system.[1]

RACE AS THE BASIS OF DEFINITIONAL SYSTEMS

A definitional system therefore represents the ideological basis of a culture or social system. Inherent in the definitional system are those beliefs and behaviors which reflect the *survival thrust* of the collection of people it represents, because it evolved from the *cumulative collective experience* or *social reality* of that particular cultural group. The definitional system thus binds the social system's membership together. It gives them their unique (distinguishable) psychosocial identity. However, it is clear that in order for the collection of people to occupy the same space (geographical relatedness) and time (historical relatedness) long enough for their definitions to achieve group relevance and consensus, necessarily requires the existence of some more concrete and fundamental force to bind them together and anchor their collective identity. Given that *race* (i.e., blood relatedness, kinship, or biogenetic commonality) constitutes the most basic and fundamental binding condition underlying human existence, and ultimately transcends all subsequent or secondary bonds of social identity, then it clearly constitutes the initial force binding people to a similar geography and history through which their similar experiences evolve into a distinct definitional system or world view.

Consequently, it is argued there that race constitutes the principal binding condition underlying the evolution of definitional systems. Such systems in their most basic and fundamental nature therefore have a "racial character." That is, they are peculiarly specific to the racial-cultural group with which they are identified. It is further argued that definitional systems reflect the distinct styles of survival maintanence characterizing different racial groups, deriving from their common geographical and historical experiences. Each racial group can therefore be regarded as having its own distinct definitional systems.

In support of this view, a concise and thorough analysis of world history readily reveals the consistent observation that groups from different races operate according to distinctly different definitional orientations (in the sense of lifestyles, social priorities, values, and so on), no matter where they are encountered in space (e.g., varied geographical regions) and time (e.g., different periods in history). By the same token, such an analysis also reveals the consistent observation that groups from the same racial backgrounds operate according to very similar definitional orientations under the same conditions of space and time noted above (see Akbar, 1973, 1976; Dixon, 1976; Nobles, 1972, 1976b, 1976c; Wright, 1974). This view is also substantiated in the fact that history further reveals that wherever in space and whenever in time the African and European worlds have encountered one another, the definitional problem, in terms of conflicting lifestyles, social priorities, and the like, has invariably arisen. It has been utterly impossible, if we subscribe to historical consistency, for different racial groups to truly integrate their respective definitional orientations and coexist harmoniously within the same sociocultural context. This has particularly been the case with European groups relative to non-European (African) groups (Nobles, 1976b, 1976c; Williams, 1971; Wright, 1974). The respective definitional systems, then, must be fundamentally different, racially specific, and, beyond that, incompatible. It is therefore apparent that the survival thrusts of the African and European worlds are distinctly different as well as incompatible (Carruthers, 1972, 1977).

This chapter thus proposes that definitional systems are indeed race-specific phenomena. We can therefore realiably speak in terms of a European definitional system as well as an African definitional system, each being distinctly different from the other in terms of basic survival thrust and fundamental character. Consequently, wherever one encounters different European groups, one will also invariably discover basic similarities between these white groups with respect to their definitional orientations. Obviously, the same observation will hold true relative to different African groups as well. While it is also true that the European world has persistently striven to psychologically devour the African world, one will nevertheless consistently observe basic definitional differences between the vast majority of African people and any European group. Such a principle naturally holds true for black people in this country relative to whites (Dixon, 1976; Nobles, 1972, 1976b). In so-called exceptional cases, one will no doubt find that the seeming discrepancies are only of a superficial— and surely pathological—nature, and are more or less consistent with the degree of psychological and social distance that exist (and have existed over time) between the racially different groups involved. This problem of race-definitional discrepancy brings us to a consideration of racial oppression as a psychological phenomenon.

CONTROLLING THE DEFINITIONAL PROCESS: RACIAL OPPRESSION

Given the thesis of this chapter, it should be obvious that all black people operate within the definitional framework of some racial-cultural system of social reality, whether it actually represents our own "African" cultural system or not. Of course, under normal and natural conditions the system of social reality controlling the definitional parameters within which we operate represents our own racial-cultural system. However, it is clear that normal and natural conditions do not characterize the situation of black people today. This is especially true for those of us who reside in the so-called African diaspora of the West. Historical circumstances, of which we are all aware, have left many of our people (again, especially those in the Western diaspora) in a rather abnormal and unnatural socio-cultural predicament. Needless to say, it is very crucial that we first recognize this *fact* if we are to realistically examine the serious problems that such a situation implies for our survival as African people. The multicultural occurrence of black people throughout the world thus indicates that we frequently reside in a general sociocultural context which is not African in its basic definitional orientation. The definitional system dominating such contexts, then, is alien to the social reality of African people. Consequently, the issue of *who controls definitions* is itself a racial issue, since actual definitional conflict invariably occurs between different racial groups where they inhabit the same social space.

History is replete with evidence which clearly reveals that whenever and wherever Europeans have encountered non-Europeans throughout the world, they have militarily striven to control the social space for themselves. They attempt to gain *psychological control* over the social space by forcing the legitimacy of the European definitional system on the non-European group. This is carried out by their formally institutionalizing only the European system of social reality. Of course, the logic of such a tactic (beyond the basic function of cultural maintenance itself) is that if one militarily contains a group which also has a functional value in one's design, then one does not effect their total elimination, but simply shifts containment to the psychological level by gaining control over their minds.[2] This, then, is where the issue of control over the definitional process becomes a principal weapon in racial oppression. Such a situation represents *psychological warfare* on a racial-cultural scale. Thus, the European group attempts to impose the European definitional orientation on the non-European group by making only the European system of social reality ultimately credible and legitimate. In other words, they in effect attack the credibility and legitimacy of the non-European group's definitional orientation by making their primary survival reinforcements (e.g., social and economic security) directly contingent upon the non-European group, subscribing legitimacy to the European system of social reality, and to only that system. Where Europeans control the general social space, such as in Euro-American society, then it is relatively easy for them to enforce this type of insidious process of psychological oppression.

In recognizing that black people in America live in a social space controlled by Europeans, it becomes clear that the dominant definitional orientation of Euro-American culture is also European in its basic nature—it projects European social reality as the center of the universe (i.e., as the universal definitional framework). Thus, the Euro-American cultural context cannot give credibility and legitimacy to the African system of social reality as well.

Particularly relevant to this problem is Wade Nobles' (1976b) discussion of what he calls the "conceptual incarceration" of black people, in which he observes that the natural consciousness of black people is forced to relate to a reality defined by white consciousness. That is, contemporary black people in the United States live in a psycho-social reality consistent [with] and supportive of white mental functioning. Such a situation is tantamount to black people living in [what for black people must be] white insanity [1976b: 26].

Euro-American culture has therefore attempted to force the legitimacy of the European system of social reality on black people, by superimposing their system on our African system of social reality. This process is carried out by their legitimatizing only European social reality through the tactic of bestowing various forms of social rewards on those of us who overtly adhere to it (in terms of our operational practices), and by punishing those of us who overtly depart from the pattern of operation projected in European social reality. In short, Europeans control the formal process of social reinforcements. Control over this vital process is the key to the power of Euro-American control over (and/or obscuring of) black people's social reality. It allows Euro-American culture to superimpose a consistent stream of Eurocentric definitions and their experiential confirmations on the experiences of black people in this society. Thus, it effectively obscures the credibility and legitimacy of African social reality by imposing punishing consequences on it; that is, by reinforcing the "illegitimacy" of African social reality for black people by making it more or less dysfunctional within the Euro-American cultural context. Figure 6.1 presents a general outline of the ramifications of this type of process.

From this illustration, we can observe that the process of psychological oppression resulting from the imposition of the European definitional system on black people can occur either through direct experience or through the observation of the experiences of others (i.e., vicariously). The important point here, however, is the assumption (as was noted earlier) that black people actually encounter the European definitional system with a *preexisting* definitional orientation that is not European in its basic nature.[3] Consequently, the European definitional system, being incompatible with the natural survival thrust (the African definitional orientation) of black people, ultimately fosters *misperceptions* and *distortions* in those of us who actually succumb to subscribing to its legitimacy relative to what our African social reality really consists of. It creates in black people a type of "altered style of consciousness" (McGee and X[Clark], 1974) relative to our natural, unaltered, style. Thus, by limiting or constraining the conceptual range of the meanings that those of us who are victimized by it will ascribe to our experiential reality, the European definitional system ultimately *misorients* (i.e., incorrectly orients) black people to their African social reality.[4] It influences black people to

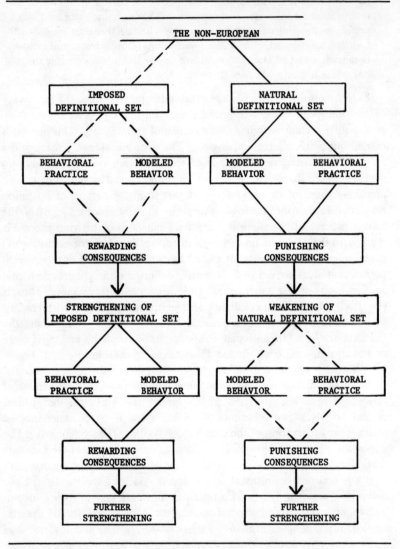

Figure 6.1: The Euro-American Cultural Context

misinterpret or to incorrectly experience their African social reality, particularly in terms of their life-survival condition and social priorities as
African people.

While there no doubt exist countless situations that would serve to
illustrate the various issues that have been raised, space will not permit any

extensive consideration of them here. It is hoped that a few of these illustrations will serve to highlight the nature of this problem. For example, the recent issue concerning the "rights of Jews" (Europeans) to African land suggests an illustrative case. This typeof situation is clearly consistent with the historical tradition of Europeans defining it as their right to take any land they can from its natural inhabitants (as in the Americas, Azania, Zimbabwe, and so on). When this type of imposition is resisted, they expeditiously define some *moral* premise to rationalize and justify their using whatever force is necessary to legitimate their definition of the situation. As in the case of the Jews, the European world has converged to support with whatever force necessary the European definition of this situation. The fact remains, however, that these people are not Africans but Europeans. Such a situation, then, clearly demonstrates how Europeans go about imposing their system of social reality on non-European cultures of the world. It precludes the legitimacy of the African's definition of this situation. This could be demonstrated very easily by having a group of black people define it to be their moral or "divine" right to take control of some land in Europe. In such an instance, we would readily see just how far our "covenant with God" would get us. The truth of the matter, of course, is that Europeans are simply militarily strong enough to enforce their system of social reality, whereas Africans are not necessarily as strong militarily. The outcome of control over the definitional process in this case, then, is to force the African world to eventually accept the legitimacy of the Jews' land claims, because the European world clearly intends to confirm the validity of this distortion of African social reality (by effectively putting down any contradictions to it).

Another relevant illustration of this problem involves the furor, primarily in the white community, over the "moral character" of former President Idi Amin of Uganda. In this particular situation, it is clear that the European community is committed to creating (in the minds of black people) a conception of Brother Amin as the most evil, destructive, and "dangerous" individual that this universe has ever witnessed. Notwithstanding the fact that Europeans, ironically, have the audacity to question the moral character of any non-European, given their own immoral and destructive history, note in particular that this kind of negative stature is being attributed to a "black" person. They even have many so-called black leaders in this country echoing this blatant distortion of African social reality, while the masses of our people in Africa appear to hold Brother Amin in the highest esteem. Of course, history readily reveals that whenever black leadership has operated firmly within the definitional context of African social reality (a la, Marcus Garvey, Malcolm X, and the like),

Europeans have defined them in similar terms. Thus, it is not surprising that many blacks in America relate to former President Amin in the same manner as do whites, given the dominance of the European definitional orientation in the American society.

Similarly, Europeans control over the definitional process can be observed in the commonly occurring situation in which whites are constantly creating what we might regard as "ego-hurdles" for black people. That is, being in control of the general social space comprising Euro-American society, whites are able to manipulate and keep black people off stride psychologically, because they can define the standards through which we achieve economic security and social mobility. In this regard, the Euro-American community is continually defining certain roles and functions as almost *exclusively white,* thereby requiring blacks to *prove* themselves worthy and capable of a particular level of performance (arbitrarily defined) in order to earn or justify their participation in such "esteemed roles." Whether the role involves that of "dog catcher," a coach in a professional sport, membership in some elite group, or various kinds of high-status jobs, it is invariably indicated that such roles and functions are beyond the initial capacity of black people to handle. Thus, we are expected to work at overcoming our initially deficient capacity until it is arbitrarily decided by whites that we have achieved the required level of performance. Our intellectual and emotional energies therefore become wrapped up in achieving the lofty status of being *the first of our race* in such-and-such a role. We erroneously assume that we have finally proven ourselves capable (equal to whites) in whatever capacity. A more accurate analysis, however, indicates that whites are simply deciding arbitrarily that we have now become capable of assuming certain roles and functions; they have the power to impose and enforce these kinds of distortions of our social reality through their control over the definitional process in this society. Clearly, then, it doesn't really matter how capable black people actually are, since we may be either as capable or even more capable than whites from the very start. Again, the crucial point is that Europeans effectively control the definitional process in American society, and therefore can arbitrarily decide if and when black people are ready for certain roles by controlling the social reinforcements associated with such roles.

A final and most crucial illustration of the psychological oppression of black people concerns the American educational process. In this regard, whites have defined the "Euro-American educational process" as the only credible and legitimate means of pursuing knowledge and enlightenment and, just as importantly, for achieving any meaningful degree of social mobility within the American social system. Given that most of us in this society are required to participate in the Euro-American educational process, especially during the highly impressionable period of childhood, this process virtually ensures that black people will be exposed to the distorted and genocidal system of social reality propagated by the European definitional system. Perhaps a good example of the genocidal consequences of this process can be observed in the area of mental health service delivery. In this type of situation, it is frequently observed that black mental health professionals, as a result of their training in the Euro-American educational process, tend to operate totally oblivious to the fact that black mental health represents a phenomenon distinct from white mental health. In their misguided attempts to treat black mental illness, rather than viewing it within the context of African social reality, many (and probably most) of these health professionals superimpose upon black psychological functioning a model of mental health derived from European social reality. Consequently, psychologically healthy blacks are typically misconstrued as being mentally ill, and vice versa, by these misguided black mental health professionals. The Euro-American educational process therefore serves as the principal institution for indoctrinating the European system of social reality in black people.[5] It is also clear that the electronic mass media have become a major institution in this regard as well.

BLACK RESISTANCE TO EUROPEAN SOCIAL REALITY

Needless to say, European definitional imposition on black people has not been a total success. It has "misoriented" black people in varying degrees; that is, from almost total misorientation to very minimal misorientation. In other words, some of us have undoubtedly suffered severe misorientation (generally as our level of education, social position, and so on, increases), while most of us have probably suffered only moderate misorientation, and others very little at all. It depends, by and large, on our individual and social circumstance. For example, in the rural South and possibly in some urban ghettos (which are farther removed from the centers of European culture and media exposure), the effects have probably ranged from moderate to little or none; whereas in the more socially integrated urban-educational areas of the country, the effects have probably ranged from moderate to severe. Thus, while the European definitional system has had some degree of influence on most black people in American society, it is clear that had black people not been to some extent successful in resisting its genocidal influences, we would not be able to observe many of the apparent vestiges of African social reality that are evident in various aspects of the Afro-American lifestyle today (Akbar, 1973, 1976; Baldwin, 1976; X[Clark] et al., 1975; Dixon, 1976; Nobles, 1972, 1974).

It is important to note, however, that black people's resistance to the European system of social reality has not necessarily been of a highly conscious form. That is, it has not generally taken the form of a carefully planned or necessarily intentional collective resistence. It rather seems to represent a *natural reaction* to an alien system of social reality. Such a situation, then, no doubt indicates just how fundamental a force our original (natural) African system of social reality is in defining the conceptual space within which black people operate. Consistent with such an observation, it has been noted that the Afro-American interaction with the African environment was much too intense and extensive to be wiped out by a few generations in an alien culture (Akbar, 1973). Notwithstanding the validity of these types of observations, it is clear, nevertheless, that *conscious, collective resistance* is ultimately required if we are to effectively combat the psychological oppression that Euro-American society imposes on black people.

Of course, it is understood that there exist a variety of instances throughout our history in Western culture which clearly indicate that black people have often consciously resisted European social reality, either in total, or relative to some particular aspect of it. For example, the various slave revolts and attempted revolts, particularly throughout the seventeenth and eighteenth centuries, the so-called black military riots of the nineteenth and early twentieth centuries, the UNIA movement and the rise of the Nation of Islam during the twentieth century, as well as the more recent RNA movement, among several others, all suggest that some degree of conscious collective resistance to European social reality has always characterized some portion of the activities of black people in Euro-American society. By the same token, however, with the possible exception of the so-called urban rioting during the decade of the 1960s, it is not clear that the activities of black people during this most recent period in our history actually represent as much a form of resistance to European social reality as a demand for greater access to it (unconsciously on our part, of course).

There is little doubt that the various wars which have occurred throughout much of the twentieth century and the overall decline of African colonialism during the early and mid-twentieth century, gave some degree of impetus to the movement in Euro-American society toward a pseudo form of social integration for black people during the decade of the 1960s. This means, in effect, that exposure to the genocidal influences of the European definitional system became available to substantially more black people than at any other time in the past. In other words, black people are now even more vulnerable to the forces of cultural assimilation—Europeanization—than ever before in our history in America. This is primarily because the Euro-American educational process, unlike in the past, when it was somewhat mitigated by relatively isolated all-black educational systems, is now directly available to all of us. Naturally, the electronic mass media (as was noted earlier) also form a basic part of the overall educational—indoctrinational—process in Euro-American society.

What all of this means, then, is that black people in America are now more likely to become victims of the European system of social reality than they have been at any other time in the past. This is due primarily to the fact that in the past we were more isolated from the European system, segregated from the social and educational centers of Euro-American culture. Thus, we were able, more or less, to avoid direct exposure to many of the forces of the European definitional process. Presently, however, this is clearly not the case (Baldwin, 1978; Nobles, 1976b; Thornton, 1977). It is therefore incumbent upon black people to maintain a vigilant posture as to the racist and genocidal nature of European social reality, and the subtle and insidious mediums through which it is presented to us. For it constitutes *an ongoing process of psychological genocide* that we must resist and combat if we are to maintain our survival in American society as African people, and ultimately achieve the fullness of psychological and physical liberation from it.

CONCLUSIONS

It is important to note that the issue of psychological control as it relates to black genocidal behavior has come under rather extensive and widespread debate in recent years throughout the black community. Much of this concern has centered around the problem of European control over "the black mind." Despite this growing concern, the black-African world has yet to be presented a meaningful analysis of psychological oppression as an ongoing—constantly operative—process. Thus, our people have had no clear frame of reference from which to ultimately examine the psychological nature of their own oppression. This chapter has attempted to clarify some of the critical aspects of that process. In this regard, a perspective on the etiology and dynamics of definitional systems as they relate to the politics of race and race relations was presented. Essentially, it was proposed that definitional systems are in effect racially peculiar phenomena and, as such, provide the dynamic context within which psychological oppression evolves as primarily a racial issue.

Needless to say, we still do not understand all of the intricate ramifications and implications of the process of psychological oppression of black people in Euro-American society. There is little doubt, however, that this process has substantially mitigated our capacity to effectively combat its genocidal effects. The extent to which this process has effectively thwarted our drive toward psychological and intellectual freedom, and ultimately toward social independence and total liberation from Euro-American society, can only be a matter of conjecture at this point. Nonetheless, it is clear that if we are to effectively combat the genocidal effects of this process, we must surely begin by understanding its nature and the subtle manner in which it operates on us. It is hoped that this discussion has contributed to furthering our understanding of these two critical aspects of this process; for as others have so aptly observed (e.g., Akbar, 1973), we have far too long defined ourselves, our "African" social reality, within the confines of an alien perspective. I cannot overemphasize the fact that the psychological survival of black people in this country and throughout the world largely depends on our understanding that we operate in a social space dominated primarily by a definitional framework which does not and cannot give legitimacy to our African social reality. It projects only European social reality as the center of the universe. Therefore, it totally obscures the natural thrust of African social reality in black people. It represents a European definition of the universe, and thus a European distortion of our African social reality.

NOTES

1. The definitional system derives its functional value in this regard from the cumulative collective experience or social reality of the group of people representing the social system. It represents those beliefs and patterns of behavior that have proven effective in their maintaining the survival of their life-cultural style. These issues will be elaborated on at a later point in the chapter.

2. The principal dynamic involved here, of course, is the maintenance of the survival thrust of the imposing racial-cultural group. In other words, enforcing the legitimacy of their own definitional system (i.e., their system of social reality) is the only way that they will be able to effectively control the social space and maintain the survival of their particular social system.

3. As I noted earlier, it is assumed that under normal and natural conditions (e.g., where each racial group controls the respective social spaces in which their cultures exist), black people operate within the conceptual framework of the African definitional orientation which derives from and thus reinforces African social reality. A couple of recent articles by Dr. Wade Nobles (1976b, 1976c) also attempt to clarify some particular aspects of this general problem.

4. The concept, "misorientation," is used here to depart from the meaning that is associated with the traditional usage of the concept, "disorientation." Whereas disorientation is usually associated with a confused and dysfunctional state of

orientation, misorientation is associated with simply an incorrect and contradictory, yet organized and apparently quite functional, orientation (that is, within the context of European social reality). Thus, a misoriented black person is one who in his own mind is neither necessarily confused about his or her identity, nor dysfunctional in his or her behavior, according to the standards prescribed by Euro-American culture. For the black person operates (thinks, feels, acts) in the manner of a European. Clearly, then, such an individual is certainly not "dosoriented" in the sense of consciously experiencing confusion and its attendant anxiety. The social cues in Euro-American society reinforces acting in such a manner. As a point of fact, however (that is, in view of the fact that he or she is actually an African), the black person is indeed "misoriented" because he or she can achieve at best only a pseudo form of European existence.

5. I discuss the problem of the educational genocide of black people more fully in another discussion (see Baldwin, 1978).

REFERENCES

AKBAR, N. [Luther X (Weems)] (1976) "Rhythmic patterns in African personality," in L. M. King et al. (eds.) *African Philosophy: Assumptions and Paradigms for Research on Black Persons.* Los Angeles: Fanon Center.
——— (1973) "Guidelines for African humanism." Presented at the International Association of Cross-Cultural Psychology, Ibadan, Nigeria.
AMINI, J. M. (1972) *An African Frame of Reference.* Chicago: Institute of Positive Education.
ASANTE, M. K. (1980) *Afrocentricity: The Theory of Social Change.* Buffalo: Amulefi Publishing.
BALDWIN, J. A. (1978) "Education and oppression in the American context." *Journal of Afro-American Issues.*
——— (1976) "Black psychology and Black personality: some issues for consideration." *Black Books Bulletin* 4, 3: 6-11.
BOTCHWAY, F. A. (1971) "Methodological approaches to the cosmological ideas of African people." *Black Lines* 1, 4: 42-46.
CARRUTHERS, J. H. (1977) "Futurity and the Black race in the western hemisphere." *Black Books Bulletin* 5, 1: 40-42.
——— (1972) *Science and Oppression.* Chicago: Center for Inner City Studies, Northeastern Illinois University.
DIXON, V. J. (1976) "World views and research methodology," in L. M. King et al. (eds.) *African Philosophy: Assumptions and Paradigms for Research on Black Persons.* Los Angeles: Fanon Center.
ERNY, P. (1973) *Childhood and Cosmos: The Social Psychology of the Black-African Child.* New Perspectives.
KUNGUFU, J. M. (1976) "Behavior and its value base." *Black Books Bulletin* 4, 3: 40-43.
MBITI, J. S. (1970) *African Religions and Philosophies.* Garden City, NY: Doubleday.
McGEE, D. P. and C. X(CLARK) (1974) "Critical elemeents of Black mental health." *Journal of Black Mental Health Perspectives* (August-September).
NOBLES, W. (1976a) "Extended self: rethinking the so-called Negro self-concept." *Journal of Black Psychology* 2, 2: 15-24.
——— (1976b) "Black people in white insanity: an issue for Black community mental health." *Journal of Afro-American Issues* 4: 21-27.

—·— (1976c) "African science: the consciousness of self," in L. M. King et al. (eds.) *African Philosophy: Assumptions and Paradigms for Research on Black Persons.* Los Angeles: Fanon Center.

——— (1974) "Africanity: its role in Black families." *Black Scholar* 5, 9: 10-17.

——— (1972) "African philosophy: foundations for Black psychology," in R. L. Jones (ed.) *Black Psychology.* New York: Harper & Row.

THORNTON, J. C. (1977) *Behavior Modification: The Road to Genocide.* Chicago: Independent Publishers.

WILLIAMS, C. (1971) *The Destruction of Black Civilization.* Dubuque, IA: Kendall/ Hunt.

WRIGHT, B. E. (1974) "The Psychopathic racial personality." *Black Books Bulletin* 2, 2: 25-31.

X(CLARK), C. (1972) "Black studies or the study of Black people?" in R. L. Jones (ed.) *Black Psychology.* New York: Harper & Row.

—— D. P. McGEE, W. W. NOBLES, and L. X[WEEMS] (1975) "Voodoo or IQ: an introduction to African psychology." *Journal of Black Psychology* 1, 2: 9-29.

7

GUILT-PROVOCATION: A STRATEGY
IN BLACK RHETORIC

Dorthy Pennington

Phenomenologically, the subject of guilt is not a new one to the human condition, especially if one considers the concept of original sin. In relations between groups, guilt often becomes the object of circular dynamics. That is, one group often attributes part of its condition to the existence of another and seeks ways to purge its system of its evil elements.

In relations between whites and blacks in America, guilt, or its implication, has not been a foreign concept. Some whites have traditionally argued that blacks were the servants referred to in the Bible and that blacks had broken covenants when they failed to obey their white masters. Blacks, on the other hand, held whites accountable for their predicament in America and felt that whites had not only violated biblical teachings, but other American principles as well. Thus, in their discursive attempts to persuade America to grant them the rights due them, guilt-provocation has been one of many strategies used by blacks. Compared to other strategies, however, guilt-provocation, if successfully effected, touches the sensibility of conscience and the fundamental emotion of pain on the part of those perceived as culpable; and just as any audience of rhetoric must be capable of mediating the change desired by the speaker, an expected and implied condition is that the audience should also come to share the basic point of view held by the speaker.

Given an objective definition of the types of guilt and the conditions under which it is said to arise, the purpose of this exposition is to show that by examining some of the views and distinctions of the types of guilt found in the literature, one can see that representative black speakers, while using the same concept, employ a basis of application structurally different from the traditional notions provided by theorists on guilt. The implication of this discovery portends difficulty for black speakers whose target audience might hold the traditional purview of guilt; diminishing the incongruous perceptions, then, would be a task incumbent upon black speakers.

The term *guilt,* or its implication in the context of black-white relations, has often been used loosely, and so it is necessary to subject its use or its implication to closer scrutiny.

Basically, guilt is said to result from acts of transgression (a point which will be later addressed). Applying this fact to the concept of original sin, we are led to assume that humans can be indiscriminately guilty because of past convenants broken with God. This is told in the story of Adam and Eve, who symbolically make possible the sharing of guilt. Coping with guilt has become emotion-laden and difficult, and so in order to seek relief or to cancel their guilt, humans have contrived victimage (see Burke, 1965: 285).

In examining the concept of guilt and the appropriateness of its use, we shall, of necessity, look at the various types of guilt and at the conditions under which guilt is believed to arise.

GUILT CONCEPTUALIZED

Jaspers (1947: 31-79) lists and differentiates among four types of guilt: criminal, political, moral, and metaphysical. Though his discussion is somewhat involved and at times elusive, the basic differentiations are these.

Criminal guilt results from crimes which can be proven in an objective sense because they violate unequivocal laws. Jurisdiction for violation rests with the courts. In terms of applying criminal guilt to another group, however, Jaspers indicates that only one individual can be a criminal, not a whole group, and, at the same time, that criminal guilt can be externally imposed; that is, one can have criminal guilt imposed upon him or her by another.

Political guilt results from the arbitrary deeds of statespersons and the arbitrary norms by which the majority of people are governed. Everyone is responsible for the way he or she and others are governed and for the deeds of the state, inasmuch as it is the state under whose order everyone lives. Political guilt can also be externally imposed, and theoretically it can be charged against whole groups, as opposed to only an individual. Jaspers, here, makes an interesting distinction in indicating that although political guilt can be externally imposed, in terms of a collective, in the political sense, *liability* is a more appropriate term than *guilt*. In other words, although the deeds of the state may be committed by a few persons in the name of the state, all citizens are liable in the sense that politically, everyone acts, whether by voting or by failing to vote. Political liability means that no one can dodge, since everyone lives by the order of the state.

Moral guilt results when an individual analyzes himself or herself and realizes that he or she has committed a wrong deed. Because moral guilt is concerned with an individual grappling with his or her own conscience, it cannot be externally imposed, but must come strictly from an inner realization on the part of the individual. Moral guilt exists for those who give room to conscience and repentance. The morally guilty are those capable of penance; that is, those who, when they committed wrong deeds, knew better, who know that they were walking in error, and yet who continue to do so. This has interesting implications for several reasons: (1) We cannot impose moral guilt upon others; its source must be internal, and (2) while in the minds of outsiders, someone may be perceived as morally guilty, unless the person himself or herself gives room for conscience, he or she cannot be considered guilty. At the same time, however, according to Jaspers, although moral guilt burdens only the individual and his or her conscience, there is still a sort of collective morality contained in the ways of life and feeling, from which no individual can altogether escape, thus giving moral guilt political significance, as well. (While the definition of this type of guilt suggests that those who do not give room to conscience and repentance could not be considered guilty, Burke, as will be later discussed, answers by saying that the capacity of humans as symbol users gives rise to conscience or a sense of obligations.)

Metaphysical guilt occurs when humans allow wrongs or crimes to be committed in their presence or with their knowledge, and yet do nothing to prevent them. Because metaphysical guilt assumes that there is a solidarity among humans which makes each coresponsible for every wrong and injustice in the world, there is virtually no escape, since whatever happens to one person has cosmic significance and effect upon all, for the ties which connect us will have been broken. Ideally, as humans, according to this point of view, we should want to live together or not at all, and such cosmic concern should extend indiscriminately to all humans, not to a select few. Jurisdiction for metaphysical guilt, unlike that for other kinds of guilt, rests not with the courts or with other humans, but with God alone; and like moral guilt, metaphysical guilt cannot be externally imposed.

Having made these distinctions among the types of guilt, Jaspers indicates that groups as collectives cannot be guilty; only individuals can be so. This has a direct bearing on our concern, for in the efforts at guilt-provocation on the part of blacks, it is interesting to note whether they indict America as a whole, or if they are more discriminating.

Just as one can make distinctions among types of guilt, one can also distinguish between guilt and related concepts, the terms for which are, according to some, more ppropriate to use in some situations than *guilt*. In its popular sense, *guilt* is more akin to *shame*: "Guilt ... results from a conflict between the ego and the super-ego and develops whenever we violate a taboo set by the super-ego. Shame, on the other hand, stems from tension between the ego and the ego-ideal and occurs whenever a goal presented by the ego-ideal is not reached. 'Guilt anxiety accompanies transgression; shame, failure' " (Halberstam, 1969: 63).

In other words, according to this point of view, not living up to one's ideals results in shame, rather than guilt. Guilt results only when one violates one's professed beliefs or actively trangresses against professed beliefs. Thus, one can only be guilty if one has harbored a certain belief, in the first place. What if one has never held such a belief? Can he or she be accused of transgression? Not according to this point of view. According to Halberstam (1969: 64), "the emotion which best fits the despairing moments of our recent racial history is shame, for it is clear that we have failed to live up to our ideals."

We can now summarize the conceptual frame established for viewing guilt: (1) Guilt results when contracts are broken and when we have violated professed beliefs; (2) criminal guilt can be imposed only upon an individual, not upon a group, as a whole; (3) political guilt can be externally imposed and each person is coresponsible for the deeds of the state by which he or she is governed; (4) moral guilt results when individuals transgress against their consciences and when they allow room for repentance; it cannot be externally imposed; (5) metaphysical guilt cannot be externally imposed, and results when individuals allow crimes or violations to occur to others and yet do nothing to prevent them, thus breaking the cosmic human link; (6) guilt, which results when individuals transgress against professed beliefs, must be distinguished from shame, which results when individuals fail to live up to their ideals; and (7) no group can be collectively guilty.

Thus, if we were to construct an imaginary continuum, we could begin with liability, and then move to responsibility, shame, and guilt, with guilt being the most extreme degree of the continuum.

We can now move toward examining the content of some of the rhetoric of black Americans, determining if efforts at guilt-provocation conform to the conceptual framework presented or whether black rhetoric suggests a different conceptual framework for viewing guilt. In case of the latter, we may assume that blacks have a different or extended concept of guilt, a fact which assumes symbolic significance if blacks are indicting America.

GUILT-PROVOCATION

An obvious basis for beginning, and one difficult to refute, is that of blacks' holding up symbols, doctrines, and principles which are dear to America and showing the contradictions between the symbols and doctrines, on the one hand, and practice, on the other. Given what is known about the function of symbols, this strategy should be successful, for "symbols and myths are an expression of man's unique self-consciousness and his capacity to transcend the immediate concrete situation and to see his life in terms of the possible" (May, 1971: 171). Therefore, people's specific nature as symbol-using animals transcends their nature as sheer animals, and gives rise to a sense of obligations (Burke, 1965); and because symbols play a part in self-consciousness and awareness, if humans appear unaffected by them, it is perhaps because they (humans) resist and thus do not want to face the truth about themselves:

> Resistance [is] an understandable part of every man's bitter struggle against the impossibly heavy and painful burden of responsibility in learning the truth about himself and of enduring the revolutionary impact on his self-image and identity. . . . Resistance is an acting-out of the conviction, 'I cannot bear to admit it is I, so I will not see it [May, 1971: 175]!

Assuming that resistance is not an immutable characteristic, blacks have appealed to the effect which symbols and doctrines should have upon the self-consciousness and awareness of America. What better symbolic doctrines to hold before America than Christianity, democracy, the Constitution, or Independence Day? In examining the rhetoric of black Americans, we find that blacks have been able to strategically and clearly identify ways in which Americans are being hypocritical in trangressing against professed beliefs.

Few black speakers better point out the contradictions between and hypocrisies surrounding doctrines and practice than does Frederick Douglass, a point made more emphatic by his strategic use of the posses-

sive pronoun "your," instead of "our" in an address delivered during the
time of slavery:

> What to the American slave is *your* 4th of July? I answer: a day that
> reveals to him, more than all other days in the year, the gross
> injustice and cruelty to which he is a constant victim. To him, your
> celebration is a sham; your boasted liberty, an unholy license; your
> national greatness, swelling vanity; your sounds of rejoicing are
> empty and heartless; your denunciation of tyrants, brass fronted
> impudence; your shouts of liberty and equality, hollow mockery;
> your prayers and hymns, your sermons and thanksgivings, with all of
> your religious parade and solemnity, are, to Him, mere bombast,
> fraud, deception, impiety, and hypocrisy—a thin veil to cover up
> crimes which would disgrace a nation of savages. There is not a
> nation on the earth guilty of practices more shocking and bloody
> than are the people of the United States at this very hour. . . . This
> Fourth of July is *yours*, not mine [Douglass, 1972: 114, 117].

We can note several interesting facts about Douglass's assertion: He uses
the term *guilty*, and according to the conceptual frame established earlier,
it is an appropriate one, since Douglass shows that the nation professes a
belief in "liberty" and "equality," but violates that belief in practice when
it comes to the needs and rights of blacks. Douglass explicitly reminds
Americans of their professed beliefs and of the fact that they are in
violation of them:

> You declare before the world, and are understood by the world to
> declare, that you 'hold these truths to be self-evident, that all men are
> created equal; and are endowed by their Creator with certain unalien-
> able rights; and that among these are, life, liberty, and the pursuit of
> happiness'; and yet, you hold securely, in a bondage which, according
> to your own Thomas Jefferson, 'is worse than ages of that which your
> fathers rose in rebellion to oppose,' a seventh part of the inhabitants of
> your country [Douglass, 1972: 126].

We find that in the mind of Douglass, America is guilty in the criminal,
political, moral, and metaphysical sense.

On the criminal level, there are the "crimes which would disgrace a
nation of savages" (Douglass, 1972), especially referring to the atrocities
of the slave trade in which one could see "human flesh jobbers, armed
with pistol, whip, and bowie knife, driving a company of a hundred men,
women, and children from the Potomac to the slave market at New
Orleans" (Douglass, 1972: 118). Clearly, the slave trade violated the
professed American belief in liberty and justice for all.

Although, theoretically, criminal guilt can only apply to individuals,
Douglass recognizes the systematization and institutionalization of slavery

being perpetuated by persons as a collective, interdependently, as opposed to its being perpetuated by individuals acting alone. This, perhaps, is a critical distinction which also suggests political and metaphysical guilt, for while all may not be guilty as a collective, persons are guilty (or certainly liable) to the extent that they identify with the deeds of the institutions or the state (political guilt), and to the extent that while not all are active participants, they, through silence and indifference, do nothing to prevent such acts (metaphysical guilt). Thus, in singling out the church as being one of the pinnacles of hypocrisy, Douglass expresses this sentiment exactly:

> The American church is guilty, when viewed in connection with what it is doing to uphold slavery; but it is superlatively guilty when viewed in its connection with its ability to abolish slavery.

> The sin of which it is guilty is one of omission as well as of commission [Douglass, 1972: 123].

Thus, the belief that silence gives consent is a real one for Douglass, and those who failed to prevent the enslavement of blacks were, in a metaphysical sense, as guilty as the "fleshmongers."

Of the church, however, Douglass makes a distinction which does not seem apparent in his broader implications regarding the national collective. He refers to the "fractional exceptions" (Douglass, 1972: 122), and wants it distinctly understood that he means the "great mass of the religious organizations of our land. There are exceptions" (Douglass, 1972). Among the exceptions, he lists such persons as Henry Ward Beecher, Samuel J. May, and the Reverend R. R. Raymond, and he sees these men as having incumbent upon them the "duty to inspire our ranks with high religious faith and zeal, and to cheer us on in the great mission of the slave's redemption from his chains" (Douglass, 1972: 124).

Like Douglass, Garnet (1972: 83) points to the "gross inconsistency of a people holding slaves, who had, themselves, ferried o'er the wave for freedom's sake." In language less sparing and more colorful than Douglass's, Garnet lambasts those who profess to be Christians and yet maintain the system of slavery, thus leaving Christianity "weeping at the cross" (Garnet, 1972); and though the system of slavery was being sustained, "Jehovah frowned upon the nefarious institution, and thunderbolts, red with vengeance, struggled to leap forth to blast the guilty wrenches who maintained it ... He who brings his fellow down so low as to make him content with a condition of slavery commits the highest crime against God and man," according to Garnet (1972: 83-84). Like Douglass, in addition to appropriately using the term *guilty* to refer to the results of America's trangression against its professed beliefs, Garnet (1972: 83) also imposes guilt from the outside, and for him, the church is guilty in the meta-physical sense because it "stood silently by."

King (1972: 972), like Douglass and Garnet, cites specific symbolic American documents which, theoretically, have assured rights to all Americans, but which have been denied to blacks, thus pointing to broken promises:

When the architects of our republic wrote the magnificent words of the Constitution and the Declaration of Independence, they were signing a promissory note to which every American was to fall heir. This note was a promise that all men would be guaranteed the unalienable rights of life, liberty, and the pursuit of happiness.

It is obvious today that America has defaulted on this promissory note insofar as her citizens of color are concerned. Instead of honoring this sacred obligation, America has given the Negro people a bad check.

It is significant to note that this promise is considered as a "sacred obligation," as if to imply that through promises a covenant had, indeed, been made, and America was, therefore, obliged to fulfill her promises.

In these speakers, we find not only a suggestion of moral and meta-physical guilt, but also a response to the theoretical assertion that neither moral nor metaphysical guilt can be externally imposed. Although in moral guilt, individuals have to grapple with the plaguing of their own consciences on an internal level, and although guilt cannot be imposed from the outside, this assertion does not preclude the possibility of having one's conscience *awakened* or *roused* from the outside. As Douglass (1972: 117) says, "the feeling of the nation must be quickened; the conscience of the nation must be roused."

It is possible, therefore, to make a distinction between rousing one's conscience and externally imposing guilt in a moral sense, although, as indicated, Douglass and Garnet clearly engage in the external imposition of guilt in the moral and the metaphysical senses in very direct styles, while the approach of King, in this case, is more indirect. Nevertheless, the postulates of Jaspers regarding the inability of guilt to be externally imposed on these levels are opposed by these speakers.

In terms of moral guilt, the need to rouse the national conscience becomes particularly significant if the conscience is definitely believed to be asleep. Similar to Douglass, King (1958: 178) holds such a perception in his advocacy of the need for blacks to use nonviolence as a means of serving as the "moral force to awaken the slumbering national con-science." Clearly, then, the question is not one of whether America has a conscience, but rather the belief that its conscience is slumbering and needs awakening or stirring.

In King we see that because the national conscience had not been roused, America had failed to perceive the oneness of mankind and the fat that whatever affected blacks also affected whites. White Americans are blind to the fact that as long as blacks suffer, they, too, suffer, an implication of metaphysical guilt:

All humanity is involved in a single process, and all men are brothers. To the degree that I harm my brother, no matter what he is doing to me, to that extent, I am harming myself. For example, white men often refuse federal aid to education in order to avoid giving the Negro his rights; but because all men are brothers, they cannot deny Negro children without harming their own. They end, all efforts to the contrary, by hurting themselves. Why is this? Because men are brothers. If you harm me, you harm yourself [King, 1958: 85].

Again, King alludes elsewhere to the metaphysical guilt which the slumbering consciences of many white Americans have prevented their seeing. Fortunately, however, there are some whites who are aware of the common plight, as King (1972: 973) asserts: "The marvelous new militancy which has engulfed the Negro community must not lead us to a distrust of all white people, for many of our white brothers, as evidenced by their presence here today [during the March on Washington], have come to realize that their freedom is inextricably bound to our freedom."

Several relevant questions now suggested themselves: (1) whether American believed itself to have entered a contract or to have made a convenant with all of its people, and (2) whether it believed itself to have trangressed against its professed principles. The issue, therefore, was not only that of America's guilt, but of her awareness of it. With most black speakers, the sentiment seemed to be a belief in America's recognition of the fact that she had made a covenant with her citizens and that she had trangressed against her professed principles. Only her slumbering conscience and the type of resistance mentioned earlier in our discussion of guilt, caused her to default on the promises made. America, therefore, needed to be persuaded of her guilt.

How, then, was the process of persuasion to be carried out?

Verbal attempts at guilt-provocation, such as those just discussed, occupied many years of black rhetoric, and the rationale behind their use is summarized by Davis (1972: 79):

We must, by every means in our power, strive to persuade the white people to act with more confidence in their own principles of liberty—to make laws just and equal for all people.

But while the color of the skin is made the criterion of the law, it is our right, our duty and, I hope I may say, our fixed determination to make known our wrongs to the world and to our oppressors; to

cease not day nor night to 'tell in burning words, our tale of woe,'
and pour a flood of living light on the minds and consciences of the
oppressor, till we change their thoughts, feelings, and actions toward
us as men and citizens of this land.

Notice the emphasis on persuading by "telling in burning words." After
the apparent inability of verbal persuasion, alone, to bring about the
desired results, the perception arose of the need for a higher form of
persuasion.

As a response to this need, King sees nonviolence as "the ultimate form
of persuasion. It is the method which seeks to implement the just law by
appealing to the conscience of the great decent majority who through
blindness, fear, pride, or irrationality have allowed their consciences to
sleep"; and he reiterates, "our ultimate aim is to persuade" (1958: 177).

Nonviolent direct action, as a form of agitation, takes the attempts at
guilt-provocation from the exclusive realm of the verbal to that of the
nonverbal, in which masses of people with their bodies united become the
message; their bodies, therefore, are the media which become the message.
The guilt of their oppressors is made to stand out in bold relief when, in
the face of violence, the nonviolent demonstrators refuse to fight back.
King (1958) hastens to point out that blacks are particularly suited for the
task of using nonviolence to persuade, not so much because they are in a
minority (in the sense that any major attempts at violence would be
suicidal), but rather because of the apparently unique "spiritual power" of
the black American, which comes from "love, understanding, good will."
Thus, by being the moral force to awaken the national conscience, the
black American "may be God's appeal to this age—an age drifting rapidly
to its doom." Forman (1971: 539) shares the view of King in calling
blacks "the most humane people within the U.S."

From this point of view, therefore, if America continues to default on
her promissory notes, it would be incumbent upon blacks to assume the
moral leadership and to once again show America the right way. And by
blacks' turning the other cheek and doing good for evil, according to King
(1958: 177) the guilt of the white American will be provoked and he will
be "glutted with his own barbarity" and "forced to stand before the world
and his God splattered with the blood of his brother." The theme of the
fortitudinous humaneness and morality of black Americans, then, taken to
its logical extent, portrays black Americans as the rightful moral leaders
and persuaders of America.

Since blacks are thought by these speakers to be more suited for
humane, moral leadership, one of the proposed aids to assist blacks in
establishing themselves in leadership positions and to assuage the "guilt"
of white America is that of finance. Thus, the request for reparations on

the part of black speakers who address the issue of guilt should come as little surprise.

Forman responds to the exigence brought on by this logical pattern of reasoning by asking for specific reparations for blacks in the amount of $500,000,000. His reasoning, as stated in "The Black Manifesto" (1971: 537-545) can be summarized as follows: (1) The United States is guilty of oppressing blacks and of denying them their equal rights; (2) not only should blacks receive wealth because they have been the most oppressed, but because they are more righteous, and it is their responsibility, as the righteous, to lead the nation and to restore it to humaneness; blacks would, therefore, be saving the country, as well as themselves; (3) to those who would ask, "What rights have blacks to lead?" he answers, "As much right as Christians had to go to Africa and capture the lives and tranquility of blacks there"; and (4) because blacks have been victims and have helped to build America, reparations are due them.

While not presented in a public address, one of the most comprehensive plans for reparations, employing a similar line of reasoning to that of Forman, is a "Freedom Budget" for all Americans (particularly the poor and underprivileged) spearheaded by the A. Philip Randolph Institute. This plan proposes ways of budgeting and distributing the national resources in order to achieve "freedom from want." Recognizing the need for an "aroused conscience of the American people," this "Freedom Budget" would "combine economic progress with moral purpose" (see A. Philip Randolph Institute, 1966: 1, 75).

These requests for reparations, therefore, grow out of a clearly established belief in the guilt of white America regarding blacks and out of the belief that blacks are, by nature, best prepared to exert moral leadership.

And because of the moral perpetuity of blacks which would awaken the consciences of whites to their guilt and to the consequent need for retribution, we may ask, from the point of view of black speakers, whether there are clearly defined responsibilities incumbent upon black Americans, themselves?

THE QUESTION OF BLACK GUILT
OR RESPONSIBILITY

While, by and large, guilt-provocation is used as a strategy of black speakers toward white America, black Americans have not been allowed to escape unscathed. They have not been absolved of their guilt for any complicity on their part with a system perceived as evil, although they are the victims rather than the perpetrators.

Historically, we see Garnet (1972: 84-89) prodding blacks into a consciousness of their responsibility to free themselves by any means necessary. From his point of view, although blacks felt a responsibility to their slave masters, they had an obligation to God which reigned supreme over their obligations to any slave owner, and it was the will of God that they should be free.

Malcolm X and King echo the same theme. While the colorful language of Malcolm X bears a striking resemblance to that of Garnet when he (Malcolm) reminds blacks of their need to actively resist any wrongs heaped upon them, King speaks in a milder tone. Malcolm (1965: 33-34) says:

> If you don't take this kind of stand, your little children will grow up and look at you and think "shame." If you don't take an uncom-promising stand—I don't mean go out and get violent; but at the same time you should never be nonviolent unless you run into some nonviolence. . . . And that's the way every Negro should get. Any time you know you're within the law, within your legal rights, within you moral rights, in accord with justice, then die for what you believe in.

And according to King (1958: 41, 173), blacks have an obligation to actively resist participating in an evil system while at the same time awakening the conscience of America:

> Often the oppressor goes along unaware of the evil involved in his oppression so long as the oppressed accepts it. So in order to be true to one's conscience and true to God, a righteous man has no alternative but to refuse to cooperate with an evil system.

> To accept passively an unjust system is to cooperate with that system; thereby the oppressed become as evil as the oppressor. Noncooperation with evil is as much a moral obligation as is cooper-ation with good. . . . To accept injustice or segregation passively is to say to the oppressor that his actions are morally right. It is a way of allowing his conscience to fall asleep. At this moment the oppressed fails to be his brother's keeper.

While there may be some question about whether guilt or only respon-sibility is being alluded to by these speakers (since the term *guilty* is never used), the assertion by King that is submitting to an evil system, the oppressed "become as evil as the oppressor" would seem to suggest guilt. And while King only makes a suggestion, Garnet (1972: 84) leaves little doubt about the possibility of black guilt, for to him it was "sinful in the extreme" for blacks to make voluntary submission to slavery.

While guilt of blacks is shown as a distinct possibility, it is, in this case, a reactionary type of guilt in which blacks would be cooperating or failing to cooperate with a system of evil already established. Nevertheless, the guilt alluded to is that of the moral and of the metaphysical types, wherein blacks would have to grapple with their own consciences and wherein they are cosmically responsible for being their brothers' keepers, respectively.

GUILT-PROVOCATION IN PERSPECTIVE

By and large, black speakers can be seen as attempting to provoke guilt in white Americans and in black Americans, as well, through both the direct external imposition of guilt, and, indirectly, by attempting to awaken the slumbering consciences of white Americans. References are made to criminal guilt in terms of groups of people, although, theoretically, only an individual can be criminally guilty. Guilt-provocation on the political level is used to a lesser degree by the speakers studied, though it is apparent; and true to the postulates of Jaspers, it is shown to be externally imposed.

Of the types of guilt mentioned, political guilt enjoys the distinction of being the one from which blacks deviated least in their guilt-provocation attempts. For although neither moral nor metaphysical guilt can be externally imposed, there are clear attempts by black speakers to externally impose both types, even if done indirectly by attempting to awaken the slumbering conscience of America. The point of significance is that black speakers are making a judgment about America based upon some criteria. And in the cases where the term "*guilty* is used by black speakers, their meaning is clear. This tendency violates the postulates of Jaspers and suggests that from the point of view of some black speakers, at least, judgments of guilt can be externally imposed upon others.

In the majority of cases, guilt, rather than shame, responsibility, or liability, is appropriately applied, in the sense that black speakers show a clear inconsistency with and transgression against professed beliefs on the part of white Americans. Though we see in King references being made to shame, rather than to guilt, shame is always closely associated with or placed within the context of guilt to the extent that the meanings of the two terms seem interchangeable. At least, distinctions between them are not readily apparent in King.

To gain perspective, we can show whether guilt-provocation as a strategy is used exclusively by a speaker or whether it is closely allied (almost inextricably, at times), with another strategy which is at least worthy of mention.

Moral guilt assumes that one has a conscience (though the conscience may need rousing). King is typical of a black speaker who designs a

two-pronged strategy through which, along with the provocation of moral
and metaphysical guilt, he also advocates withdrawal of blacks from the
system until its ills are remedied. Thus, while this withdrawal shows some
degree of responsibility as being incumbent upon blacks, it simultaneously
wreaks economic suffering for the businesses from which the patronage is
withdrawn. The economic effects of such a strategy seem to go beyond the
realm of moral suasion/guilt-provocation, alone.

While the provocation of moral guilt is based upon the assumption that
the c 'er has a conscience, such as in the case of the black speakers who
attempt it, not all black speakers share this assumption. For example,
Malcolm X (1965: 40) states his disbelief in America's possessing a
conscience: "And that whole thing about appealing to the moral conscience of America—America's conscience is bankrupt. She lost all conscience a long time ago. Uncle Sam has no conscience. They don't know
what morals are."

Black speakers who hold this point of view are less likely to rely upon
guilt-provocation as a strategy, particularly the provocation of moral guilt.
They are likely to resort, rather, to perceiving the relations between white
and black Americans as involving a power play in which white America is
not moved so much by conscience as by such things as economic and
political threats. Thus, on a continuum ranging from "conscience" to
"lack of conscience," with the notion of "slumbering conscience" in the
middle, guilt-provocation could be placed on the end under "conscience,"
while the more power-oriented strategies could be placed at the opposite
end, under "lack of conscience."

conscience	slumbering conscience	lack of conscience
(guilt-provocation)		(economic, political power)

REFERENCES

A. Philip Randolph Institute (1966) A "Freedom Budget" For All Americans. New
    York: Author.
BURKE, K. (1965) Permanence and Change, An Anatomy of Purpose. Indianapolis:
    Bobbs-Merrill.
DAVIS, S. H. (1972) "We must assert our rightful claims and plead our own cause,"
    in P. S. Foner (ed.) The Voice of Black America. New York: Simon & Schuster.
DOUGLASS, F. (1972) "The meaning of July fourth for the Negro," pp. 114-117 in
    P. S. Foner (ed.) The Voice of Black America. New York: Simon & Schuster.

FORMAN, J. (1971) "To the white churches and the Jewish synagogues in the United States of America and all other racist institutions, Black Manifesto," pp. 537-545 in J. L. Golden and R. D. Rieke (eds.) *The Rhetoric of Black America.* Columbus, OH: Charles E. Merrill.

GARNET, H. H. (1972) "An address to the slaves of the United States." pp. 83-89 in P. S. Foner (ed.) *The Voice of Black America.* New York: Simon & Schuster.

HALBERSTAM, M. (1969) "Are you guilty of murdering Martin Luther King?" *New York Times Magazine* (June 9): 63.

JASPERS, K. (1947) *The Question of German Guilt.* New York: Dial Press.

KING, M. L., Jr. (1972) "I have a Dream," pp. 972-974 in P. S. Foner (ed.) *The Voice of Black America.* New York: Simon & Schuster.

——— (1958) *Stride Toward Freedom.* New York: Ballantine.

MALCOLM X (1965) "The ballot or the bullet," pp. 33-34 in G. Breitman (ed.) *Malcolm X Speaks.* New York: Grove.

MAY, ROLLO (1971) "Guilt and awareness," pp. 171-175 in R. W. Smith (ed.) *Guilt: Man and Society.* Garden City, NY: Doubleday.

8

RACIAL PERSPECTIVES IN ECONOMICS

Thaddeus H. Spratlen

One of the major intellectual developments in economics during the 1960s and 1970s was the increased recognition of racial issues and perspectives in relation to resource use, ownership, and control. A new journal (*The Review of Black Political Economy*) was started in 1970 with almost exclusive coverage of race-related problems and issues in the discipline. Since 1969, participation by Black economists in the annual meetings and proceedings of the American Economic Association has increased markedly. A professional organization of black economists (National Economic Association) has focused attention on the presence and substance of alternative perspectives in the discipline. As referenced here, numerous articles and books have appeared on topics related to race and economics. Nevertheless, conventional theory and analysis in economics largely ignore the substance of the contributions and challenges made by alternative interpretations of the meaning and relevance of the black economic experience.

This chapter interprets the main characteristics of racial perspectives in economics and marketing, especially as they challenge or alter traditional ways of thinking about and responding to racial issues in the world of economics. Ideology, theoretical content, and institutional relevance of the alternative thinking are noted in an attempt to highlight the contributions and challenges made by emerging racial perspectives in economic thought.

MEANING AND IMPORTANCE OF
RACIAL PERSPECTIVES

Introducing racial perspectives in a discipline involves the explicit recognition that race, color, and ethnicity are factors in determining the opportunities, choices, or outcomes of actions available to individuals. For economics this occurred most formally in the work of Gary Becker (1957). Although the differential economic status between blacks and whites has long been recognized and documented, the matter did not have formal status as an issue in theory and analysis prior to the 1950s. A generation later, the prevailing view in conventional economics and among white economists generally is that race as a social and cultural concept does not represent a fundamentally unique theoretical problem. Neither does it appear to deserve independent theoretical status. It is more commonly regarded as a subset of some other category of problems: poverty, education, social stratification and the maintenance of social boundaries, traditional privileges, or the like. The traditional conceptual frameworks of economic analysis have been racially or ethnically neutral. If race/ethnicity explained anything about economic relationships, it was for the sociologist, social critic, or some other analyst to discern.

Aspects of the meaning and importance of racial perspectives can be further illustrated by the concepts and relationships outlined in Table 8.1 (Exhibit 1). With reference to the nature of economic relations, in the classic descriptions of the marketplace, individuals are expected to make their choices so as to gain the greatest satisfaction from the use of available resources. Merit, efficiency, and reason establish the norms for choice selection. Such expectations are for all times and places. Yet, the very nature of racial discrimination is such that personalized choices are made. Becker (1957: 13-17) suggests a "taste for discrimination" as the underlying rationale. Particular groups of individuals are singled out for treatment which contradicts the conventional assumptions regarding marketplace behavior.

Structure in racially neutral, conventional analysis defines basic rules regarding expectations, explanations, and observations pertaining to resource-use behavior. As to expectations, the tools of conventional analysis focus on mechanisms and institutions for the creation and control of individual and social opportunities (Smith, 1974: 320). Conventional explanations and observations are developed primarily for the elucidation of problems, not their elimination (Smith, 1974: 321). Racial perspectives require that the structure of economic analysis reflect explicitly the motivational and behavioral conditions which cause discrimination, as well as the consequences of discrimination that can be observed in the economy and society. The boundaries of the discipline become indeterminate, since historical, moral and other cultural forces are just as much matters of economics as the statistical, technological, and computerized manipulations of data on market transactions. Such an interpretation is obviously subject to dispute. As noted by Sowell (1971: 3), moralistic evaluations of economic problems fall outside the boundaries of economic analysis. The interpretation presented here recognizes that the structure of economic analysis with racial perspectives is more interdisciplinary than conventional analysis. One reason for this is that it permits a more comprehensive assessment of the causes and effects of cumulative inequities experienced along racial lines in the economy.

In process terms, conventional economic analysis focuses on the presumed aims and requirements for making choices for the alternative uses of resources. The choice process involves the mobility and substitutability of resources as well as people. Yet, immobility and nonsubstitutability are the realities of market processes when racial discrimination is practiced. Unless racial perspectives are introduced or incorporated into economic analysis, there are gross omissions of the well-established practices, customs, and laws that define opportunities and results in terms of race (Vowels, 1971: 6). A point made earlier regarding the ahistorical character of economic analysis with racial perspectives, should be recalled. Other ethnic groups in the United States (meaning particularly whites) have advanced into the higher-income sectors over a period of two or three generations (Sowell, 1975). By contrast, "blacks have been at the bottom of the economic ladder as long as data and descriptions have existed" (Fusfeld, 1970: 62). Hence, it is through the development of racial perspectives that economic analysis can be effectively reoriented to address the realities and concerns of a system in which race is, in fact, an important determinant of economic outcomes and relationships.

The ideological content of conventional analysis is fundamentally supportive of the existing economic order. It defines who gains, who loses, and how much, with respect to the presumed conditions of access to information, resources, and opportunity, in general. It assumes away the major contradictions which an analysis from a racial perspective would consider essential. From a racial perspective, the question is asked: How (are, can, should) choices for alternative uses of resources (be) made, given that racial factors greatly influence opportunities and outcomes in the marketplace? Thus, incorporating racial perspectives into economic analysis should lead to challenges of the existing economic order as well as to analytic prescriptions for system reform in order to improve the accuracy and applications of economic knowledge.

The last two categories of criteria for comparing the dimensions of economic analysis in terms of racial perspectives—methods, focus, and scope of the analysis—can be more thoroughly discussed in relation to the theoretical content of the analysis. The following section concerns this aspect of the topic.

THEORETICAL CONTENT OF RACIAL PERSPECTIVES

Racial perspectives broaden the concerns and scope of the discipline. They are described here principally in terms of the various dimensions which are emphasized. The scope and focus of analysis represents one heading under which basic theoretical content is discussed. The other identifies methods and approaches of analysis.

FOCUS AND SCOPE OF THE ANALYSIS

Racial and interdisciplinary aspects are the two main areas of emphasis to be discussed.

Racial Emphasis. The specialized research and analysis of the economics of discrimination offer several ways of explaining racial discrimination, especially in labor or job markets. Besides the "taste-preference" basis identified earlier in the work of Becker (1957), others fall into the broad categories of market failure, monopoly, and other institutional constraints (Stiglitz, 1973: 289). Underlying reasons may include lack of information, control of entry by unions in apprentice programs, government credentials, and certification practices which perpetuate racial discrimination as well as other hiring and placement practices. The analysis is sufficiently technical that little of it has filtered into the general discussion of economic problems and issues. Yet, some have strong empirical support (Smith, 1974).

The taste-preference idea is probably most widely generalizable. This is especially true regarding the widespread practice of racial discrimination in housing markets. Less well known are practices which have similar results in insurance, home mortgage lending, and capital resource markets for minority business firms. The adverse effects of such practices are of sufficient magnitude that the resource allocation process is distorted: Blacks pay relatively more for housing than similarly situated whites; upward mobility of blacks tends to be more limited and, hence, both credentials and experience may bring a smaller return to blacks than to whites, and so forth. Conventional analysis should reflect such relationships.

TABLE 8.1   Exhibit 1: Selected Fundamental Premises of Economics
With and Without Racial Perspectives

Without a Racial Perspective (conventional analysis)	Criteria	With a Racial Perspective (political and institutional analysis)
Universal and impersonal	Nature of economic relations	Personalized and particularistic
Interactive, independent, and interdependent units with determinant boundaries and patterns of interaction	Structure	Interactive, independent, and interdependent units with indeterminant boundaries and patterns of interaction
Motivated by the pursuit of self-interest, individualism, and materialistic priorities	Economic processes	Motivated by maintenance of status and privilege based on racial restrictions and exploitation
Conservative and status-quo-oriented	Ideology	Change-oriented; challenge and reform of existing inequities
Objective or positive, with an emphasis on observed behavior and measurable data	Methods of analysis	Subjective or normative; acceptance of explicit value judgments and qualitative as well as quantitative types of analysis
Technical precision is emphasized more than institutional relevance; descriptive explanations and techniques stressed	Focus and scope of the analysis	Institutional relevance is emphasized; prescriptive or policy formulations stressed

Interdisciplinary Emphasis. In order to be properly conceptualized and interpreted, the complex set of forces that create and sustain racial discrimination requires a comprehensive framework of analysis. The narrower confines of conventional economics are not sufficient for a thorough and realistic analysis. An economic interpretation of discrimination is strengthened by an understanding of concepts from other social sciences. Social stratification, alienation, social disorganization, and other processes that affect the acquisition and use of resources in relation to discrimination suggest that important insights can be gained from incorporating racial perspectives into the analysis.

A general framework of analysis can be linked to the tradition of social and political economics. This is in contrast to the narrower technical focus of conventional economic analysis. Power, privilege, and social class are examples of factors that influence economic opportunities. Conventional analysis is largely silent on such dimensions of economic and social life.

METHODS AND APPROACHES

The manner or techniques by which concepts and relationships are analyzed can also be extended when racial perspectives are introduced. The dimensions discussed here include those which are: (1) quantitative and empirical; (2) qualitative and ideological; and (3) institutional, bicultural, and ecological.

Quantitative and Empirical Dimensions. In their quantitative and empirical dimensions, racial perspectives require the use of techniques for measuring racial disparity or black-white differentials with respect to income, wealth, or other expressions of resource access, ownership, and control. The purpose of such measures is to quantify the pervasive and persistent disparity, inequality, and related disadvantages between blacks and whites in the economy and society (Alexis, 1978; Anderson and Wallace, 1975; Flax, 1971; Freeman, 1973; Stiglitz, 1973; and Swinton, 1975). However, it should be noted that important aspects of some relationships get omitted, even in the extensions of conventional economic analysis. There may be exclusions from some of the data—the averages of income from the black middle class who experience the greatest economic advancement may obscure the continued stagnation of the underclass laborers in the urban core; or the unemployment figures may not count the discouraged black worker who is no longer seeking work and is by definition not in the labor force. But the more serious limitations occur with respect to the limiting assumptions needed to apply most of the statistical models in conventional analysis—e.g., information, substitutability, and mobility.

Qualitative and Ideological Dimensions. Analysts who wish to explain economic relationships involving racial perspectives often turn to qualitative and ideological factors. Conflict between various groups, common interests and attitudes, and sources of political control are examples. A representative framework for analysis is the colonial analogue (Tabb, 1970; and Harris, 1972). The inner-city enclaves or ghettos where most blacks live are viewed as at least quasi-colonies and less-developed small countries. As Tabb (1970: 21) suggests, "the black ghetto is best viewed from the perspective of development economics. In its relations with the dominant white society, the black ghetto stands as a unit apart, an internal colony exploited in a systematic fashion. There are limits to such a parallel, but it is helpful as an organizational construct. Through it, current policy alternatives may be viewed in a more meaningful perspective than heretofore." He goes on to identify the parallel elements in the analogy: low per-capita income and high birthrates; lack of skills, capital, and managerial know-how; one principal source of export income (e.g., labor services employed in businesses, government agencies and other organizations outside the ghetto); and related conditions which inhibit growth and development. Such an approach seeks to define the nature and effects of economic subjugation and control. Alternative strategies are then formulated for economic lberation from poverty and external domination of the ghetto economy (Harris, 1972; Henderson and Ledebur, 1970).

Institutional, Bicultural, and Ecological Dimensions. These terms reflect a diverse range of constraints and characteristics which define the racial dimensions of economic life for blacks. Each is illustrated below.

Institutional factors encompass established patterns and relationships as well as organizations that make up the structure of opportunities and outcomes available to blacks. The available schools, public transportation, and government and community service agencies are familiar examples. Given the widespread pattern of segregation and discrimination which exists, blacks, for the most part, function in a dual economy. The world of the inner city and the local institutions (business, social, cultural, and otherwise) are linked to, but are distinct from, the larger surrounding community and society. This dualism impacts black economic life in a variety of ways. Its structure, style, and operations are sufficiently different to have some recognition in economic analysis.

Bicultural dimensions of economic relationships are rooted in the institutional arrangements and experiences which collectively define black economic life. There is an inescapable duality in the combined mixture and separateness of being black in white America. The essence of the relationship has been described by Dixon (1970: 425) as being diunital in nature--apart (black or white) and united at the same time (fusion of blackness and whiteness); or, alternatively, "a union of opposites without inherent antagonism." However, contradictions do have to be reconciled, such as

- when a black gets a better job and higher salary, yet still finds that opportunities may be more limited for him or her than for whites in similar circumstances;
- when a black is asked to buy from a black business (or actually has few alternatives to doing so), yet realizes that the price paid may be higher than would be paid in other parts of the city;
- when a black has a strong aspiration to find a way out of the ghetto, yet recognizes that only 5 percent of the black population lives in the suburbs; or

- when a black desires to remain in the inner city because of friendships, preferred lifestyle, and familiar surroundings, yet finds exploitation from inside the area by hustlers, rackets, and fencers as well as deteriorating structures, along with exploitation from merchants and employers on the outside.

Such conditions and experiences pose distinct challenges for those who recognize the need to reconcile conventionality and duality in economic relationships.

Ecological is used here in reference to the interplay of forces among individuality, ethnicity, and the environment in which economic activities take place. This dimension involves recognition that the factors influencing economic relationships involving race, have added dimensions of complexity, multiethnicity, and multidimensionality. Currently, the levels of theory and analysis do not recognize the ecological issues involved. Yet, in the framework of racial perspectives a combination of individual, situational, and institutional factors needs to be understood in order to develop more accurate explanations of economic behavior. Answers are needed to such questions as: How can the diverse influences on such behavior be more accurately specified? How can the formulations of expected behavior take duality (as well as other dimensions noted here) into account in future economic studies? Until such questions are answered there will continue to be considerable hidden inaccuracy and uncertainty in the generalizations made about choice processes for alternative resource uses whenever racial issues are involved.

INSTITUTIONAL RELEVANCE
OF RACIAL PERSPECTIVES

The extent to which race and responses to it are rooted in the institutions of society was stated most memorably by Wicker (1968: vii). In the introduction to the Kerner Commission report on urban riots, he observed that the causes of and conditions in the ghetto are not understood by white America. Yet, "white society is deeply implicated in the ghetto. *White institutions created it, white institutions maintain it, and white society condones it*" (1968: vii).

The basic logic of his assertion holds for racial discrimination. Whites gain from it, albeit despite aggregate and opportunity losses to the economy as a whole (given that resources are misallocated when choices are made on grounds unrelated to efficiency, competition, and so on).

Developing racial perspectives can also be linked to other applied and policy concerns in economics. As with many other applied areas of the discipline, racial perspectives tend to reflect an institutional emphasis. Actual practices, processes, and real-world relationships, along with socially conditioned patterns of racial behavior, form the basis of theoretical and policy formulations. As noted above, the environmental and institutional setting of market relationships involving race subverts the general norms implicit in mutually beneficial contractual relationships. Various constraints, including a preassigned status of blacks, are integral parts of job, housing, and other transactions in the marketplace.

Institutional relevance takes on added significance in racial terms because of the changing roles of institutions in economic life. The changing importance of sectors should be noted.

The private sector is necessarily dominant in a private market economy. However, there are changing role expectations. Corporations are expected to provide investments which support innovation and technological change. But equal employment opportunity, affirmative action, and jobs for the disadvantaged are other social contributions and responsibilities of the private sector.

Policies for income redistribution and the reduction of inequities represent important goals which have a direct bearing on race-related aspects of economic relationships. Through a variety of programs, government assumes roles ranging from consumer advocate and insurer to entrepreneur and economic developer.

The third sector consists of foundations and a wide range of nonprofit organizations whose operations and programs encourage social change in a variety of forms. Their is a supplemental role to both private- and public-sector activities. Many black community institutions, such as community development corporations, cooperatives, and the like, have received sustaining investments from third-sector organizations.

Self-help activities in a variety of forms are linked to community groups. As a political and economic response to disparity, there is more of a need for direct community involvement in activities which support the economic development process.

A graphic way of describing the major sectors and their roles in the economic process is presented in Figure 8.1. Because of increasing scale, expansion of social objectives in economic performance, and constraints imposed by general economic developments, the roles of each of the other sectors are being enlarged relative to the private sector. While such changes are by no means unique to a black perspective, generally they would be viewed positively rather than negatively, as is likely to be the case in conventional economic analysis.

Learning and borrowing from the international development experience is also likely to become influential in formulating policies and guiding

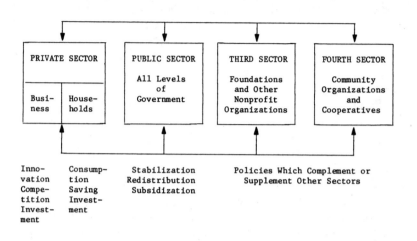

Figure 8.1: Major Sectors and Their Role in the Economic Process

institutional practices. The resulting cross-cultural dimensions should bring even greater institutional relevance to the process of analysis using racial perspectives. Some examples of this potential can be found in the work of David (1975), Ijere (1972), and Osagie (1973).

CONCLUSIONS

The conventional wisdom in economic analysis presents a universally applicable and impersonally oriented technological framework of theory and institutional arrangements. Except for the specialty subject area of the economics of discrimination, the general analysis is racially or ethnically neutral. The analysis presented here has emphasized some of the limitations of such a framework. It is at many points discrepant with racially determined outcomes and opportunities in the economy and society.

Alternative extensions of conventional analysis have been illustrated at the conceptual level. Racial perspectives can make many positive contributions toward understanding the nature and magnitude of race-related choices and relationships associated with alternative uses of resources. A framework of analysis augmented by racial perspectives would provide greater comprehensiveness, institutional relevance, and reform potential for addressing race-related issues in the economy and society.

Intellectually, there is a need to recognize racial differences and diversity as well as disadvantages and disparity. There is more to be analyzed than poverty and related forms of economic pathology. Different priorities, time horizons, and value-oriented choices deserve greater theoretical and analytic interest. Furthermore, the challenges of reflecting duality in race-related economic issues open up a broad range of ecological dimensions. There is a largely unexplored but unique interplay among individuality, ethnicity, and environment surrounding race-related issues in the economy and society.

Finally, evolving racial perspectives in economic thought provide a more holistic and comparative mode of analysis. No claims are made for statistical or technological elegance. That has reached the ultimate in complexity and sophistication in conventional analysis. Insight, priorities, and reorienting the uses of knowledge represent more pressing concerns, at least when economic issues and relationships are viewed in a racial perspective. The province of economic society can be enriched in many ways by the positive and persistent exploration into a fuller understanding and application of racial perspectives as an integral part of economic analysis.

REFERENCES

ALEXIS, M. (1974) "The political economy of labor market discrimination: synthesis and exploration," in A. Horowitz and G. von Furstenberg (eds.) *Patterns of Discrimination.* Lexington, MA: D.C. Heath.
––– (1978) "The economic status of blacks and whites." *American Economic-Review—Papers and Proceedings* 68 (May): 179-185.
ANDERSON, B. E. and P. A. WALLACE (1975) "Public policy and black economic progress." *American Economic Review—Papers and Proceedings* 65 (May): 47-52.
BECKER, G. (1957) *The Economics of Discrimination.* Chicago: University of Chicago Press.
BELL, D., Jr. (1971) "Bonus schemes and racism." *Review of Black Political Economy* 2 (Summer): 110-114.
DAVID, W. L. (1975) "Alternative paradigms in economics and the study of development and underdevelopment." *Review of Black Political Economy* 6 (Fall): 72-89.
DIXON, V. J. (1970) "The Di-unital approach to 'black economics.'" *American Economic Review—Papers and Proceedings* 60 (May): 424-429.
FLAX, M. J. (1971) *Blacks and Whites—An Experiment in Racial Indicators.* Washington, DC: The Urban Institute.
FREEMAN (1973) "Decline of labor market discrimination and economic analysis." *American Economic Review* 63 (May): 280-286.
FUSFELD, D. R. (1970) "The basic economics of the urban and racial crisis." *Review of Black Political Economy* 1 (Spring-Summer): 58-83.
HARRIS, D. J. (1972) "The black ghetto as colony: a theoretical critique and alternative formulation." *Review of Black Political Economy* 3 (Summer): 3-33.
HENDERSON, W. L. and L. C. LEDEBUR (1970) *Economic Disparity—Problems and Strategies for Black America.* New York: Free Press.

IJERE, M. O. (1972) "Whither economics in a black studies program?" *Journal of Black Studies* 3 (December): 149-166.

MARSHALL, R. (1974) "The economics of racial discrimination: a survey." *Journal of Economic Literature* 12 (September): 849-871.

OSAGIE, E. (1973) "Guidelines for an African economic ideology." *Journal of Black Studies* 4 (June): 418-440.

SOWELL, T. E. (1975) *Race and Economics.* New York: David McKay.

——— (1971) "Economics and black people." *Review of Black Political Economy* 2 (Winter-Spring): 3-21.

SMITH, V. L. (1974) "Economic theory and its discontents." *American Economic Review—Papers and Proceedings* 64 (May): 320-322.

STIGLITZ, J. E. (1973) "Approaches to the economics of discrimination." *American Economic Review—Papers and Proceedings* 63 (May): 287-295.

SWINTON, D. H. (1975) "Factors affecting the future economic prospects of minorities." *American Economic Review- Papers and Proceedings* 65 (May): 53-58.

TABB, W. K. (1970) *The Political Economy of the Black Ghetto.* New York: Norton.

VOWELS, R. C. (1971) "The political economy of american racism—nonblack decision-making and black economic status." *Review of Black Political Economy* 2 (Summer): 3-42.

WICKER, T. (1968) "Introduction," in *Report of the National Advisory Commission on Civil Disorders.* New York: Bantam.

WILSON, W. J. (1973) Power, Racism, and Privilege—Race Relations in Theoretical and Sociohistorical Perspective. New York: Macmillan.

9

BLACK AWARENESS AND AUTHENTIC
BLACK/BLACK RELATIONS

David R. Burgest

Since the decline of the Black liberation movement of the sixties, there has been a deemphasis of and decline in the creation and maintenance of Black awareness, Black identity, and Black consciousness in the Black community. There are Blacks who are quick to refer to the concept of Black consciousness and Black identity as stemming from a time when Blacks were forced into a new day with different approaches and attitudes. There are those who believe that we (Blacks) have outgrown the heyday of the sixties and must move to another level. It is not really clear yet what that new level is, but it rests somewhere between the notion of individualism (achievement through one's own merit and skills) and a heavy religious orientation which suggests the fifties and the years preceding. Black awareness and Black consciousness, which premeated the dress, hairstyle, speech, and the total lifestyle of many Blacks during the sixties, is limited now to the study of Black and African history and culture. However, many Blacks who experienced the sixties and its upsurge of pride, dignity, and identity continue to maintain the assumptions which emerged during that time, even though they do not overtly manifest signs of the handshake, dress, and hairstyle. Most of those Blacks are parents today, and they are attempting to develop Black awareness, Black consciousness, and Black identity in their children.

On the other hand, there is a group of Blacks who were not affected by the sixties. They continue to maintain the assumptions of race awareness which were prevalent during the forties and fifties—that it was better to be light-skinned, curly-haired, and imitate whites. Much of the reason that the notions of Black awareness and Black consciousness have gone underground could rest with the fact that no one has come up with a definition which is agreeable to all Blacks. What is Black consciousness and Black identity to one person may not be Black awareness and Black identity to another. In other words, there is no agreement on what it is to "think Black," "act Black," and "live Black"; yet, "thinking Black" or "thinking from a Black perspective" is a component which is seen as real.

We may never develop an adequate definition of Blackness which may be acceptable to all, but we can identify the assumptions, myths, and stereotypes which Blacks hold about other Blacks, Blackness, Black culture, whites, whiteness, and white culture which may block the development of authentic interpersonal relationships between Blacks and Blacks. At the same time, we can identify the necessary assumptions, myths, and stereotypes that Blacks should possess to *facilitate* the development of authentic interpersonal relationships with other Blacks. It is safe to say that the assumptions Blacks hold about Black people, Blackness, and Black culture provide an indication of how that person sees him- or herself.

This Black awareness self-examination exercise is based on the general premise that in order for Black individuals to truly accept themselves, their identity, their culture, and other Black people, they must destroy all of the negative myths, stereotypes, and assumptions regarding Blackness, Black people, and Black culture which have been created by white America. At the same time, they must do away with all the racist positive myths, stereotypes, and assumptions about whiteness, white people, and white culture. In other words, Blacks must do away with the "what white is" and "what Black is not" syndrome that is prevalant in all facets of this American society. By the same token, this chapter is based on the premise that Blacks must develop authentic interpersonal relationship with other Blacks prior to engaging in the development of authentic relations with whites. Much of this has to do with the fact of the difficulties Blacks experience in relating to each other are directly related to the problems of racism and white supremacy in the American society. Therefore, they must purge themselves of the effect that Blackness has on them before they can attempt to engage in authentic relations between Blacks. It is not suggested, however, that this self-examination exercise on Black awareness cannot be useful as a tool in getting whites to look at their perceptions of how they assume Blacks should think.

This self-examination is divided into two topics: (1) assumptions Blacks make, and (2) behaviors of Blacks. In each case, one has to choose whether the statement indicated either block and/or facilitate the development of

TABLE 9.1   Assumptions of Blacks Regarding the Development of
Black Awareness

Assumptions Blacks Make	
I happen to be Black.	Some Blacks hold racist attitudes toward whites as well as Blacks.
I am Black first and an educator second.	People are people, regardless of the color of their skin.
I am different from other Blacks because. ...	I can't help that I'm Black.
All Blacks don't deserve respect because they don't respect themselves.	I am pro-Black.
	The problem with us (Blacks) is Black self-hatred.
Black is beautiful but white can be beautiful.	All Whites are racists.[a]
I am human first and Black second.	Blacks really don't have much of which they can be proud.
No Black person is free until all Black people are free.	The Black militants are the trouble-makers.
Blacks are individuals.	I believe in "every person for him- or herself."
All Blacks are oppressed.	
Anything that is all Black is usually no good.	
We need to "off" all "Uncle Toms."	

a. Source: Betram M. Lee and Warren H. Schmidt, "Toward More Authentic Interpersonal Relations Between Blacks and Whites," *Training News*, 1977, 13 (National
Training Lab Institute, Washington, D.C.).

authentic interpersonal relations between Blacks and Blacks by placing
"F" or "B" in the box indicated. This process of identifying the assumptions and behaviors which may block or facilitate the development of
authentic relations between Blacks will stimulate an exchange between
Blacks which will increase their sensitivity to and awareness of one
another. However, there will be an analysis and interpretation of each
statement indicating the appropriate assumption Blacks should hold. In
addition to the above, it is important to note that all behavior is based on
assumptions. The assumption may be either conscious or unconscious, but
the fact remains that assumptions predict behavior. By the same token,

TABLE 9.2   Behaviors of Blacks

Behaviors of Blacks	
Avoidance of contact[a]	Let's act as though we are as good as whites.
Treating Blacks and whites on a one-to-one basis	Viewing self as better than other Blacks because. . . .
Showing annoyance at behavior which differs from your own[a]	Assisting other Blacks in developing Black consciousness
Black is beautiful and we don't need to prove it.	Race (color) is important in interpersonal relations between Blacks and whites.
Treating whites on an individual basis	Seeing self as Blacker than other Blacks
Identifying with the positive qualities of whites	
Proving that we are Black	If I were white I'd have it made.
Being concerned about what white society think of us	A brother will let you down when things get tough.
My approach is the best approach to handling whites.	Assisting whites in understanding racist behavior of which they are unaware
Talking to other Blacks about white behavior rather than talking to whites concerned	We are no better or worse than the least of our brothers and sisters.
	Going an extra mile to help someone who is Black.

a. Source: Betram M. Lee, and Warren H. Schmidt, "Toward More Authentic Interpersonal Relations Between Blacks and Whites," *Training News*, 1972, 13 (National Training Lab Institute, Washington D.C.).

there are behaviors which Blacks manifest in their relationships with other Blacks which are detrimental to the development of authentic interpersonal relationships between Blacks and to Black awareness.

ASSUMPTIONS BLACKS MAKE

I Happen To Be Black (block). Too often Blacks view themselves as "happening to be Black." Usually, the comment is in reference to a noted Black scholar, figure, or individuals whose achievements are considered

worthy. In such instances, there is a blatant apology for the color of one's
skin and a subsequent acceptance of the racist premise that "white only"
is worthy, good, or valuable, and Black is unworthy, bad, and valueless. At
the same time, there is a deemphasis of color or race. The other side of the
coin is, "I happen to be Black; thus I 'could have been white.' " By the
same token, such Black individuals have accepted the negative definition
of Blacks and Black culture as defined by white racist America. Above all,
there is a view that the color of one's skin and race is accidental or
circumstantial.

The other side of the coin on "happening to be Black" is used by
Blacks who consider themselves worthy, to Blacks who are considered
unworthy and have been excommunicated from the Black race. That is,
they will say that this person "happens to be Black." Such an approach is
taken because many Blacks view the negative behavior of other Blacks as
reflecting on the entire Black community or Black race.

Seldom, if ever, do whites abdicate the positiveness attributed to
whiteness by stating that others of their race "happen to be white." The
rare occurrence of such comments from whites is limited to conversations
in the presence of Blacks in an attempt to apologize for the negative
treatment of Blacks by whites. The purpose of the statement at that time
is to identify with the humanness in Black people and to imply the
possibility of having been Black. In this instance, to be Black is to be
human and to be white is to be nonhuman, and the white person is
identifying with Black qualities in this situation to make him or her look
favorable. However, there is no other circumstance where whites view
being white as a misfortune or happenstance, whereas Blacks are constantly attempting to escape the negativism implicit in the concept
"Black." This is not to imply that *because* whites do not abdicate their
whiteness, Blacks should not abdicate their Blackness. This is to suggest
that once an individual or person is able to accept his or her culture,
lifestyle, customs, and color, there is no need to apologize for race, for
one's racial identity is God-given.

I am Black First and an Educator Second (facilitate). It is not infre-
quently that we hear Blacks who say, "I am a doctor first and a Black
second," or "I am a Social worker first and a Black second." In most cases,
Blacks identify with their professions more than they identify with their
Blackness. In essence, Blacks are placing the greatest emphasis upon their
acquired professional skills and deemphasizing color or race. The fact of
the matter is, many such Blacks have assimilated the negative myths,
stereotypes, and assumptions about Blackness, Black people, and Black
culture created by white racist America. Consequently, in an effort to

move closer to that which is identified as being white-oriented, they indentify with their professions first and their race second. At the same time, Blacks who identify with their professions first, do so because they have a need to be identified with a league of white professionals. By the same token, many Blacks deemphasize color and race out of a fear that to limit themselves to being *Black first* is to limit their scope of their contribution. Many Blacks take this perspective to the extreme, in that they prefer not being looked at as, for instance, a *Black doctor* but as a *doctor* or *lawyer* or *teacher*. There is a fear that their identity will somehow be diminished by being identified as Black.

On the other hand, whites do not experience the ambivalence of being identified as *white* and *educator* or *white* and *teacher*, because it is generally assumed that the two are equivalent. That is, white America sets this society's standards and parameters of education, and there is no dissassociation of being *white* and being an *educator, doctor,* or *lawyer*. In that many Blacks identify their professions as being white-oriented and dominated, they prefer to be more closely identified with their professions than with their racial origin. However, there should not be a dichotomy between being Black and being a professional. If such a distinction is to be made, Blacks should identify with their God-given identity first, and their acquired profession second. In this way, it is clear where the Black person places his or her greatest emphasis and commitment.

I am Different From Other Blacks Because. . . . (block). Each person is a unique individual and differs from other individuals in some aspect. However, it is the view of many Black individuals that they differ *from the masses of other Black people*. The emphasis here is being placed on the notion that one Black person feels as though he or she possesses unique qualities which somehow are not attributable to "other Black people" or to the masses of Black people. In other words, some Blacks may feel that they have liberated themselves from behaviors and attributes which are identified as being Black behavior, and that they are thereby different from other Blacks. This is not to suggest that they are not different from other individuals. However, it does imply that all the behavior manifested by Black people, negative as well as positive, must be viewed in the context of Black behavior. This includes the behavior of Blacks who have adapted to and assimilated the white culture, as well as the behavior of Blacks who maintain ties with the Black culture and community. This includes Blacks who are lazy/smart, prostitutes/ministers, pro-Black/antiwhite, Uncle Toms/militants, and others. Given the impact of racist/white supremacy upon Blacks and the domination of a Western world-view culture, the range of Black behavior is varied. The point being made, nonetheless, is that Blacks who view themselves as differing from other Blacks have identified themselves as being "above" what has been identified as Black behavior, and such a view is destructive to the notion of Black unity as well as the development of Black consciousness.

All Blacks Don't Deserve Respect Because They Don't Respect Themselves (block). The premise that there are Blacks who do not respect themselves is more prevalent than the assumption that whites do not respect themselves. The truth of the matter is that all individuals are deserving of respect, regardless of their race or position in society. One should not assume that another individual, because he or she is Black, does not respect him- or herslef. The other part of this assumption is that Blacks are not worthy of respect. This view is held by whites as well as Blacks, and such a view is destructive to the development of Black identity, Black consciousness, and Black awareness.

Black is Beautiful But White Can Be Beautiful (facilitate). In the Black Community, "Black is beautiful" is a popular saying. Many Blacks have come to accept this as reality more than a slogan. This is good. On the other hand, there are many Blacks who have adopted the view that "Black is beautiful" but "white is not." There are antiwhite feelings existing under the assumption that *only Black* is beautiful. Yet, antiwhiteness is still no indicator of pro-Blackness. In other words, "everyone that hates white people does not necessarily love Black people," even though there may be slogans and cliches utilized to express antiwhiteness. Thus, we must move to the level of consciousness where we can recognize that "Black is beautiful" but "white can be beautiful." In this way, *Black* pride will not exist and thrive on the negative assessment of another race; the beauty of Blacks will stand alone on its own merit. Too often, the love of self is dependent on the hate of someone or something else. This is not authentic love of self. Consequently, we as Black people must recognize the potential of beauty in whites which exists in many Blacks. In this way, there it will be possible to develop Black awareness and authentic interpersonal relations between Blacks and Blacks.

I am Human First and Black Second (block). In the usual context of the statement "human first and Black second," there is a blatant apology for the color of one's skin or the race of an individual, and a deemphasis of color or race. At the same time, there is a concentration on the "humanness" or "humanity" of the individual. Yet, to become "legitimized" into the "human" race is equivalent to becoming white, given the white society's definition of whiteness and Blackness. In the Euro-America culture, to be Black is to be nonhuman and to be white is to be human.

Therefore, many Blacks see a contradiction in being Black and being human. In an effort to resolve the contradiction, they view themselves as being human first and Black second. By identifying with being "human" first, Blacks see themselves as being able to align themselves with a core that encompasses the attachments of whites. Yet, there is no physical or psychological process by which one can separate *humanness* from *Blackness*. A distinction between being Black and being human need not be made. A Black individual is a *Black human being*.

No Black Person is Free until All Black People are Free (facilitate). There are many Black individuals who hold the view, "I am free." That is, they do not recognize any barriers created by the white society that in any way prohibit their growth and development as individuals, based on their color. They may have the financial resources, education, home, care, and other material necessities and social contacts with whites and other Blacks which may suggest to them that they are free individuals. They may feel that they have not experienced racial prejudice or discrimination based on color or race. Nonetheless, there are Black people who have been and are currently being victimized by racism, racial predjudices, and discrimination. The individuals who view themselves as being "free" reply that such Blacks can overcome such obstacles through either education, assimilation, or integration. They do not recognize that the threat or perpetuation of racism, racial prejudice, or discrimination against any Black person in the world is an indictment against all Black people. In other words, as long as racism is alive, no Black person is free. Consequently, no Black person is free until all Black people are free. This is the proper attitude and assumption to possess for the maintance and development of Black consciousness, Black identity, and Black awareness.

Blacks are Individuals (facilitate). There are those (both Black and white) who wish to look at Blacks as a group rather than as individuals. Thus, many whites have developed the concept, "all Blacks look alike," to suggest that there is no individuality. On the other hand, many Blacks, during the height of the Black identity regeneration of the sixties, suggested that Blacks must not look at themselves as individuals but as members of a group. That is, they must not act as individuals or think as individuals but should always think about themselves as members of the Black community. In most instances, it is good to be group-conscious, but the fact remains that Blacks are individuals with their own unique qualities, styles, personalities, and functioning. If we remember this, it is impossible to apply stereotyped behavior to Blacks. Blacks must be looked at as individuals, even though they may possess group unity.

All Blacks are Oppressed (facilitate). In the same manner that no Black person is free until all Black people are free, no Black person is free from oppression until all Black people are free from oppression. Consequently, all Black persons are oppressed, whether they recognize it or not. There are many Blacks who prefer to believe that they are not victims of oppression. Even though a Black individual may be a millionaire in the American system, with the purchasing power to buy and go where she or he pleases, the fact remains that such persons are subject to the same elements of racism, prejudice, and discrimination based on his or her color and race. I can recall Black politicians and judges who were subject to the same search and seizure tactics applied to all Blacks of the Black community, as they attempted to enter the Black community to negotiate with the Black looters and rioters of the sixties. Once a Black millionaire is removed from his or her immediate environment and placed in Black and white society, he or she is subject to the same racial oppression that any ordinary Black person may be subject to.

There may be Blacks who, based on personal experience, do not recognize that all Blacks are oppressed. That is, they have not encountered any experiences which would indicate that they are oppressed; therefore, they do not assume that all Blacks are oppressed. Nonetheless, if the least one of us (Blacks) are oppressed because of color anywhere in the world, it is a threat to the welfare of Blacks everywhere. When a Jew is being oppressed in Russia, Germany, or any other place or country in the world, the Jews all over the world become upset and attempt to negotiate the resolution of the difficulty, because they clearly recognize the implication that all Jews are oppressed when one Jew is subject to oppression. We must become that aware and conscious of our relationship, and that our existence is dependent upon the survival of all Blacks.

Anything that is All Black is Usually No Good (block). There is an assumption in the Black community that anything which is usually all Black is not any good; therefore, Blacks do not frequent all-Black stores, shops, restaurants, schools, or organizations. If whites are not present in some capacity, usually with a share in defining the direction of the facility, Blacks as well as whites assume that there are deficiencies in the structure of that facility. Much of this has to do with the fact that Blacks are considered inferior, by the white society's definition of things, and many Blacks have assimilated the definition in the American culture of "what Black is not" and "what white is." Thus, an all-Black school is considered innately inferior to a school where there are white teachers and students. Many Blacks will not send their children to an all-Black school for this reason. This is not to suggest that an all-Black situation is innately superior to an all-white situation, but it does suggest that Blacks, and whites, for that matter, should do away with the assumption that just because something is all Black, it is inferior in quality and service.

We Need to "Off" All "Uncle Toms" (block). There is a view within the Black community that "Uncle Toms" are responsible for all of the difficulties Blacks experience in their efforts to gain liberation, as well as responsible for all the difficulties inherent in Black-white relations. This is not true, for it is white racism which is responsible for the difficulties inherent in Black-white relations, as well as the difficulties Blacks experience in their efforts toward liberation. However, "Uncle Toms" may be destructive in that they ingratiate themselves with whites and create a false stereotype in the minds of whites concerning how Blacks respond and carry information to whites on the planned activities and strategies of Blacks. The ultimate goal of the "Uncle Toms" is to gain the favoritism of whites. The goal of the "non-Uncle Toms" is similar, in that they are attempting to affect the behavior of whites, but it is based on the principles of equality in the relationship, rather than subordination. Both "Uncle Toms" and "non-Uncle Toms" want primarily the same thing, but their approaches are different. Thus, it should become the responsibility of the "non-Uncle Toms" to develop self-awareness in the "Uncle Toms," to show that there is another, more human, approach to affecting the behavior of white society. As the Black militants used to say during the heyday of the sixties and Black awareness, "every Uncle Tom is a potential revolutionary."

Some Blacks Hold Racist Attitudes Toward Whites as Well as Blacks (block). There is no such entity as "Black racism," whether it is supposed to be geared toward other Blacks or toward whites. Yet, there is the opinion that Black racism exists in relationships between Blacks and in relationships between whites. First of all, whites (Europeans/Greeks) are the creators and perpetuators of racism. American racism is originally based in the presence of African slaves in white America and continues through the process of segregation and discrimination based on color and race. Consequently, it is the natural response of a people who are oppressed, victims of prejudice, segregated, and discriminated against to react negatively to that experience. Those negative reactions are real and have results in the destruction of property and lives of white people, but those reactions can not be interpreted as racism, even though the same elements of white behavior and assumptions that have contributed to white racism, may be present in Black behavior and assumptions. Instead, Black behavior must be viewed as merely a reaction to the historical and contemporary treatment Blacks have received.

Many whites are ready to define the reactions of Black revolutionaries and militants to white oppression as Black racism. It is easy to see how individuals, both Black and white, are able to make this mistake. However, there is no mistaking the behavior of an individual who is bound and gagged and is struggling for freedom as a reaction to his or her oppression, not an exhibition of the same behavior as that of the person who has done the gagging and binding.

On the other hand, there is the view that Blacks demonstrate racist behavior toward other Blacks. That is, Blacks discriminate, segregate, and have feelings of racial prejudice against members of their own race. This is true. Many Blacks have the same stereotypes and negative assumptions of Black people, Black culture, and Blackness that whites hold. There are Blacks who prefer to live in an all-white community, send their children to all-white school, and who refuse to rent or buy from other Blacks. In this instance, it is clear that such Black persons have been innoculated with the values of white society. Nonetheless, they can not be called Black racists; even though the symptoms of whites and Blacks may be similar, the dynamics are different. Blacks must be viewed as victims of a white racist society in that they have bought the definition of "whiteness" and "Blackness" created by white society and they have been successfully indoctrinated into the white culture. Consequently, they are responding to the racism of the American society rather than being racist. Racism must be viewed as a phenomenon which occurs between two different races, as opposed to a phenomenon which occurs within races, although biases and prejudices exist within races of all groups.

People are People, Regardless of the Color of Their Skin (facilitate). There is no individual or face that is inherently evil or inherently good, even though as we analyse the historical relationship between Blacks and whites, many Blacks as well as whites would think that about each other. There is good and bad in each and every individual and race. Therefore, people are people, regardless of the color of their skin or racial identity. To think otherwise, one would be put in the position to assume that the destruction of a total race is necessary for the implementation of equality, humanness, and harmony within the universe. This is not true, even though it appears that the white race is bent on the perpetuation of racial prejudice and of disharmony between Blacks and whites, as well as other races and ethnic groups. By the same token, it appears that the exploitation of the minority groups is done at the expense of capitalistic gains and technological advancements within the society. Nonetheless, the relationship among Blacks, whites, and other minority groups are relatively young, and the potential of unity and harmony between races, colors, and ethnic groups is real.

I Can't Help That I'm Black (block). Living Black in white America has a way of causing Black individuals to think, "I can't help that I'm Black," as if to say, "I an not to blame for being Black; therefore, I should not be required to suffer the agony experienced as a result of being Black." It is certainly true that one has no power over his or her racial identity, for this most surely must be predetermined by divine forces. Nonetheless, it is a negative and destructive view of self and the universe to adopt the notion that there is something wrong with being Black. This is what is explicit in the assumption, "I can't help that I'm Black." The fact of one's Blackness is absolute and nonnegotiable, in the same way that one's whiteness is absolute and nonnegotiable. Thus, there is no need to attempt to compromise one's Blackness by stating that it "can't be helped." Such a statement is indicative of hopelessness and despair.

I am Pro-Black (facilitate). Many Blacks resist the notion of being pro-Black and identify pro-Blackness with being negative. There is the assumption that there is something wrong with being pro-Black—that people should be prohuman and do away with any distinctions relating to color or racial identity. This would be ideal in a society where all is equal; however, all is not equal. On the other hand, there are many Blacks who hold the view that to be pro-Black is to be antiwhite, which is not necessarily true. There are some Blacks who do feel that being pro-Black is directly congruent with being antiwhite. It is necessary for Black people to operate out of an attitude of pro-Blackness, that is, to buy Black products and to support Black functions, operations, and organizations for Black survival. This is not to say that one is antiwhite because one believes in supporting Black pride, Black consciousness, and Black awareness. It is the same behavior which is manifested among Jews, Germans, and other ethnic and religious groups. Yet, it is probably among the Black-American groups where the awareness that works to develop Black institutions and Black causes, functions least.

The Problem with Us (Blacks) is Black Self-Hatred (block). There is an assumption existing in the Black as well as the white community that the major problem with Blacks is Black self-hatred. In other words, if Black people did not hate other Black people, they could make progress socially, economically, and politically. Black self-hatred has been attributed to crime in the Black community, drug addiction, suicide, breakup of the Black family, and all other social ills of the Black community. Black self-hatred has even been attributed to the riots of the sixties and the existence of antiwhite feelings in Blacks. Aggressive behavior as well as submissive behavior on the part of Blacks has been attributed in part to Black self-hatred.

Nevertheless, the major problem that Black people fact is not Black self-hatred. However, this is not to suggest that some Black people do not hate themselves; to a very large degree, the concept of Black self-hatred, which emerged during the early sixties, is primarily a white society's interpretation and definition of Black behavior, which places the burden of the social ills in the Black community upon Blacks and denies the role white society plays in creating the ills. Looking at the historical relationships between Blacks and whites, we can find many such concepts to explain and interpret Black behavior. At first, Blacks were considered savages or barbarians who were in need of socialization by white society. The "inferior" behavior of Black people was attributed to the fact that they were savages. However, after the so-called emancipation, Whites apparently could not justify coexistence with savages; consequently, Blacks were defined as innately inferior, and this was attributed to the fact that they were unable to develop and progress within the American society. As time went on, segregation and discrimination were considered to be the causes of the "inferior" behavior of Blacks. Finally, the concept of Black self-hatred emerged. It is clear that the Euro-American's underlying definition of Black behavior has not changed; only the labels have changed. Thus, the problems Black people face stem primarily from the inability of white society to abolish the notion of white supremacy/Black inferiority and racism.

All Whites are Racists (facilitate). Many Blacks do not feel that all whites are racist and most whites do not feel as though all whites are racist. There are both Blacks and whites who reject the notion on the general premise that "all" are included. They hold the view that to say "all" invalidates the premise. On the other hand, there are Blacks who hold the view that they have come in contact with whites whom they would not define as racist, prejudiced, or biased against Black people. By the same token, there are whites who hold the view that they harbor no negative feelings, racist feelings, or prejudiced feelings against a people based on color. All of the above may very well be true. Nonetheless, white individuals are products of a white racist society as well as a benefactors of institutionalized and individual racism against Blacks and other minorities. Consequently, they are unable to be free of racism until the concept of racism has been abolished in the universe. It is one thing for whites to be friendly with Blacks and not harbor any negative, racist, or prejudiced feelings against Blacks, but the responsibilities of whites do not end there. It is the responsibility of whites to work with other whites for the total destruction of racism and they cannot be viewed as free from racism until the job is completed.

In many instances, it is easy for Blacks as well as whites to identify with the notion that "all" Blacks are victims of racism, whether individual

Blacks, recognize it or not. At the same time, the question of invalidity does not occur with the premise that "all" are included. Yet, when the premise applies to whites being racist, the notion of invalidity applies. Yet, it seems logical that if no Black person is free until all Black people are free or all Black people are oppressed by white racism in America, then it seems logical that "no white person is free of racism until all whites are free of racism." This is not to suggest that whites and Blacks should not establish relationships with each other, nor should this assumption alter any any relationship existing between Blacks and whites.

Blacks Really don't have Much of which They can be Proud (block). There are Blacks who do not feel as though there is much of which they can be proud. Much of this feeling stems from the fact that there has been an inadequate interpretation of Black history in America and Africa. Black history has been distorted, "lost, stolen, and Strayed." Second, Black people in America have generally limited their study of Black people to the continent of the United States and see themselves primarily as products of this continent. Third, Blacks have been portrayed by the media, radio, and motion pictures in a negative sense. Fourth, many Blacks highlight their victimization by white racism as slaves and insubordinates, as the major focus of their history.

Yet, Blacks have a heritage of which they can be proud when they look at their roots in Africa and analyse the many contributions that Africans have made to the development of Eastern ideology and the Eastern world, the many contributions which Blacks have made in America, and the contributions Africans and Blacks have made to the world. History informs us that civilization began in the Nile Valley in Egypt. In addition, Blacks in this country have made a major impact on the advancement of medicine, science, art, music, religion, and politics, to name only a few areas. The fact that Black people have survived the oppression of white America is a tribute which can be made to every Black man, woman, and child today.

The Black Militants are the Troublemakers (block). There are many Blacks who feel that it is the "Black militants" who are responsible for most of the difficulty inherent in Black-white relationships. There are whites who hold the same views. The assumption seems to be that "everything would go along fine between Blacks and whites if it were not for the 'trouble makers.' " Black militant behavior is considered disruptive because it further alienates whites from Blacks and may create a "white backlash." At the same time, such behavior supposedly alienates Blacks from other Blacks with different views on race relations. On the other hand, there are whites who are more readily able to compromise with

Black moderates after a confrontation with Black militants. By the same token, there have been strategies of the sixties with which the so-called militant and moderates cooperated, to the advantage of all Blacks. The militants kicked down the door and the moderates followed with a milder approach, negotiation and compromise. Thus, Black militants as well as Black moderates play a significant role in Black-white relations. The whites who retreated into a "backlash" in reaction to militants could not have been very sincere and authentic with Blacks in the first place.

White society has labeled and categorized the behavior of aggressive Blacks as "militants" and set them apart from other Blacks as a means of diminishing their effectiveness. Therefore, the negative image of the "Black militant" is created as a means of discrediting Blacks within the white as well as the Black community.

The Black militants are not "troublemakers," in that they are responding to the problems created by white society, rather then creating the problems. It is the creators and perpetuators of racism who are responsible for the problems, and if the term *troublemaker* applies anywhere, it should apply to white racist America.

I Believe in "Every Person for Him or Herself" (block). There is a prevailing assumption unique to Western (European) thought that each person will "make it" on his or her own unique individual qualities, skills, and talents. In the Black society, where acquisition to the resources and benefits of white society are few, many Blacks have adopted this same notion. That is, they must not be concerned about the welfare of another Black person because it is assumed that the Black individual who is less fortunate is in that position because he or she has not been able to develop or utilize his or her skills and talents due to some inherent deficiency. This attitude may be partly true for individual whites who do not experience prejudice, bias, or discrimination based on color, but it is most definitely not true for Blacks. The white-American institutionalized system will only accommodate so many Blacks at one time, irrespective of their qualifications. This is true in universities as well as in the job market, where the quota system is in operation. Recently, in a Supreme Court decision, a white individual (Bakke) felt as though he had been discriminated against because of a quota system set up for Blacks and the Court upheld his position. Consequently, "every person for himself or herself should be abolished in the thinking of Black individuals.

Blacks should recognize that the survival of individual Blacks is intricately tied into the survival of Black people as a whole. Consequently, Blacks who have unique qualities, skills, talents, and resources should use those resources and talents for the enhancement of the Black community.

We cannot adopt the attitude of "I got mine; now, you have to get yours." During the bombing of Pearl Harbor, all Japanese were incarcerated. They did not differentiate between the militant, moderate, "Uncle Tom," Christian or Muslim Japanese. The same is true for Black people: Their lives interlock, and Blacks must respond to each other recognizing that their lives are intricately interwoven. This is not to say that Blacks should not take advantage of the resources of white society because other Blacks may not be able to do so. Rather, it is to say that Blacks must do what they can to assist other Blacks.

BEHAVIORS OF BLACKS

In the same way that there are assumptions, stereotypes, and myths which out of which Blacks operate that block or facilitate the development of Black awareness, Black identity, and Black consciousness, both in the self and within the Black community, there are behaviors of Blacks in Black/Black relationships which may block and/or facilitate the development of authentic interpersonal relations between Blacks. In this section we will look at such behavior and its implications for Black/Black relationships.

Advoidance of Contact (block). It is the behavior of many Blacks to avoid contact with other Blacks. Much of this has to do with the fact that there are Blacks who stereotype other Blacks in the same way that whites stereotype Blacks. The fact of the matter is that many Blacks accept the stereotypes and myths about Black people which have been created by whites. Such Blacks have not lost their physical identity as Black, but they have rejected what has been traditionally defined as "Black behavior" and have modified their behavior accordingly. Consequently, they avoid contact with Black people.

On the other side of the coin, there are many Blacks who hold the view that they are not to congregate or assemble in a group consisting of white people. They do not want to be labeled as segregationist, antiwhite, or separatist. Consequently, Blacks in the midst of a large group of whites often speak not to each other but, rather, spend their time mingling and mixing with whites. In this way, they avoid being labeled or categorized in a negative sense. It is true that there are whites who view the congregation and assemblings of Blacks in a large group of whites as separatist, antisocial, and possibly anti-white. The notion of separatism and antisocial behavior is not equally distributed, in that most whites present in a large group of Blacks do not hold the view that they must disperse and mingle with the Blacks present in order to avoid being considered a separatist. By the same token, it is commonplace to see whites in a large group of Blacks to be sitting or standing together. It appears from the prevailing assumption on the part of whites that it is the responsibility of Blacks to demonstrate and prove that their motives are pure.

Treating Blacks on a One-to-One Basis (facilitate). It is necessary for Blacks to treat other Blacks on a one-to-one basis. Too often, Blacks react to other Blacks on the basis of stereotypes developed by white America, as well as on the basis of the stereotypes they have created on their own.

In the eyes of many whites, all Blacks are the same. It has come to the point that many whites say that "they all look alike." To suggest that Blacks relate to Blacks on an individual basis is not to imply a deemphasis of unity. Blacks are individuals, the fact that Blacks are of the same race, does not imply that all Blacks are going to be able to get along with each other. By the same token, the existence of differences and personal preferences among Blacks in developing and establishing relationships does not suggest that some Blacks are better or superior to other Blacks. The matter of personal choice in selecting friends, acquaintances, and associates within the race of Black people is a phenomenon which cannot be overlooked. Blacks as well as whites must treat Blacks on an individual basis.

Showing Annoyance at Behavior Which Differs from Your Own (block). Often individuals show annoyance at behavior which differs from their own. They feel as though their behavior is the more acceptable behavior and behavior contrary to theirs must be put down and destroyed. This is true in Black/Black relationships. In the eyes of many Black people, what is considered proper and improper Black behavior is directly related to what is considered proper or improper behavior in white society, or is based on white society's definition of what is proper or improper for Black people. In other words, there are many Blacks who adapt their behavior to what white society thinks. I can recall the reactions of many Black politicians and social scientists to the many motion pictures which were created by Blacks during the seventies. One Black man indicated that he was ashamed after viewing one motion picture created by Blacks, which he considered perpetuated the image that all Black females were prostitutes. His greatest fear was that whites would begin to think of all Black women as being prostitutes. My response is that the Black individual should recognize the realities about Black women, based on his own experience in the Black community. What the Black individual knows to be reality should not be determined or dictated by what whites may think. Too often, Blacks respond to each other based on what whites think, as opposed to what the realities are. Consequently, behavior which differs from their own seems to threaten the way all Blacks might be viewed by whites.

As Black people, we must recognize that there are individual differences among Blacks and it is the prerogative of Blacks to respond as individuals. Once this is understood, Black individuals can more appropriately respond to other Blacks whose behavior differs from their own. It should not be the burden of Blacks to abolish the stereotypes of whites by accommodating their behavior.

Black is Beautiful and We Don't Need to Prove It (facilitate). There are many Blacks who "jump on the bandwagon" to illustrate that "Black is beautiful." They respond as though this is a revelation. They feel as though they have to prove that "Black is beautiful." That is, they have to convince themselves as well as "prove" this to whites. The fact of the matter is that whether whites think Black is beautiful or not is not really pertinent. Black society does not need to seek the agreement of white society that "Black is beautiful" before they are able to accept this fact. Yet, many Blacks may unconsciously see this as necessary. Second, "Black is beautiful" does not necessarily mean that white is not, even though there are many Blacks who have adopted this attitude. Finally, any efforts to "prove" the obvious are an indication of insecurities about the matter. Yes, Black is beautiful; we do not need to prove it to ourselves or anyone else.

Treating Whites on an Individual Basis (facilitate). There are many Blacks who look at whites in the same way that many whites look at Blacks. That is, Blacks look at whites as one large mass of people without individual differences and uniquenesses. Whites differ in attitude, disposition, and behavior to the same degree that Blacks differ in attitude, disposition, and uniquenesses. All whites are not the same in regard to their view of Black people. This is not to say that all whites are not racist because they differ in their approach to Black people, nor is this to suggest that all Blacks are not oppressed, even though their behavior, attitude, and disposition may differ. The fact that one Black individual is discriminated against due to race suggests that no Black person is free until all are free. By the same token, as long as white racism is alive and well within our society, no single white individual is free from it until all whites are free. The above is not to suggest that Black people should not treat whites on an individual basis in the same way that they treat Blacks on an individual basis.

Identifying with the Positive Qualities of Whites (Block). There are Black individuals who adopt the view that they can "improve themselves" by identifying with the positive qualities of whites. They see this as an indication of cultural growth and awareness. The problem with this approach is that there is an underlying assumption that "positive qualities" are somehow associated with white people and white culture. This implies that "positive qualities" are unique to white society and does away with the notion that they are a human phenomenon that cuts across all racial, ethnic, and religious grounds. There are qualities which people admire, but these qualities must be associated with human qualities and not the white race.

It seems logical that many Blacks adhere to the notion that they must adopt the positive character of whites given the definition in the American culture of "what white is" and "what Black is not." Given this definition, there are many Blacks who do not see Blacks as possessing any positive qualities. On the other hand, there are many Blacks who identify certain behavior in Black people as "white." By the same token, Blacks will say to other Blacks, "Now you are acting like a 'nigger.' " (*Nigger* in this sense is defined as describing behavior which is uniquely "Black.") The fact of the matter is that Blackness and whiteness are both real issues, but not the basis on which to determine behavior. This is not to suggest that Black people do not have a culture or do not have a lifestyle which is uniquely theirs, nor is this to suggest that whites do not have a culture and lifestyle of their own. It is true that each has a culture of its own; however, there is a thin line between behavior/culture and the instinctive forces which dictate and determine behavior. Nonetheless, the major premise here is that Blacks should not accept the notion that they will receive the positive qualities of life only by identifying with whites, thus placing themselves in their culture in a subordinate position. They should identify with the qualities they deem as necessary for their survival and the survival of their children. Those qualities are universal and not specific to a racial group.

Proving that We are Black (block). Blacks should not be put in a position in which they feel as though they have to prove their Blackness. By the same token, whites should not be put in a position in which they have to prove that they are nonracist or free from racism. This would be similar to being put in the position of having to prove one is human. Once Blacks engage in the process of proving that they are Black, it is more than likely an indication of their uncertainty and insecurities about the issue. Once you are sure where you stand, you do not have to prove anything.

For Blacks who engage in the above process, it is destructive in that the boundaries and parameters are not clear-cut, and one can always suggest that the behavior being manifested is not "Black enough." The dialogue and interaction that accompany such a charge are debilitating in group meetings among Blacks and are also destructive in Black-white relations.

Blacks do not need to prove to whites how Black they are, or the fact that they are Black. First of all, the fact is obvious, and any interpretation beyond that point is fruitless.

Being Concerned About What White Society Thinks of Us (block). There are many Blacks who are acutely concerned about how they may be viewed by the white community as individuals, and there are Blacks who are concerned about what the white society thinks about Black society. The Black individual's concern supersedes the way he or she may be viewed as an individual but relates to how he or she is thought of as a *Black person.* That is, Black individuals are concerned about whether they are projecting the proper images and attitudes as a *Black persons.* Much of this has to do with the fact that many Blacks have a need to seek the approval of whites on anything they may do. Ultimately, they request approval to be Black with an Afro and a dashiki. If whites say they like it, the Blacks are satisfied. On the other hand, if whites disapprove, the Black person is hurt and modifies his or her behavior.

By the same token, there are Blacks who are concerned about the images of the Black community from the white perspective. I have often heard Blacks who expressed grief when a Black person rapes someone white, or commits mass murder, because they are fearful of the images that white society will get. That is, they fear that whites are going to adopt the perspective that "they are all like that." However, Blacks must come to realize that they cannot be responsible for either the individual or the collective behavior and actions of other Blacks. Above all, they cannot control what white society may think about Black people. The fact of the matter is that what white individuals and society think about Black people tells one more about those particular white persons than it does about Black people. Yet, we have the responsibility to explore and sensitize whites to racism, when the situation arises. This is different from being overly conscious about what they think about us as individuals and/or collectively.

My Approach is the Best Approach to Handling Whites (block). Often, Blacks encountered other Blacks who feel as though they have the best solution to the problems of Black-white relations. They adopt the view that their approach in handling whites is the best approach and no other approach is feasible or workable. This is not to suggest that Blacks cannot learn from each other in their approach to handling difficulties in race relations; Some strategies may be more appropriate at a given time than other strategies. But the fact remains that no single Black individual has a monopoly on the best approaches to handling whites. An individual with such an ethnocentric view is not open to learning other possibilities and options. Above all, there is no fair exchange of ideas which can facilitate learning.

Talking to Other Blacks About White Behavior Rather Than Talking to Whites Concerned (block). Blacks are able to discuss, analyze, and interpret the behavior of whites but often find it difficult to confront whites on an individual basis or collectively about the issues concened. Many Blacks fear that their behavior or motives may be misinterpreted or they feel inadequately prepared to defend themselves in case that the white individual refutes the concerns being raised. Nonetheless, those fears are not present while they are in the company of other Blacks who show approval as well as disapproval of the analysis and interpretations being made.

It is necessary that Black individuals begin to spend less time ventilating with other Blacks and spend more time dealing directly with what they perceive to be the source of their problem. In many instances, there are Blacks who can give a vivid description of what they should do or what they in fact are planning to do, but much of what is discussed is often not realized. In the company of other Blacks, there are many Blacks individuals who are able to "move motivations" in regard to their treatment of Blacks but often such Blacks are "morse" in the presence of whites. This is not to suggest that Blacks should not converse with other Blacks about their relationships with whites or their analysis of white behavior; however, this is to imply that Blacks are not to limit their concern to ventilating to other Blacks.

Let's Act As Though We Are As Good As Whites (block). There are many Blacks who adopt the view that they are as "good as whites" or that they can "act as though they are as good as whites." Implicit in this assumption is the view that whiteness is good, while Blackness is bad. There is the ever-present assumption that white behavior is to be emulated because such behavior is equivalent to goodness and superiority, while Black behavior is to be rejected because it is equivalent to bad and inferiority. Consequently, many Blacks see it as appropriate to "act like whites." Once Black people liberate themselves from the negative stereotypes and myths in the American culture about Blackness and Black people and abolish all of the racist positive myths and assumptions in the American culture about whiteness and white people, the Blacks will be able to look more realistically at each other as well as whites. At the same time, whites will be better able to look more realistically at themselves and at Black people and Black culture.

Viewing Self As Better Than Other Blacks Because. . . . (block). Once Blacks begin to look at themselves as being better than other Blacks because . . ., they are using the same tactics to discriminate and justify their prejudices that they complain about in whites. This is not to imply that all Blacks are the same or that Blacks should view their behavior as similar, even though there are distinct differences in Black behaviors. However, those behaviors which differ from one's own should be looked at as merely different, not inferior or superior. When one takes this attitude there is no need to persuade all Blacks to be the same, nor is there a need to eliminate or discriminate against the behavior of Blacks which is not similar to one's own. On the contrary, it is quite appropriate to recognize characteristics within Black individuals that may vary. It is acceptable that likeness attracts and that Blacks gravitate to other Blacks who have similar goals, aspirations, and behaviors to their own, but it is inappropriate to separate oneself from other Blacks who may differ in behavior, aspirations, and values.

Assisting Other Blacks in Developing Black Consciousness (facilitate). In the same manner that Blacks should make white individuals aware of their racism, Blacks have a responsibility to assist other brothers and sisters in their development of Black consciousness, Black awareness, and Black identity. It is the process of sharing between Blacks and Blacks that continues to develop Black awareness and Black consciousness. It would be ideal if Blacks developed their Black identity and Black awareness mutually. However, the process does not always operate in this manner.

Black scholars, educators, and social scientists should develop Black awareness kits for use in elementary schools, high schools, colleges, and the community as a whole.

Race (Color) is Important in Interpersonal Relations Between Blacks and Whites (facilitate). There are many Blacks as well as whites who hold the view that color or other factors of race are unimportant in interpersonal relationships between Blacks and whites. An informed survey (discussion, in a classroom situation, between Blacks and whites) I have conducted shows more whites than Blacks to hold the notion that color is unimportant in interpersonal relations. Blacks seem to want their color to be recognized as important, while whites prefer to ignore color. At the same time, Blacks tend to want to recognize whiteness as a factor in establishing a relationship with whites, and they see the whiteness of the individual as being significant.

As we analyze this situation further, it becomes apparent that whites wish to ignore color or see color as unimportant; they say that they "look at the individual." When the point is made that they are looking at a Black individual, they ask why that is important. Further interpretation of this fact will reveal that whites wish to ignore color because in the minds of many whites the mere act of identifying color somehow implies discrimination or prejudice. There is a fear on the part of some whites that to identify race or color as important is to generate all of the negative myths, stereotypes, and assumptions existing about Black people. Therefore, in order to avoid this premise, many whites avoid considering color to be important. There are also some whites who are able to ignore color because they see a certain Black person as just another "white" individual.

However, an individual's race and color are important, and recognizing them demonstrates acceptance of that individual's total identity. It implies the recognition and acceptance of differences rather than the need to create or develop sameness in order to develop or maintain a relationship. This is true for Blacks as well as whites, for there are many Blacks who prefer to ignore color in their relationships with whites. Much of this has to do with the fact that Blacks attempt to make such whites into "Blacks" as a means of accepting them. The recognition of color as important implies that one is comfortable with his or her racial identity and comfortable with the race or color of another whose physical appearance and culture differs from one's own. In conclusion, however, color should not be important in relationships with members of the same race.

Seeing Self As Blacker Than Other Blacks (block). The "Blacker than thou" syndrome is destructive to the unification of Black people in the same manner that proving you are Black is destructive. Rhetoric and verbal exchange among Blacks that accompanies this syndrome is merely an indication of their insecurities in the area of their Black awareness. If one is secure with one's identity, there is no need to engage in fruitless dialogue—to maintain, for example, that one is "Blacker" than another Black individual. Yet, the practice was widespread during the sixties and is prevalent today. In addition to individuals, there are Black organizations and institutions which engage in the same dialogue. If a Black person feels that he or she has some expertise or knowledge to offer the Black community, he or she should make this knowledge known. However, if that expertise is not needed or required, the Black individual should find the organization or institution which can best use it.

If I Were White I'd Have It Made (block). There are Blacks who would prefer to be white, given what appears to be the privileged position that whites have within this society. Thus, they feel as though they would be really "getting over" as whites, given the talents, skills, and energy they possess as Black individuals. On the other hand, there are Blacks with undeveloped skills and talents who hold the view that they would "have it made" as a white person because of the readily available resources for white people. Yet, Blacks with such an attitude place the greatest emphasis on the acquisition of material goods; they equate material wealth with "having it made" and deemphasize the quality and essence of their individual identities. In other words, they have identified with the benefits accorded white America based on the white American's exploitative nature and racism. There is no inherent quality relating to white humanity which Blacks do not have, for ultimately the oppressor is as oppressed as the group or individuals whom he or she oppresses. Both are captives. If the analogy of the white man standing with his foot on the Black man's back is an indication of racism, then it takes as much energy, if not more, for the white man to keep the Black man down as it does for the Black man to attempt to get up.

A Brother Will Let You Down When Things Get Tough (block). There is a particular assumption in the Black community that a Black man will let another brother down in a crunch, particularly when the situation involves confrontation with whites. Thus, Blacks operate out of fear and paranoia when they work with other Blacks in planning streategies against white society. This view is also held when Blacks operate within groups, among themselves. This is not to suggest Blacks have not let other brothers down when the going gets tough; however, this myth is not reality, and it is destructive to the development of Black awareness and Black consciousness. Blacks should look at Blacks on an individual basis and not perpetuate a stereotype which is destructive to Black unity.

Assisting Whites in Understanding Racist Behavior of Which They are Unaware (facilitate). During the sixties and the height of Black consciousness-raising, many Blacks held the view that it was not their responsibility to educate, teach, or sensitize white people. This view declined at the decline of the Black liberation struggle. Nonetheless, there are still many Blacks who hold this point of view.

Once we accept the fact that being Black is not equal to being antiwhite and, for that matter, that being antiwhite is not necessarily equal to being pro-Black, then we can accept the fact that we have a continuing responsibility to make whites conscious of areas of racism of which they are unaware. This is not putting oneself in the position of a guinea pig, as is thought by the Blacks who refuse to make whites aware, for it should be the responsibility of any individual to make other individuals aware of where they may be going. This is no more than the communication which should take place between two authentic adults. Yet, the view remains that the whites who claim to be aware should make other whites aware. This is true; however, the only way that most whites can get to the point that they can educate other whites is through contact and sensitivity from Blacks.

We are neither Better nor Worse Than the Least of Our Brothers and Sisters (facilitate). It is a fact that Black people have thought of themselves as being better than other Blacks for various reasons. Some Blacks have considered themselves better than other Blacks because they may have lighter complexions, are more educated, have more money, associate with whites, live in a certain neighborhood, and so on. The fact is, however, that no Black person is better or worse than the least Black among us. Our lives are intricately tied into the lives of all other Blacks. Consequently, Blacks can not engage in the better/worse paridign. This is not to suggest that Blacks are not different from one another or that they do not possess individuality, but the fact remains that we are neither better nor worse than the least among us. Ultimately, in the eyes of white America this is true. The FBI's suspicion and surveilance of the NAACP, SNCC, and the Black Panther Party are a clear-cut indication of this. In *The Man Who Cried I am,* John A. Williams revealed a plan whereby all Blacks would be incarcerated if a full-scale Black revolution emerged. This plan included the "best" and "worst" of the Black community.

Going an Extra Mile to Help Someone Who is Black (facilitate). There are Blacks who have done away with the concept of color, and look at an individual as an individual. They do not hold any allegiance to Black people because they are Black. Consequently, they will not go an extra mile to help someone who is Black. Whites view the behavior of whites who will go an extra mile to help someone Black as reverse racism. Many cases in the courts today regard this very same issue.

Some Blacks go to the opposite extreme. They will vote for someone Black "just because he or she is Black," without regard to the background or qualifications of the person concerned. The implications are that the candidate is better because he or she is Black. This is not necessarily true. By the same token, there are whites as well as Blacks who vote for whites primarily because they are white. This reason is inadequate, for whenever a person is elected because of his or her race or color alone, a total injustice has been perpetuated upon the election system. It occurs often. However, we as Black people must look at what is going to be best for us and elect the person who can accomplish it. Yet, we must go an extra mile with the Black person. That is, we must find a Black person we want to represent us. We must assist in cultivating and refining the Blacks who may not meet all of our standards and qualifications as candidates. We must go that extra mile with Blacks.

PART III

THE SOCIOLOGICAL DIMENSIONS

Fundamental to an understanding of the nature of intellectual thought in contemporary society is the proper analysis of social phenomena. Sociology, as it has been developed, deals with the intricacies of human socialization and institution-building. In one sense, it is the social science which best fits the category of social science; in another sense it is the least unified of the social sciences. Our authors demonstrate the unity inherent in the new perspectives operating in the field.

In this section our authors provide penetrating analyses of five major social issues: (1) media technology, (2) television effect, (3) church, (4) criminal behavior, and (5) health care. Howard's chapter demonstrates the effect of media technology on human sociology. She is most precise in her understanding of the impact of the technology on African Americans. In fact, this is a pioneering work on the relationship of media to society, because Howard takes the technology of media and demystifies it. Asante discusses the impact of television on African-American children. His work reinterprets data presented by some researchers and affirms others. Wilson's brilliant work on church participation is a return to a subject which has long fascinated social and behaviorial scientists interested in interpreting African-American life. Wilson's work is a singular effort to lay open the relevant demographics of the situation, to explain how participation in the church relates to social development. Following Wilson is Johnson's sound study of alcoholism in regard to the recidivism question. He categorically denounced any relationship between criminal repeaters and the addiction to alcoholism. Johnson's work has implications for all students of crime and rehabilitation. These studies add to the body of contemporary explorations in sociology.

10

MEDIA TECHNOLOGY AND
AFRICAN-AMERICAN SOCIOLOGY

Juanita Howard

As by Merton (1968: 475), the self-fulfilling prophecy is generally based on and is best understood in terms of the Thomas Theorem: "If men define situations as real they are real in their consequences." This theorem, in application, was and indeed remains a significant determinant in the struggle between blacks and whites in America. From the 1700s when blacks' condition as slaves determined their inferior status in the social structure, on through to their statutory emancipation in 1865 and to the 1954 Supreme Court decision declaring the inequality inherent in the educational separation of blacks, whites have unswervingly held and still hold to the concept that blacks are innately inferior to them (Frederickson, 1971; Jensen, 1969). This most historically prevalent of American attitudes has promoted and installed a socioeconomic-political environment which has denied blacks equal opportunities in every socializing particular—most meaningfully and consequentially in education and employment. Indeed, denial of this particular combination of needs still powerfully operates to fulfill the historical white prophecy (and too often to induce black acceptance) of black illiteracy and that pervasive hopelessness among blacks carelessly characterized as "laziness" (Merton, 1968: 475).

However, Merton (1968: 477-478) points out that

> the self-fulfilling prophecy is, in the beginning, a *false* definition of the situation evoking a new behavior which makes the originally false conception come *true*. The specious validity of the self-fulfilling prophecy perpetuates a reign of error.... As a result of their

failure to comprehend the operation of the self-fulfilling prophecy, many Americans of good will (sometimes reluctantly) retain enduring ethnic and racial prejudices. They experience these beliefs, not as prejudices, not as prejudgments, but as irresistible products of their own observation. "The facts of the case" permit them no other conclusion.

It is obvious that so much of the worst social prophecies concerning blacks in America could not have been fulfilled without dedicated cooperation of institutions composing the American social whole; and as unintentional and unconscious as this whole negative prophetic process might have become, examination of the history of blacks in America reveals that the consequences for blacks have been no less negative and indeed might now be even worse. For example, progressive technological development of the means of communication, from the printing press to the television tube, may on balance be viewed as at best a mixed blessing by those historically, intellectually, and morally interested in a progressively positive social position for blacks in America and throughout the world.

Advancing technological development of radio and motion pictures has, in turn, either more and more effectively advanced the distortion and ridiculing of blacks' disadvantaged social position, or more and more effectively ignored it. Media stereotypes of blacks characterized as coons, toms, mammies, bucks, and tragic mulattoes were predominantly developed for and projected by motion pictures (Bogle, 1973). These characterizations not only negatively affected how generations of whites historically viewed blacks but, even more important, how generations of blacks perceived themselves (Cripps, 1977; Bogle, 1974; Noble, 1974).

Historically, an inverse relationship appears to exist between ongoing development of media technology and objective media treatment of blacks (Cripps, 1977; Barnouw, 1977). Consistent with this phenomenon, there seems to be a direct general relationship between media projections of blacks and the unvaryingly negative perception of the black American community by the white American community (Cripps, 1977; White, 1969).

Recognizing the coercive, pedagogical role of media technology, this chapter will address itself to media reflection of black stereotypes and their sociological implications for relationships between blacks and whites in America. Specifically, a description and discussion of technology as employed by college students studying mass media and its relation to black Americans will be explored.

Crucial to their examination of the latter relationship, the students sought to answer the following questions: (1) Why was it important and crucial for white America to reinforce negative images of blacks? and (2) By what means were these negative images communicated?

Research has revealed that, indeed, the extent to which blacks internalized these images all but excluded development of feelings other than inferiority, negative self-concept, self-hatred, and intragroup conflict (Clark, 1965; Murray, 1973). In a way perhaps totally unforeseen, these abasing projections, in the broadest sense, negatively affected relationships between blacks and whites.

Concerted efforts have since been made to examine the effects of images of blacks as portrayed in the print media, in films, and now more particularly in television, which has used, learned from, and now replaced motion pictures as the most effective, technologically advanced, mass-educational teaching tool—subliminal and overt.

The message expressed in every form of communication, be it verbal, the printed word, or visual, has been that blacks are inherently inferior to whites in every way—physically, intellectually, and culturally—leaving whites helplessly superior in all ways. Jordan (1969) found that attempts were made to legitimize these perceptions first by popular and common use of biblical allegories, such as the curse of Ham, or by the postulation that the dark tribes of Africa were fated to be "hewers of wood and drawers of water." Jordan examines the development of these antiblack perceptions in depth. His thesis is a perceptual dissertation on the arguments upon which the white male has built his theories of racial superiority.

I believe it is fair to say that some whites developed these arguments to convince each other (Myrdal, 1962: 60). They had to believe these theories or else they would not be able to convince other generations of whites of the "validity" of their case—nor adequately develop a negative self-fulfilling prophecy of black racial disabilities for black consumption (Merton, 1968; Frederickson, 1971: 245-255).

Jordan further indicates that beginning with the description of blacks and their cultures by early white explorers of Africa, we find continuous confusion about the black skin color. Was it the result of overexposure to the sun? Was the blackness carried in the blood like a sickness? After pseudo-scientific probings, but with no acceptable answers to these and other questions, theories were developed to support white presuppositions about the black man's inferiority. They were based on skin color as a different and unknown quantity because skin color was such an obvious observable difference, which could be exploited on many levels (Myrdal, 1962: 97). Thus, for over four hundred years, erroneous theories regarding blacks' innate inferiority have persisted, and negative images of blacks have been projected by whites to whites and blacks alike (Lyons, 1970).

Clearly, it is difficult to exploit or enslave someone whom you recognize as a person, as a human being. It would mean constantly contending with the individual's feelings, pain, humanity. But if you can convince yourself through scientific theories and "corroborated" biblical research that that individual is not a person but an inhuman, savage, uneducable, and treacherous animal, then you can do anything—treat the person in any fashion you choose, like a chair, tobacco, cotton, things that are inanimate—much like any other commodity traded in the slave period (Myrdal, 1962: 103).

The documented history of slavery in America attests to the complete acceptance of these theories of black inferiority not only by the slave traders, but by the majority of the white population, who did not participate in the slave trade but who benefitted from the national economic advantage enjoyed as a result of the slave business (Meier, 1976).

From as early as the 1700s, the American black man's social reality has been described and projected in the print media always in the most narrowly ideological and negatively subjective, traditional American terms. Indeed, the historical media projections of blacks as bestial or savage almost inevitably institutionalized such projections as classic stereotypes, and reinforced the variety of antiblack preconceptions.

The newspaper was the primary commercial medium of communication prior to the abolition of slavery. Printing was introduced in England in the late 1400s and newspapers were printed in the 1600s. But it was not until the early 1700s that what was called the "colonial press" developed in America (DeFleur and Ball-Rokeach, 1975). It was in these newspapers that slaves were advertised along with all other cargo being shipped into the colonies. Descriptions were given as to the slaves' general physical condition—their strength, sturdiness, and fecundity.

In addition, the politicization propagandistically characterized the slaves' inherent emotional makeup as lazy, treacherous, and sullen. This would alert the buyer and indeed the whole culture of slavers to the temperament not only of the individual slave but of his race. This would then dictate the nature of the restraints needed to ensure productive handling of both the slave and his race.

Wax (1969) presented some graphic examples of how the sale and general dispositions of blacks of the period were reported. What is significant is the consistently negative bias coloring all media reporting about blacks—then as now, a pervasive factor, instrumental in setting up fear in whites and in reinforcing previously accepted negative images and attitudes about blacks (Myrdal, 1962).

An interesting related phenomenon is that illiterate whites during that period relied for their information solely on the folkloric tradition (oral history, if you will). There are several instructive dissertations on the point (Turner, 1965; Spaulding, 1972; Perdue, 1971). The significance is that such whites understood the black only as the stereotypes described to them, and were thus literally given the images which preconditioned their attitudes toward blacks before they ever saw a slave. Rosenberg (1970) found in researching the image of blacks in white folklore that they were in some instances quite pathological, as so many of the images held by whites dealt in obsessively lascivious detail with myths about black sexuality and appetites.

Needless to say, for the free blacks in the North who had learned to read and write, the need to strike out in print against the total institution of slavery was imperative. As a direct result, *Freedom's Journal* was founded on March 16, 1827. This newspaper's black cofounders, Russworm and Cornish, first and foremost called for the abolition of slavery. In addition they decried the misrepresentations of blacks and asserted the need for educating blacks and for civil rights for blacks. As an organ of abolitionism, Frederick Douglass's newspaper, *The North Star*, also championed the same struggle. Douglass's newspaper sought above all to project black people as other than the caricatures so common to white media of the time (Dann, 1972).

Unfortunately, the effects of the long conditioning of whites against blacks had by then routinely expressed themselves in acts of brutality and menace, particularly by slave owners and their overseers. Brutality and menace became the commonest of American antiblack instruments. Floggings, beatings, brandings, mutilation, lynchings, and cross-burnings served to condition the minds of blacks to understand the source of this brutalization as all-powerful (White, 1969). The consequent psychopolitical development laid the social foundation for black fear of, deference to, and dependency on that very power, with resulting loss of black self-esteem, lowered black self-concept, and finally the development of black self-hatred (Kardiner and Ovesey, 1966).

Another element which played a crucial and significant role in subverting black social existence was and still is the high contrivance by whites which effect the pervasive social "invisibility" of blacks in America. It was obvious on the plantations and as depicted in the colonial press that slaves were property and not people to be seen, touched, or humanely considered. What was reported about them in the newspapers of the period only related to their salability or concerned the offering of a reward for an escaped slave.

It is important to point out that although during slavery some free blacks printed their own newspapers and began the struggle for equality in print, they were a very small minority compared to the number of blacks who were slaves and so could not read and avail themselves of even that small black media message.

In addition, the gatekeepers—that is, those whose sole purpose is maintenance of the status quo—understanding the importance of preventing slaves from propagating revolutionary ideas, were particularly vigilant in their menace and brutalization of slaves who either attempted to learn to read, to write, or to escape (Aptheker, 1968: 595).

Therefore, the tactic of "contrived invisibility" was related to keeping blacks from becoming a part of any organized society by denying their social and thus their human existence. This allowed blacks to be maids, butlers, cooks, nursemaids, and all other types of service functionaries—people to be given orders but who were not permitted to question anything. Thus, slaves were looked over, around, and through, as if they did not exist (Kardiner and Ovesey, 1966: 42-43).

Ellison's (1952) classic work examines this concept in great social depth. Another interesting study analyzed the role of the press in reporting about blacks in Los Angeles from 1892 to 1968 (Johnson et al., 1971). Their research revealed that blacks were virtually "invisible" to whites based on newspaper reporting of black activities, up to and including the period immediately preceding the Watts riot in 1965. Interviews with whites selected at random revealed that many had never been in a black neighborhood, did not see a black more than once a week, or blocked blacks out of their consciousnesses even when they may have encountered a black person.

The Los Angeles *Times* and the Los Angeles *Herald Examiner* averaged less than 1 percent print space to black news coverage from the period from 1892 to 1954. (The later date marked the period of the Supreme Court school desegregation decision.) When these newspapers did report information concerning blacks, it was usually related to a negative incident.

The 1950s saw a slight increase in news coverage of blacks. The riot in Watts positively affected the extent of coverage of black activity, although the news again was of a negative nature—primarily of interracial conflict. The study showed that within a short period of time after the riot, news coverage of blacks again returned to the pre-Watts riot level.

It is important to note that during Reconstruction, because of the educational programs of the Freedman's Bureau and other organizations, illiteracy decreased among blacks. Many more blacks were then able to read and so were acutely aware of how they were being depicted in the press, and of the negative attitudes that were always developing. Black editors continued to oppose these negative projections in their own newspapers, which proliferated after the Civil War and into the twentieth century (Williams, 1976).

Toward the end of the nineteenth century great strides had been made in the ability to transmit sound by means of electrical systems and project moving images on a screen. Before these two technological phenomena were synchronized, people watched silent motion pictures. Two early films which strongly angered blacks were Edwin S. Porter's *Uncle Tom's Cabin* in 1903, which featured a white actor in stereotype, burnt-cork black face, portraying the black man as idiotically docile and inappropriately compassionate, and D. W. Griffith's *Birth of a Nation* in 1915, perhaps the most powerfully influential antiblack film ever made (Mapp, 1971). This latter film's theme was related to the Civil War, its causes and its effects upon the South. The blacks were again stereotypically depicted by white actors using burnt cork on their faces. Their portrayals venomously stereotyped blacks, and basically established the kind of roles blacks would ultimately play in films (Cripps, 1977). So violent were reactions of white audiences to the depiction of a young white southern girl being chased through the woods and menaced by a lustful "black" soldier (a girl so fearful of and repulsed by the menacing black that she leaps from a cliff to her death) and to another scene of marauding "black" Union soldiers plundering and burning white southern homes, that blacks were beaten in the streets and lynched, black homes were burned, and Ku Klux Klan crosses were burned in the yards of black families. Again, whites deliberately employed gross media distortions, brutality, and menace to reinforce their social and political omnipotence (Landay, 1973: 26).

Mapp's (1972) definitive research again demonstrates that during the pre-World War II period, blacks were as a matter of course depicted in a derogatory manner in American as well as European films.

From the 1920s, when sound was synchronized with motion pictures, until the present, the movies have been the most powerful attitude-shaping, behavior-modifying, teaching tool invented. Looking at the movie screen, the masses of blacks could escape neither their American degradation nor the cruelly caricatured images held of them by the white society (Cripps, 1977). There blacks saw the unvarnished American perception of them as buffoons and clowns, as stupid, laughing, praying, pimping, whoring, as killers of other blacks. Blacks learned to hate themselves (Kardiner and Ovesey, 1966).

Through the same screen the mass of whites in turn learned to laugh at blacks and to hate them. The projected stereotypes reinforced old antiblack attitudes or developed new negative ones. Unfortunately, in due course it was black actors who were employed to portray these stereotypes on the screen. Many blacks, of course, disapproved of this. They felt such black actor's portrayals totally subverted all the positive efforts made by other blacks to overcome the bombardment of negative images of them (Patterson, 1974).

Ironically, during the period 1882-1927, over 5000 people were lynched in America, and of that number 3500 were recorded as being blacks. During the period 1920-1927, blacks were not only being lynched figuratively on the motion picture screen but quite literally by marauding whites who felt encouraged to do so by the assurance that the act would be done with impunity (White, 1969: 172).

Although lynchings subsided and decreased markedly, the negative images of blacks in the media did not. This, of course, provokes the obvious and often-asked question—what were the blacks doing over this 200-year period? Why for example, did they not use the media to project more positive images?

The fact is, of course, that blacks did rebel against their oppressive conditions, and in many instances were successful in escaping to the North or West primarily by means of the Underground Railroad. After the Civil War, during Reconstruction, blacks were instrumental in the successful passage of the Thirteenth, Fourteenth, and Fifteenth Amendments. During that period there were black senators and congressmen seated in southern state capitols and in Washington, D.C. But white hostility and resentment over what many whites felt was discrimination in reverse—a phrase with a certain current familiarity—because of the educational and employment programs which they felt benefitted blacks more than whites. Such white hostility spilled over to become the all-too-common lynchings pervading the earlier period referred to (Meier and Rudurich, 1976).

At the time of the Depression, during the 1920s and 1930s, blacks began migrating North and to the Midwest. There again they met with violent white hostility. Because of the scarcity of jobs, blacks were seen as a threat to stable employment and wages. Factory owners were known to hire blacks at lower wages and as scab labor when there were strikes.

Consequently, at the turn of the century and until the mid-forties, lynchings of blacks and race riots were almost commonplace. However, blacks were better capable of defending themselves. And they did. Many blacks and whites were killed and wounded in these riots. Concerned whites and blacks (for example, the NAACP) realized that these killings had to end. The NAACP fought for legislative passage of an antilynching law. However, it was not until 1937 that a similar bill was passed by the House of Representatives, but not the Senate. Although it did not become law, this bill caused a more positive response to the principle of civil rights and human dignity for blacks.

Still, a continuing crucial problem was, and remains, media projections of unrepresentative, negative black images. Historically, the NAACP has been visible in organizing demonstrations, picketing plays and motion pictures in which blacks were being misrepresented. The NAACP and many other black organizations have pressed for the hiring of black media technicians, writers, and directors who would provide some significant input into characterizations of blacks in media and so promote more positive images (Noble, 1974).

We can infer from this overview that research of—and related to—the development of stereotypes of blacks in media shows that each media-technology advance, from newspapers to television, more than anything else made it possible for both black and white American communities to view and hear ever more clearly the qualitatively unchanged, negative projections of blacks. Burdened with this "clarity of misperceptions," both communities are then coerced into forming additional opinions and values about black America—or into reinforcing old ones—based essentially on the spectrum of media stereotypes.

In the fall of 1976, as an innovation, fifty-two students taking the course "Mass Media and the Black American" were assigned to in-depth research of the range of mass-media stereotypes of blacks. This exploration was undertaken in recognition of the by now common appreciation of media's uncommon power as a sociocultural determinant. The course, "Mass Media and the Black American," had been designed and developed as a part of the Black and Hispanic Studies curriculum at Baruch College, in major part to address and explore this ongoing relationship. The specific task of the class as a whole was to use data gathered to present a historical overview of the status and treatment of blacks in the form of an audio-visual exposition to which the entire student body and faculty of the college would then be invited to record their criticism and commentary.

The content of the standard "Mass Media and the Black American" course first of all requires general examination of the nature and basic elements of communication (DeFleur and Ball-Rokeach, 1975). That information is then used as background for specific examination of the black role in media, including the uses of black stereotypes, and for understanding the psychosocial implications of these projections for blacks in America (Clark, 1965).

However, as part of my redesign of the course, in addition, black personalities in media were invited to discuss their experiences, status, and roles as, essentially, blacks in white media. Among several guests who appeared were Harry Belafonte, actor/director, Charlayne Hunter-Gault, New York *Times* reporter, David Lampel, director of news for station

WBLS, and Jimmy Hicks, editor of the New York *Amsterdam News*. Slides and films depicting the range of black stereotypes were, of course, also analyzed. These processes provoked lively discussion. However, it soon became apparent that proper understanding and appreciation of the social, ideological, political, and economic significance of media's powerfully subliminal influence on blacks crucially prerequire in-depth examination of the relationship between the historical progression of the overall social image of blacks in America and the historical treatment of blacks by each medium as it developed. Certainly no less critical to this understanding is study of the historical development—or nondevelopment—of black media in America, and of the latent as well as the manifest uses to which both media images continue to be commercially and ideologically put (Myrdal, 1962; Dann, 1972).

Students were therefore assigned the historical research of black stereotypes as a class project. The data gathered were then used as the material basis of a mass-media exposition entitled "Blacks in Media: Yesterday, Today and Tomorrow." The Students were solely responsible for the research and for the scripting or writing of all information about all materials displayed. The instructor served as a resource person—for example, lecturing on related sociological theories primarily having to do with race relations and communication theory.

The students worked in six teams composed of seven or eight students each, with one team for each of the five major media: newspapers, magazines, radio, films, and television. The sixth team explored live theater. The students felt that although it did not represent the popular concept of mass media, live theater is nevertheless a powerful means of cultural communication and one with which the black community is becoming increasingly involved (Patterson, 1974). Historically, live theater, of course, provided the learning environment for many successful black actors and actresses in films, not the least among whom were and are, Paul Robeson, Canada Lee, Diana Sands, James Earl Jones, and Ossie Davis (Landay, 1973).

Each team met, decided upon specific tasks for each member, and set deadlines for selection and analysis of all materials. At the times decided upon, technical and sometimes technological decisions were made regarding, for example, materials best suited for presentation as slides or as videotapes.

The classroom lectures gave historical background which complemented the research material secured by the students. If, for example, the lecture concerned the American press of the mid- or late-nineteenth century, students on the newspaper team would discuss, and so in discussion more compellingly demonstrate, the critical necessity for concurrent development of the black press as a parallel structure, and the singular power for change that, as an institution, it might accomplish (Blackwell and Janowitz, 1975).

Close classroom examination of documents such as *Freedom's Journal,* published by John Russworm and Samuel Cornish in 1827, or Frederick Douglass's newspaper, *The North Star,* graphically communicated the sense of the dangerous historical environment in which blacks lived and managed to survive in America. It was in these discussions that the project's productivity was appreciated. It was apparent in such exchanges that the students were better able to understand and discuss the interdisciplinary concepts of alienation, social isolation, racial segregation, and discrimination. They also more readily grasped sociological theories associated with communication concepts, such as functional analysis, dysfunction, manifest and latent functions, conflict theory, and the self-fulfilling prophecy.

To give clearer understanding to the general student body and faculty viewing and listening to the exhibits, the class provided a written introduction to the overall production. In addition, separate written introductions were also provided for each medium researched. The completed production included over 200 photographs and pictures, 50 slides, videotapes of prominent black media personalities from each medium, recordings of Paul Robeson, Bessie Smith and the cast recording of the Broadway play, "For Colored Girls Who Have Considered Suicide When the Rainbow Is Enuf'."

There were copies of approximately 35 separate black newspapers from across the country, in addition to magazines representing and covering areas of special interest to the black community. There were presentations of blacks in media, from the most abasing stereotypes to black producers and directors. And no attempts were made to minimize the problem of continued stereotyping of blacks in contemporary media (Bogle, 1974). As an epilogue, in summary, the project addressed the role black communities must assume in attacking perceptions which allow young blacks in particular to accept the commonly projected stereotypes as valid and viable modes of behavior (Howard, 1975).

This production provided a learning experience that was informative and indelible beyond any participant's most optimistic anticipation. For example, as students worked together in the groups composed of males and females, they found themselves confronted with and discussing sex roles. The males unquestioningly expected the females to do the typing of all information. Enjoying a somewhat more heightened awareness, the females refused the traditional honor (Wolosin, 1974). Everyone who could type was expected to type his or her own material, following a specific format for uniformity. When the work was completed, the males in particular were rather proud of their newfound self-reliance.

Since the production required interdisciplinary efforts and expression in constant crossovers between sociology, black history, media technology, and pedagogy, it particularly stimulated the interest of faculty members and students with academic interests and investment in those areas. The written comments from students and faculty were overwhelmingly positive. Many confessed the appalling degree of their general unawareness of the pervasiveness of negative projections of blacks in media, and of blacks' continuing, but desperately unavailing, efforts to substitute more representative black images. The students were observably proud of their efforts and more than gratified by the congratulatory comments of their fellow students and the faculty.

At the last session, the students then evaluated the project and the course. The students indicated the following:

(1) Those who had never taken sociology felt more comfortable with the course because they had a clearer understanding of the concepts.

(2) Researching the material themselves brought them into contact with other related information which added to their knowledge and understanding—not least, of the course.

(3) All students, whites and blacks, expressed greater understanding of the racial problems in America—greater empathy with the efforts of, for example, Dr. Martin Luther King, Jr.; and, in particular, greater appreciation of the historical causes of employment now plaguing black youth.

(4) Man of the black male and female students were particularly chastened by the information and experience. Their self-concepts, their degrees of self-awareness relative to their ages, their education, their vocational choices, and their interpersonal relationships were all brought into question.

(5) Media's responsibility for projecting the ongoing, negatively distorted programming about blacks without some balance of representative black programming, also came into question.

(6) All were concerned about eliminating inconsistencies relating to the well-advertised equal availability of at least opportunity to all American citizens.

(7) In conclusion, the students recognized black sociology and the black community as shaped in large part by the deep American internalization of negative images essentially projected by media.

They also suspect and fear that the larger American society's prejudices and hostilities vis-á-vis black America are in no small way reinforced by the media's bombardment of America with negative black images.

Finally, the class recognized their responsibility as students, as members of the media audience, and as members of society at least to write to offending newspapers or television stations when, as is the common case, grossly unrepresentative images are projected in the media. Conversely, where they see representative programming, letters of commendation and encouragement should be sent. Both responses could have some reforming effect on the media's tendency toward misrepresentation and derision of blacks.

The results of the project revealed that a larger and more practically consequential problem exists: Basically there are still too few blacks in top-level decision-making positions in the media; and even they suffer from the lack of capital accumulation sufficient to finance media projects which would project the images and substance necessary to reverse severe damage already done to the image of blacks and to replace the inimical stereotypes with more representative black reality.

Dodson and Hachten (1973) concluded that ownership of the means of communication is power for any group. In their analysis, Africans and Afro-Americans are equally negatively affected by total control of the media by outsiders. These outsiders select, edit, and shape all news and media projections coming into black communities or, in the case of Africans, into the particular black country.

Furthermore, the lack of trained journalists and skilled technical personnel for electronic media cripplingly handicaps the African and the Afro-American alike. Also, the problem of reduced language facility in America and the lack of a common language in Africa impede interaction with the larger society and communication on the international level.

An ultimate goal, therefore, is for blacks to own a representative part of the means of media communication, particularly in the area of broadcast media. This would provide the resources for developing the many other concepts involved in successful broadcasting.

It is my belief that this goal will be addressed only when those members of the black community who are able to finance such projects finally come to the understanding that black media ownership is absolutely crucial to their personal interests and to the survival of the black community (Merton, 1968: 478). It is hoped that the product of this analysis can be the basis for giving productive direction to the formulation of new images, to the end that the coming generations, black and white, will be able to understand and preserve a more sanguine and less narrowly parochial society. In a word, we look forward to the creation and projection of a positive, self-fulfilling prophecy.

REFERENCES

APTHEKER, H. (1968) *A Documentary History of the Negro People in the United States, 1910-1932.* Secaucus, NJ: Citadel Press.

BEGLIS, J. F. and A. A. SHEIKH (1974) "Development of the self-concept in Black and White children." *Journal of Negro Education* 43: 104-110.

BARNOUW, E. (1977) *Tube of Plenty: The Evolution of American Television.* New York: Oxford University Press.

BLACKWELL, J. E. and M. JANOWITZ (1975) *Black Sociologists: Historical and Contemporary Perspectives.* Chicago: University of Chicago Press.

BOGLE, D. (1974) "Uptown Saturday night: a look at its place in black film history." *Freedomways* 14, 4: 320-330.

––– (1973) *Toms, Coons, Mulattoes, Mammies and Bucks: An Interpretative History of Blacks in American Films.* New York: Viking.

BOND, J. C. (1975) "The media image of Black women." *Freedomways* 15, 1: 34-37.

CLARK, K. (1965) *Dark Ghetto: Dilemmas of Social Power.* New York: Harper & Row.

COLE, B. C. (1970) *Television.* New York: Free Press.

COLLE, R. D. (1968) "Negro image in the mass media: a case study in social change." *Journalism Quarterly* 45: 55-60.

COOPER, L. and L. S. HAVERKOS (1973) "The image of American society in popular music: a search for identity and values." *Social Studies* 64-65: 319-322.

CRIPPS, T. (1977) *Slow fade to Black: the Negro in American film, 1900-1942.* New York: Oxford University Press.

––– (1969) "Movies in the ghetto, B.P. (before Poitier)." *Negro Digest* 8: 21-27, 45-48.

––– (1967) "The death of Rastus: Negroes in American films since 1945." *Phylon* 28: 267-75.

DANN, M. E. (1972) *The Black press, 1827-1890: the quest for national identity.* New York: G. P. Putnam.

DeFLEUR, M. L. and S. BALL-ROKEACH (1975) *Theories of Mass Communication.* New York: David McKay.

DODSON, D. and W. A. HACHTEN (1973) "Communication and development: African and Afro-American parallels." *Journalism Monographs:* 28-33.

DWORKIN, M. S. (1960) "The new Negro on the screen." *Progressive* 24: 39-41.

ELLISON, R. (1952) *The Invisible Man.* New York: New American Library.

FRANKLIN, J. H. (1974) *From Slavery to Freedom: A History of Negro Americans.* New York: Knopf.

FREDERICKSON, G. M. (1971) *The Black Image in the White Mind: The Debate on Afro-American Character and Destiny.* New York: Harper & Row.

GATES, H. L. (1976) "Portraits in Black: from *Amos 'n' Andy* to *Coonskin.*" *Harpers* 242, 1513: 16-25.

HATCHER, R. G. (1973) "Mass media and the Black community." *Black Scholar:* 2-10.

HIRSCH, P. M. (1968) "An analysis of Ebony: the magazine and its readers." *Journalism Quarterly* 45: 261-70, 292.

HOWARD, J. R. (1975) "Sitting, eating popcorn as alienation grows." New York Times (August 12).

HUGHES, L. and M. MELTZER (1956) *A Pictorial History of the Negro in America.* New York: Crown.

JENSEN, A. R. (1969) "How much can we boost IQ and scholastic achievement?" *Harvard Educational Review* 39: 1-23.

JOHNSON, P. B., D. O. SEARS, and J. R. McCOHAY (1971) "Black invisibility, the press, and the Los Angeles riot." *American Journal of Sociology* 76, 4: 698-721.

JONES, R. L. (1972) *Black Psychology.* New York: Harper & Row.

JORDAN, W. D. (1969) *White Over Black: American Attitudes Toward the Negro, 1550-1812.* Baltimore: Penguin.

KARDINER, A. and L. OVESEY (1966) *The Mask of Oppression: Explorations in the Personality of the American Negro.* New York: World Publishing.

KEY, W. B. (1972) *Subliminal Seduction.* New York: New American Library.

KLEIN, W. (1968) "News, media and race relations: a self-portrait." *Columbia Journalism Review* 12: 3.

LANDAY, E. (1973) *Black Film Stars.* New York: Drake.

LINCOLN, C. E. (1967) *The Negro Pilgrimage in America: The Coming of Age of the Black American.* New York: Bantam.

LYMAN, S. M. (1972) *The Black American in Sociological Thought: A Failure of Perspective.* New York: G. P. Putnam.

LYONS, C. H. (1970) "To wash an Aethiop white: British ideas about Black African educability, 1530-1865." Doctoral dissertation, Columbia University.

MAPP, E. (1972) *Blacks in American Films: Today and Yesterday.* Metuchen, NJ: Scarecrow.

McCOMB, M. E. (1968) "Negro use of television and newspapers for political information." *Journal of Broadcasting* 13: 26.

MEIER, A. and E. RUDURICH (1976) *From Plantation to Ghetto.* New York: McGraw-Hill.

MENCHER, M. (1969) "Journalism: the way it is, as seen by Black reporters and students." *Journalism Quarterly* 96: 499-504, 554.

MERRILL, J. C. and R. L. LOWENSTEIN (1973) *Media Messages and Men. New Perspectives in Communication.*

MERTON, R. K. (1968) *Social Theory and Social Structure.* New York: Free Press.

MIDURA, E. M. (1971) *Why Aren't We Getting Through: The Urban Communications Crisis.* Washington, DC: Acropolis.

MOSS, C. M. (1963) "The Negro in American films." *Freedomways* 3: 134-142.

MURRAY, J. (1973) *To Find an Image: Black Films from Uncle Tom to Superfly.* Indianapolis: Bobbs-Merrill.

MUSGRAVE, P. W. (1965) *The Sociology of Education.* New York: Methuen.

MYRDAL, G. (1962) *The Negro Problem and Modern Democracy: An American Dilemma.* New York: Harper & Row.

NOBLE, G. (1974) "Who controls media information?" *Freedomways* 14, 4: 317-319.

NOBLE, P. (1970) *The Negro in Films.* New York: Arno.

OLMSTEAD, M. S. (1959) *The Small Group.* New York: Random House.

PATTERSON, L. (1974) "Black theater: the search goes on." *Freedomways* 14, 3: 242-246.
——— [ed.] (1968) *Anthology of the American Negro in the Theatre. A Critical Approach.* New York: Publishers Company.
PERDUE, C. L. (1971) "Movie star woman in the land of the black angries: ethnography and folklore of a negro community in rural Virginia." Doctoral dissertation, University of Pennsylvania.
PLOSKI, H. A., O. J. LINDENMEYER, and E. KAISER (1971) *Reference Library of Black America.* New York: Bellwether Publishing.
ROSENBERG, N. Y. (1970) "White folklore about Blacks." Doctoral dissertation, Indiana University.
RUDWICK, B. M. (1971) *The Black Sociologists: The First Half Century.* Belmont, CA: Wadsworth.
RYAN, W. (1971) *Blaming the Victim.* New York: Vintage.
SHOOK, M.S.W. (1972) "Changing the racial attitudes of white students toward Blacks using commercially produced films." Doctoral dissertation, Duke University.
SPAULDING, H. D. (1972) *Encyclopedia of Black Folklore and Humor.* Middle Village, NY: Jonathan David.
TURNER, F. W. (1965) "Badmen, black and white: the continuity of American folk traditions." Doctoral dissertation, University of Pennsylvania.
VALENTINE, C. A. (1976) "Using small group methods for social education." *Clearing House* 50: 115-116.
WANDER, B. (1975) "Black dreams: the fantasy and ritual of Black films." *Film Quarterly* 29: 2-11.
WAX, D. D. (1974) "The image of the Negro in the Maryland Gazette, 1745-75." *Journalism Quarterly* 46: 73-80, 86.
WHITE, W. (1969) *Rope and Faggot: A Biography of Judge Lynch.* New York: Arno.
WILLIAMS, J. D. (1976) *The Black Press and the First Amendment.* Washington, DC: National Urban League.
WOLOSIN, R. J. (1974) "Group structure and role behavior." *Annals of the American Academy:* 158-172.
WRIGHT, C. R. (1959) *Mass Communication: A Sociological Perspective.* New York: Random House.

11

TELEVISION'S IMPACT ON BLACK CHILDREN'S LANGUAGE: AN EXPLORATION

Molefi Kete Asante

The great bulk of literature on television's impact on children has dealt with aggression and violence. Since the late 1950s, a considerable corpus of research has issued forth, like some massive wave, in an unending effort to link the behavior of children to television. Almost none of the hundreds of experimental studies have tested hypotheses derived from communication theories or studied black or other minority children. Research on television and the minority child has been a vast wasteland. Moreover, while there exists general psychological interest in the developmental and socialization problems of black youth, no substantial data exist on how black children are affected in their language socialization by television. The works of Brody (1964), Erikson (1964), Hauser (1971), Pettigrew (1964), and Taylor (1976) have added to the psychological development literature on black children, but so far few works have considered television's impact on the language of our children.

This chapter proposes a heuristic device for the study of television's influence on the language socialization of black children. Essentially, three

AUTHOR'S NOTE: This chapter was originally prepared for UCLA's National Institute of Mental Health Conference on Television and the Socialization of the Ethnic Minority Child, April 27 and 28, 1978.

assumptions support my inquiry into the nature of television's influence on the language socialization of black children:

(A1) The strongest unit of linguistic control for an individual is the reinforcing speech community.
(A2) Television serves as an influence mediator for black children.
(A3) The impact of television on black children's language socialization is compounded by culturoenvironmental factors.

A person's speech community constitutes his or her principal reinforcing agency. Such a community supports the accepted and demonstrates the acceptable rules of language usage. Comprised of one's siblings, parents, and peers, the reinforcing speech community may exist within the general speech community and yet be touched by that community in only insignificant ways. Parents are the primary models for infants and young children; they represent the standards of communication and social conduct. Normally what passes for acceptability among members of the speech community influences the young child.

Children are members of at least two speech communities, i.e., the immediate speech community and the general speech community. When the immediate speech community reinforces the general speech community, uniformity results. On the other hand, diverse speech communities produce critical tension. The ability to evaluate and judge is a necessary skill when one lives in two speech communities. Although a child may recognize differences and be unable to explain them, the awareness alone introduces critical tension. A sort of bilingualism emerges. Yet, it is the dominant speech community which constitutes the main social agency for language reinforcement.

The language of speech communities contains two elements: (1) structure and (2) meaning. *Structure* refers to the basic syntactical and grammatical principles of the language; *meaning* is the intent or purpose denoted by a unit of language. It is the speech community which demonstrates most effectively the critical difference between black and white communication behaviors. Kochman (1972) and Smith (1973) have shown that blacks and whites tend to have perceptual variances because of cultural factors. The difference between the signification for guilt and innocence among blacks and whites is an area of cultural dissimilarity explored by Kochman. Erickson's microanalysis reveals that blacks and whites tend to be out of synchrony when speaking to each other, but in excellent synchrony when communicating within their own groups. The work of Smith (1973) and Taylor (1976) has served to establish the cultural differences which emerge in interracial interactions. Rich (1974), Daniel (1972), and many other scholars have advanced reasons for difference as well as ways to achieve communicability. Structure and meaning become for intercultural scholars elements of languaging to be analyzed in any intercultural meeting. Television, as a political as well as technical achievement, combines consciousness-raising with structuring of audience territories (Asante, 1976). It highlights differences in communities and promotes the imperialism of image.

Despite the many misunderstandings about the code-switching abilities of black, Chicano, or Japanese-American children because they exist within two language communities, perhaps the first assumption posited should be considered in light of semantic and structural switching. When a certain black person says, "ain't got no money" you cannot translate that "I do not have any money." To do so would be to obtund the expression by obliterating a whole history, personal and collective, of deprivation. "Ain't got no money" means "I ain't got none now, ain't had none, and if I get some I won't have none, because its gone before I get it." It is too easy to infer from the common translation, "I do not have any money" that "I may have some one day." This is to miss the language. Code-switching cannot always be a one-to-one relationship. The young black child who says, "I'm fixner go" knows precisely what she means, and it is not "I am getting ready to go." *Fixner* implies that you are already ready and that you are indeed on your way.

Greenberg and Dominick (1969) show racial difference in television use with Mexican-American sixth- and tenth-graders and their Anglo peers. Mexican-Americans are said to watch more television. Similarly, the same researchers have shown that low-income black teenagers watch over six hours of television a day, while low-income whites watched only four and one-half hours. Liebert et al. (1973) suggest that such differences exist regardless of economic background. Given this information, we can assume that television constitutes a larger window for Mexican-Americans and African-Americans. Furthermore, through television these minority teenagers are more likely to have greater exposure to world affairs and domestic affairs than their white peers. This being the possible case, the data gathered by Greenberg and Dominick have far greater significance than a record of use; it is likely that the sociopolitical maturity of minority children is greater than that of white children. In fact, we may have crossed the threshold into visual literacy, with minority children outdistancing their white counterparts in TV analysis. Gerbner (1975) asserted that anyone not viewing at least four hours of television is out of touch with society. Nevertheless, the impact of this viewing on language development would have occurred much before the high school years. Despite the racial difference in use data at the teenager level, there appear to be no clear differences in terms of use at the earlier ages. Children at the

earlier ages seem to view about the same amount of television. At that age
the critical difference in language development is most probably the
immediate family.

As the first assumption of my inquiry, the contention that the speech
community is the strongest reinforcing agency has definite implications for
research into television's impact on the black child. Conceivably, if it
exists, television's influence on the language socialization patterns of black
children is a secondary rather than a direct influence. What influence does
a sibling parent or peer have on a child? Listening to and watching
television may have some influence, as we shall see, but television reinforced by parents probably has more impact on language socialization than
television unreinforced by the speech community. There is no evidence to
suggest this with any strength at this time. It is raised here as an alternative
answer to the influence question.

Television's role as influence mediator for black children has not been
studied in any great detail. In 1961, Schramm et al. wrote *Television in the
Lives of Our Children,* in which they explained a demonstration project
called Teletown and Radiotown. The efficacy of a video-audio program
was demonstrated when children who were regular television watchers
scored higher on a standard vocabulary test. Depending upon whose data
are analyzed, it is possible to come up with almost any interpretation of
television's impact on children. The work by Klapper et al. has concentrated primarily on patterns of television use. Only Greenberg, however,
has dealt extensively with use of television by what he calls the disadvantaged or urban poor. Nevertheless, few of the studies of television's
influence seem rooted in hypotheses derived from communication. This is
not to minimize the value of the works mentioned, but to point to a
serious flaw. Thus, combined with the lack of emphasis on black children,
the absence of communication theory-derived hypotheses indicates that
television's influence on studies of black children's language socialization is
nearly nonexistent.

To speak sensibly about communication is to recognize that the *creation, presentation,* and *reception* of symbols constitute the core of the
process. The nexus of presentation and reception becomes a historical
event. Such a historical event possesses the markers to identify the communicative situation as *influential, persuasive, entertaining,* or *informative.*
Combinations of these purposes exist within most communicative situations. Understanding communication in this way, I view all communicative
acts as persuasively designed to modify beliefs, attitudes, values, and
behaviors. Any communicative event designed to entertain or inform
transforms its audience in some way. Measuring the extent of the transformation has consumed a large portion of our communication research.

Television represents the most potent symbol-creating and -presenting device yet developed. In its symbol-producing and symbol-manipulation roles, television manages to create its own audiences. Perception, visual discrimination, color sensitivity, and listening skills are integral factors of audience appreciation of televised messages. The function of television as a mediator of symbolic messages is more significant in social development than its McLuhanesque technological contribution to society. In one sense, the technological device has taken its place alongside the ten billion other artifacts of our natural and technical environment. One cannot minimize the instrumental importance of the machine, but what it *does* apart from its technical existence is more significant for persuasion. It is much like the son who received a telegram which read "Mother is better." Because his mother had been seriously ill and he had awaited word from his sister, when the telegram finally arrived, he framed it and hung it over the mantle. The telegram as instrument appeared to loom larger in his mind than the actual fact of the recovery of his mother. As an instrument for message delivery, the telegram's primary importance is in rapid long-distance transmission. Similarly, the television is an *instrument* for transmission of symbols. Yet it is in its production and presentation of those symbols that television assumes its real significance. It is, in fact, one of two contemporary architectonic devices—the other being the computer.

A considerable bibliography of work exists in response to television as a technical instrument. For example, research on use, rate of viewing, number of sets per household, relationship between use and economic status, represents work on characteristics of the intrument's impact, rather than characteristics of communication message. Although research has been accomplished dealing with messages, the hypotheses have not been adequately formed to suggest generalizable conclusions about language acquisition of minority children.

The saturation of the American society with television sets means that black children have about equal access to the symbols of television. Virtually all black children have some access to television. We seem to know how much and what kind of use is made of television by black children, but we do not yet know what linguistic acquisitions or modifications take place.

We assume that television's impact on black children's language is primarily linguistic. This assumption is logical, given the nature of the communicative process. Television socializes through speech as well as through action. We also know, however, that the minute displays of emotions such as affection, pride, guilt and anxiety (rather than the words used, the meanings intended, or the philosophy implied), transmit to the child the outlines of what really counts in his (sic) world (Erikson, 1964).

Emotional expression, with or without accompanying language, serves to influence the child's socialization. It is a form of social influence which, although possibly ineffable in a language sense, provides a cognitive reservoir for expression at some later time. Whether specifically linguistic or more generally symbolic, television's role in the socialization process appears to be persuasive. Bogatz and Ball (1972) have shown that black and white children's vocabularies benefit from *Sesame Street*. Interestingly, the study also demonstrates that *Sesame Street* has influenced behavior, attitudes toward school, and attitudes toward people of other races. By providing meaningful warrants for action, television utilizes the basic needs of individuals as it influences society. All persuasion is grounded in human needs; thus, functionalism is enthroned in any persuasive situation.

The black child's language behavior, therefore, may be described in a functional sense as instrumental, ego-defensive, value-expressive, or knowledge-seeking. According to Katz (1960), these four classes represent the individual needs of human beings. To influence the socialization of children it is necessary, in a strict functionalist view, to change the motivational and personality needs of the children. If we accept the above classifying criteria for human behavior, then it is clear that either of the classes may represent the black child's response to television at any given time. For example, the instrumental function of attitude is served when a child who regularly views television maximizes his or her ability to secure parental favors by repeating that "nationwide is on your side," or the ego-defensive language mechanisms which may be influenced by television in such statements as "express yourself," where the ventilation of one's internal feelings helps to discharge inhibited influences in order to change ego-defensive attitudes. The value-expressive function is served when a child seeks to enhance self-identity and self-image. Television may conceivably produce identity confusion in black children. Thus, a black child who identifies with the characters or personalities of a television program may be induced to adopt the language patterns of the characters. When the characters are unrepresentative of the child's actual self, physical and psychological, a dissonance is created. The kind of communication banter which typifies most black children's interactions is generally not heard on television. Consider the following dialogue I overheard between two of my cousins:

"Git out the way ole fat girl."
"Don't say nothin' to me."
"You goin' do something about it."
"You can't make me."

Or the statement, "If you had asked me before I might of could but I'm tore up now," for the refusal of a drink. Television dialogue, in its soulest moments, does not approach the authenticity of such interchanges. I cannot believe that black writers are not writing this dialogue. Value-expression, then, is a function which may be achieved more through peer relationships than television influence. Children learn what language cues and communication behaviors are representative of the speech community. Therefore, an elongated vowel, as in *long* train or *ugly* boy, is more likely to come from parents, siblings, and playmates than from television's *Sesame Street*.

Serving as the frame of reference giving meaning to a child's ambiguities and complexities, the knowledge-seeking function of behavior is inextricably joined to value-expression. Who we are and what we will become can be clarified by the reinstatement of cues associated with our previous histories. In this way, any ambiguity for a child by new knowledge acquired outside the home can be reinforced or not reinforced by television. A friend of mine who teaches at Howard University told me that she had to take her son to Maryland and Virginia periodically because at eight years of age he had begun to think that the whole world was black. Living in Washington, even watching Washington television, you can get a distorted view about America. Thus, cues have to be reinstated and concepts have to be restated in order to maintain a consistent defense against crippling ambiguity.

The third assumption is that the impact of television on black children's language is compounded by other factors. This may account for the lagging research in this area. Furthermore, the impact of black language behavior on television is without calculation. All of the irony, much of the syntax, and most of the popular expressions from the black community tend to become victims of television's rapacity. The intertwining of the black influence on television writers with the influence of television on the American society complicates the process of assessing just how much television is responsible for black language socialization. While the finished product may not assume the exact characteristics of the source, there appears to be enough borrowing for one to recognize the root. Polishing the authentic black word becomes a productive part of television. Thus, in order to measure the impact of television on the black child's language development, it would be necessary to control all extraneous factors. Obviously this is not possible. We cannot totally isolate children from their environments. Nevertheless, it is possible to hypothesize about the impact of television programs on black children's language. Harold Lasswell's classic statement regarding communication was who

says what

to whom

in what channel

with what effect?

Assuming the difficulty of measuring the effect of television on the language socialization of black youth, I attempted to answer some of the fundamental questions regarding black children's perception by asking for their responses to five communication-based statements.

The results and implications of a recent Buffalo survey with black youth provides direction for a heuristic. Greenberg and Dominick reported three projects involving the use of media by the poor. Although none of these studies was meant to treat language socialization, one of the reported studies dealt with the functions television performed for disadvantaged children. In this study Greenberg and Dominick (1969) asked black and white youngsters whether or not they perceived some similarity between the world portrayed on television and their world. Five agree-disagree statements were used. Typical of the statements were:

— Families I see on television are like my family.

— The programs I see on television tell about life the way it really is.

Race and income differences showed; however, blacks were said to perceive television as more realistic than whites. Among the conclusions one can draw from this project is that black children are more inclined to view the language of television as more realistic as well. At least, such a conclusion is possible if one argues that children are influenced by the physical symbols as well as the verbal symbols which are transmitted by television. What a child hears becomes equal to what he or she sees. For young children the ability to separate language from other cultural aspects of life does not develop, in any analytical sense, until early adolescence.

The Buffalo survey utilized five communication-oriented statements of the agree-disagree variety to test whether black elementary school children from an inner-city school perceived similarity between the language used by people on television and their own communication patterns. Statements employed in the study were:

(1) The way people talk on television sounds funny.
(2) The way people talk on television is the way I try to talk.
(3) Television news reporters talk like my mother and father.
(4) Programs on television remind me of the way my friends talk.
(5) I like the way people talk on television.

Subjects were 65 girls and 35 boys from the fourth grade (range - 9, 9-10, 8) of the Buffalo Build Academy, a predominantly black elementary school in the inner city. All subjects were black. The subjects were given questionnaires during regular class time in February 1978.

The questionnaires were administered by the researcher. Each student was allowed as much time as possible to complete the questionnaire. The longest completion time was five minutes. Each child indicated that a television set was available in the home. This project was concerned only with perceived language reality. Students were told that they should be as thoughtful as possible in their answers. In addition, I had the children indicate which television programs they watched the most.

Response scores to the five items were computed in strict percentages in order to provide an indication of survey results. The results obtained in percentages (see Table 11.1).

While this preliminary survey cannot be considered conclusive, it can be seen as an indication that black children at this particular school do not see television language as their reality. The cumulative index of perceived language reality indicates black children do not perceive the language of television as reality. Such results imply that Greenberg and Dominick's finding that black children perceived *television* to be more real than do white children may be misleading. There exists no single television reality; many factors constitute the real for television viewers and listeners. Language reality could conceivably be isolated from the generic television reality. Furthermore, what has been considered perceived reality of television may have more to do with images, symbols, and ideas than with the spoken language utilized by television characters and personalities. Another implication of this study is that television's impact on black children's language may be more *idiomatic* than *structural*. A child may employ idioms, colloquials, expressions from children's programs, cartoons, and commercials, but not be impressed by the structural linguistic content of regular adult programming. Indeed, the idiomatic expressions may only appear in the child's language for a brief period of time, corresponding with the popularity of *Dr. Who, Wonder Woman, The Electric Company, Sesame Street,* or *Fat Albert.*

IMPLICATIONS

The implications of this discussion are enormous for any theoretical heuristic device. How do minority children make sense out of the television symbols and signals they receive? Such a question assumes, quite

TABLE 11.1

Statement	Yes	Don't know	No
1	63%	7%	30%
2	29%	11%	60%
3	52%	0%	48%
4	38%	12%	50%
5	51%	0%	49%

plausibly, however, that sentencehood comes through external reinforcement. People make sense out of the world for children. Yet, equally plausible is the belief that the knowledge of making sense with sentences comes from deep inside children. If this is the case, then phylogeny announces ontogeny as much as ontogeny recapitulates phylogeny.

BEHAVIORIST IMPLICATIONS

According to the behaviorist perspective, language is a learned phenomenon and can be acquired in the same manner that anything else is learned. Thus, a child is a *tabula rasa* at the initial stage of language acquisition. There is nothing necessarily inherent in the child which makes him or her more capable of language development. The principles of learning are universal and can be applied to all experiences of raw data. Children choose the principles which give them results; they are rewarded for conformity and penalized for aberrations. Therefore, from a behaviorist's perspective, imitation becomes significant. The questions raised in the study reported above are addressed to issues of imitation. Yet, the evidence on imitation is difficult to interpret. Wardhaugh (1976: 143) argues that children do not repeat all the utterances they hear; are not very good imitators if perfect reproduction is used as a criterion; and they produce in imitation only the forms they would say in spontaneous speech. In Wardhaugh's judgment, if children are asked to use types they are not yet using, they fail badly ("The boy the book hit was crying" is imitated as *"Boy the book was crying"*) or they change what they hear to conform to what they can say. Consequently, imitation does not appear grammatically progressive but is used only to give practice to what has already been learned and not to try out new forms. Acceptance of this view means that television can provide any child only with opportunities for practice. What the child does in response to the language transmission of television can be predicted, according to this view, by analyzing the child's prior language capacity. Practice makes perfect only insofar as the child is capable of repeating what he or she hears.

The behaviorist view, relying heavily on imitation, is an important perspective for developing a heuristic. In fact, the importance of environment, the significance of data-gathering, and the access which a child has to the language, enrich the learning experience but cannot explain all the issues in language acquisition. Thus, in terms of the black child exposed to television it is possible that the perception of language reality is of no consequence to the developmental question. Indeed, television itself may prove to be a force retarding the natural learning experience. Only in the sense that television provides a considerable amount of spoken items to be imitated can it be considered contributive to learning. All verbal statements are not religiously repeated or imitated by children, black or white. In fact, there appears to be a cultural mechanism which prevents black children from using "gee whiz," "golly," or "Jesus," as interjections.

NATIVIST IMPLICATIONS

This view holds that children are specifically endowed with certain innate abilities to acquire generative-transformational grammar. Without this mentalistic ability, children would not be able to convert the degenerate stimuli from the environment into meaningful sentences. According to the nativist perspective, perception, categorization, and the capacity for transformation are biologically given. This view is almost diametrically opposed to the behaviorist perspective. B. F. Skinner, a leading proponent of the behaviorist school, has been attacked by David McNeill and Noam Chomsky, champions of the nativist perspective. The nativist position seriously questions the television-influence view. Innate mechanisms for language acquisition operate without regard to environmental conditions.

RESEARCH ON PROSOCIAL EFFECTS

Several studies (particularly Ball and Bogatz, 1970; Fowles, 1971; Bogatz and Ball, 1972) have examined the relationship of children's programs on educational television to learning. As alternatives to the violence and mayhem which continue to appear on commercial television programs geared toward children, Sesame Street and The Electric Company have become exceedingly desirable. These programs have benefited from planning, monitoring, and ongoing evaluations. Sesame Street grew out of the combined efforts of public and private agencies to establish the Children's Television Workshop. In 1969 the program was first aired, and its concentrated planning and development helped to make it an instant success. The Electric Company was also a Children's Television Workshop project, aimed primarily at improving the quality of reading among chil-

dren. *Sesame Street* and *The Electric Company* used educators to participate in identifying curricula strategies, evaluating effectiveness, and assessing basic instructional procedures.

Research based on both *Sesame Street* and *The Electric Company*
seems to indicate that the programs on educational television do succeed
in making a difference in a child's abilities to recognize the alphabet, write
their names, develop or improve their reading skills (Liebert et al., 1973:
106-107). How much of this difference can be attributed to normal
maturation is not known. What has been established is that children who
watch *Sesame Street* and *The Electric Company* tend to achieve higher
scores on alphabet recitation and the writing of their names than children
who do not. The effect of television in this case is that it serves as an
avenue for a deliberate pedagogical endeavor, and the endeavor seems to
be succeeding.

On the side of commercial television, CBS established an ongoing
committee under the direction of Gordon Berry to assess the educational
and social value of *Fat Albert and the Cosby Kids*. But this example is not
often repeated among commercial networks. Public television, not commercial television, has provided our most comprehensive rationale for
studying the impact of television on the language socialization of minority
children.

Inasmuch as any heuristic device must be grounded in some theory, it is
necessary to understand how communication as a process underscores our
search for implications. In the classic Berlo (1960) SMCR model, the
source encodes and sends a message through a channel to a receiver. The
black or minority child who receives a message decodes it before acting
upon it. If the message is a recitation of the alphabet, the child must
decode that message before he or she is able to understand it. This does
not mean that the message is unrepeatable, only that unless the child
decodes, he or she will not know that he or she is repeating. All of us have
had experiences with young children who seem to know so much for their
age. Children can imitate their parents or television speakers; in many cases
the language may be "over their heads," but it can be repeated by children
who have mastered the appropriate phonemes.

Normal children who are exposed to language will begin to talk. In fact,
"no special teaching is necessary for the emergence of language" (Lenneberg, 1967: 135-137). Yet, environment seems to influence language
development. That is to say, a deprived environment leads to poor language development and an enriched environment leads to improved language development. We must be careful, however, not to equate deprivation
with minority, or enrichment with white. The fact is that different
experiences at home, whether through the media or parental teaching,

appear to influence vocabulary growth (Smart and Smart, 1972: 265). The National Institute of Mental Health's *Cognitive and Mental Development in the First Five Years of Life* (1970) points to home environment, parental attitude, child's exposure to the wider world, and quality of child-parent relationship in the early cognitive development of the child. If all of these factors in addition to the child's own innate patterns for languaging influence linguistic development, then it is, as I have assumed, quite impossible to isolate television's impact. What we do see and respond to are the children's visible and vocal communication cues.

My heuristic assumes: (1) The strongest unit of linguistic control for a child is the reinforcing speech community; (2) television serves as an influence mediator; and (3) the impact of television on black children's language socialization is compounded by other culturoenvironmental factors. Furthermore, the theoretical base of all research must be in communication theory with emphases on principles of information-dissemination and -reception, audience analysis, message presentation, and purpose. In this respect, scholars may bind implications for future research for a more adequate understanding of the relationship of television to language socialization.

However, the continuing presence of numerous uncontrollable variables of the culturoenvironmental variety makes it extremely difficult to obtain significant and practical results at a level equal to the researcher's investment of time and energy. Results will always seem to be highly specific to the situation, group, or television program. I believe that is one reason we have not had the kind of substantial data necessary for a productive theoretical generator. We live within the very few generalizations which have been ventured, knowing full well that the cast is not complete and the table of contents for an all-powerful, architectonic theory of impact on minority children is still being assembled.

REFERENCES

ASANTE, M. K. (1976) "Television and Black consciousness." *Journal of Communication* (Autumn): 137-141.

BALL, S. and G. A. BOGATZ (1970) *The First Year of Sesame Street: An Evaluation.* Princeton, NJ: Educational Testing.

BERLO, D. (1960) *The Process of Communication.* New York: Holt, Rinehart & Winston.

BOGATZ, G. A. and S. BALL (1972) *The Second Year of Sesame Street: A Continuing Evaluation.* Princeton, NJ: Educational Testing.

BRODY, E. B. (1964) "Color and identity conflict in young boys." *Archives of General Psychiatry* 10 (April): 354-360.

DANIEL, J. (1972) *Black Communication.* New York: Speech Communication Association.

ERIKSON, E. (1964) "Memorandum on identity and Negro youth." *Journal of Social Issues* 20 (October): 30.

FOWLES, B. (1971) "Building a curriculum for 'The Electric Company,' " in *The Electric Company: An Introduction to the New Television Program Designed to Help Teach Reading to Children*. New York: Children's Television Workshop.

GERBNER, G. (1975) "Institutional forces and the mass media," in M. Cassata and M. K. Asante (eds.) *The Social Uses of Mass Communication*. Buffalo, NY: Communication Research Center.

GREENBERG, B. and J. DOMINICK (1969) "Racial and social class differences in teenagers' Use of Television." *Journal of Broadcasting* 13: 1331-1334.

HAUSER, S. T. (1971) *Black and white identity formation*. New York: John Wiley.

KATZ, D. (1960) "The functional approach to the study of attitudes." *Public Opinion Quarterly* 24: 163-204.

KOCHMAN, T. (1972) *Rappin' and Stylin' Out*. Urbana, IL: University of Illinois Press.

LENNEBERG, E. H. (1967) *Biological Foundations of Language*. New York: John Wiley.

LIEBERT, R. M., J. NEALE, and E. DAVIDSON (1973) *The Early Window: Effects of Television on Children and Youth*. New York: Pergamon.

National Institute of Mental Health (1970) *Cognitive and Mental Development in the First Five Years of Life*. Rockville, MD: Author.

PETTIGREW, T. F. (1964) "Negro American personality: Why isn't it more known?" *Journal of Social Issues* 20 (April): 4-23.

RICH, A. (1974) *Interracial Communication*. New York: Harper & Row.

SCHRAMM, W., J. LYLE, and E. B. PARKER (1961) *Television in the Lives of Our Children*. Stanford, CA: Stanford University Press.

SMART, M. and R. SMART (1972) *Children: Development and Relationships*. New York: Macmillan.

SMITH, A. L. [M. K. ASANTE] (1973) *Transracial Communication*. Englewood Cliffs, NJ: Prentice-Hall.

TAYLOR, O. and D. FERGUSON (1975) "A study of cross cultural communication between Blacks and Whites in the U.S. Army." *Linguistic Reporter*. (CAL Research Report 2)

TAYLOR, R. L. (1976) "Black youth and psychosocial development: a conceptual framework." *Journal of Black Studies* 6 (June): 353-372.

WARDHAUGH, R. (1976) *The Contexts of Language*. Rowley, MA: Newbury.

12

CHURCH PARTICIPATION IN A
COMMUNITY OF BLACK INMIGRANTS:
A SOCIAL SPACE ANALYSIS

Bobby M. Wilson

The religious life of any people is profoundly social. Vital religious devotion, or worship, is a personal experience, but even when a person is alone his or her religious behavior rests upon values and sentiments—i.e., significant symbols—shared with other people. Religious beliefs and actions are largely a product of a process of learning from significant others, which is influenced by past experiences. For a large segment of the black population, religion represents a significant symbolic form that is used to organize a self-concept and to guide relationships with others in the environment.

Based on the unique situation that black inmigrants have faced, the church, relative to other social institutions, has offered and continues to offer certain unique amenities. Historians have shown the importance of the church within the black community (Fauset, 1944; Frazier, 1964). Even during the time of slavery, religion played a leading role in sub-stantiating the hope of many blacks. Hence, today, even though black people participate in other social institutions, it is suggested that there still appears to be a strong tendency on the part of some blacks, especially rural inmigrants, to identify with religious institutions.

The influx of black inmigrants into northern cities during the 1900s saw the creation of a large number of black religious movements (McNeal, 1969; Myrday, 1944). The growth of storefront churches in cities during this period has been studied by Daniel (1940), who traces the development from the South to northern cities (1940). Frazier has identified the storefront church "as an attempt on the part of the rural in-migrants to re-establish a type of church in the urban environment to which they were accustomed" (1964: 53). This attempt to reestablish the rural church was a reaction against the impersonal social structures of urban churches. This is not just a characteristic of the urban church, but of most urban institutions (Wirth, 1938: 1-44).

Studies that have dealt with church attendance have indicated some major differences between black and white churchgoers, and differences related to migrant status. Lazerwitz (1961: 301-309) found that of the black Baptists, 84 percent attended church regularly or often, in contrast to 69 percent of the white baptists. The relationship between migrant status and church attendance has been studied by Jitodal (1964: 261-268), who examined the percentage of white non-Catholics who attend church frequently, standardized by migrant type, by region, and by length of reisdence. He found that rural migrants from the South who have been in Detroit at least eleven years have a higher rate of attendance than that of the native population and that of their urban and rural counterparts from the North. Since the urban black church has been defined as a prototype of the rural black church, it becomes a very important place of activity[1] for those rural inmigrants wishing to maintain and reinforce a rural "self."

CONCEPTUAL FRAMEWORK

Assuming the church to be a dominant reference group for a certain group of black rural inmigrants, this study examines the influence that church participation may have on the behavior in space of these migrants within Bedford-Stuyvesant, a predominant black section located in central Brooklyn, New York. The concept of social space, elaborated by notions derived from the theory of symbolic interaction, and reference group theory were used to formulate an integrative framework for studying this influence.

In order to better understand the relationship between the sociopsychological characteristics of people, i.e., the inner self, and their overtly expressed spatial patterns of behavior, i.e., activity space, the research considered two central indices of social space: (1) its spatial *extent* as defined by a set of locations, e.g., relatives, friends, social and economic institutions, and the like, that an inmigrant may select out of the opportunity surface which best serves his or her needs; and (2) a generalized *surface* specifying the preference level associated with each place (Horton and Reynolds, 1971: 36-48). This allowed for an investigation of the spatial extent of the inmigrants' overtly expressed spatial behavior and needs; and to place this within the meaning context of the inmigrants' lived experiences.

It is the assumption that one's behavior in space is influenced by the "self." The discriminating process used by an individual or group of individuals to select out certain places in space is a function of the self which is generated through both social and spatial interaction. People's entire lived experiences involve, to a certain extent, trying to establish some degree of symmetry between their inner selves and their external behavior in space. How successful they are in achieving this symmetrical relationship determines to an extent their success in eliminating environmental stress or alienation.[2] The importance of defining the relationship between one's inner self and one's overt behavior is best exemplified by Mead's (1934) description of the *total* self. It is a

> character which is different from that of the physiological organism proper. The self is something which has a development; it is not initially there at birth, but arises in the process of social experience and activity, that is, it develops in the given individual as a result of his relations to that process as a whole and to other individuals within that process.

The self that tends to exist among church members of a black migrant community is one that helps in cushioning the impact of a sudden transition from past rural experiences to the lifestyles demanded by the urban environment. The development and maintenance of this self, however, is made possible through a *communal*, intragroup relationship that often characterizes black churches, as opposed to an *associational* type of relationship (Nelson, 1971: 102-110). The communal church recruits its members from a given and clearly defined territorial base. The church is also seen by its members as contributing to the symbolic and social well-being of the community. The communal relationship that exists in some black social groups has always been a trait of black culture. Some students of black culture have suggested that such a trait represents a form of "African survialism" (Nobles, 1973: 11-31). Rural migrants who experience this kind of communal relationship within their church are able to develop and maintain significant values and express their spatial patterns of behavior as a group. The manifestation of such shared values in patterns of spatial behavior defines the church group's social space, which tends to be rural in nature. The associational church does not recruit its members from a given territorial base, but is composed of members from a widely dispersed area. The church is perceived by its members as providing a very specialized function of serving just the religious needs of its members.

Such a church would be characterized by a number of different self-images within the church group. The manifestation of these self-images tends to be reinforced by the great deal of sociospatial variance which prevails among individual church members.

Works in perception have shown that overtly expressed spatial patterns may have different meanings for different societies (Burton and Kates, 1964: 412-441). Also, it has been shown on a micro-level that human spatial patterns and the schema which is responsible for their formation could vary according to membership in particular groups (Buttimer, 1972: 279-318; Shibutani, 1955: 562-569). However, the role of any group in one's lived-experiences will determine its influence on one's behavior in space. By studying inmigrants' social spaces as they relate to two types of church relationships, it was hoped that the relative role of the church in the sociospatial experiences of two groups of inmigrants within Bedford-Stuyvesant, New York, could be identified.

THE STUDY AREA AND SELECTION OF SAMPLE POPULATION

Today, Bedford-Stuyvesant, a section of Brooklyn, New York, is considered to be the largest black slum/ghetto[3] in the United States, with the highest concentration of blacks within a single circumscribed area (see Figure 12.1). The area traces its origin as a ghetto to the Barbadians who acquired private houses in the quiet middle- and upper-middle-class neighborhoods of central Brooklyn in the 1890s. This area, once populated by wealthy families of Dutch and English background, became the overcrowded repository for space-seeking black inmigrants from overcrowded Harlem and from the South (Etzkowitz and Schaflander, 1969: 3-5).

Besides the push-pull factors that stimulated southern blacks to migrate to Bedford-Stuyvesant, two major developments can be cited as providing the stimuli for the mass migration of blacks from Harlem. First, there was the development of a large number of residential homes in Bedford-Stuyvesant between 1879 and 1930; thus, during the Depression the area had an oversupply of homes for sale. Second, in 1936, the city of New York extended a new subway line to Bedford-Stuyvesant which provided a rapid-transit link with Harlem. As a result of the availability of homes and the transit link with Harlem, a migration of the more prosperous blacks from Harlem to Bedford-Stuyvesant occurred (Etzkowitz and Schaflander, 1969: 3-5).

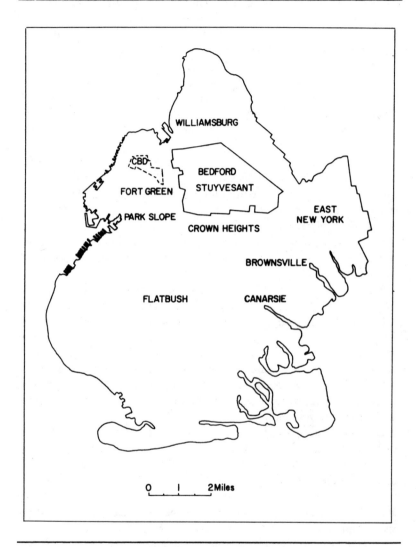

Figure 12.1: Location of Bedford-Stuyvesant Within the Borough of Brooklyn

By 1955, Bedford-Stuyvesant had experienced a growth somewhat similar to that of Harlem. An area once almost entirely white, its population had grown from 200,000 to 250,000 persons, about 150,000 of them blacks (Etzkowitz and Schaflander, 1969: 3-5). At the time of the 1960 census, the area had become 74 percent black, and in 1970 it is estimated that approximately 95 percent[4] of the population was black. Other estimates, alleging a serious census undercount in ghetto districts because of wary enumerators and suspicious residents, say the population of Bedford-Stuyvesant was almost double the census figure. The Bedford-Stuyvesant Restoration Corporation[5] calculates the area to have a total of about 500,000 persons, 95 percent of them black.

Within the last two decades, the percentage of blacks migrating from the British West Indies is significantly greater than the percentage of southern blacks migrating to Bedford-Stuyvesant (New York Times, 1955: 25). However, intraurban movements explain a large part of the migration process.

As a result of the area being defined *racially* more often than *geographically,* many inconsistencies exist with respect to what its boundaries are. Like Harlem, the name "Bedford-Stuyvesant" is often perceived by individuals as incorporating those sections, contiguous with Bedford-Stuyvesant, where blacks have moved in and about. Because of the invasion and succession process occurring in these sections, it is not infrequent that a person will refer to these sections as part of the Bedford-Stuyvesant community.

The observations on which the analysis of this study is based are drawn from a survey of 62 black inmigrants who attended two churches located within the Bedford-Stuyvesant area of Brooklyn, New York. A sample of 28 was chosen from one church within which interpersonal relationships were assumed to be communal, and a sample of 34 was selected from the other, within which relationships were assumed to be of an associational nature. Such assumptions were based on the writer's personal involvement in the two churches, and the observed intensity of face-to-face interaction of the two church groups.

On what appeared to be a typical Sunday, and with the permission of each minister, a brief description of the nature and purpose of the study was presented to the two congregations. Members who consented to the interview were asked to give their names, addresses, and telephone numbers. These respondents were later contacted and asked to give a convenient time at which the questionnaire could be administered. Each interview lasted approximately forty-five minutes and contained both structured and unstructured questions covering very specific areas designed to shed light on the central questions of the study.

METHOD OF ANALYSIS

The research involved two major tasks: (1) analyzing the extent of each group's behavior in space; and (2) developing a composite preference scale.

Eight types of place activities that tend to characterize the everyday activities of migrants were analyzed as points in a geometric space (Table 12.1). By placing a Cartesian grid over the general area of a group's activity space, it is possible to record all spatial interaction with regard to an x/y coordinate system. The technique used to record this interaction is the standard deviational ellipse, which best describes the spatial extent of the activity pattern (Bachi, 1963: 83-132; Brown and Holmes, 1970). In order to count for both spatial and social interaction, each place activity was weighted according to frequency of use. Places were weighted according to the following scale: once/week to several times/week (3.0), less than once/week (2.0), once/month or less (1.0).

From individual preference ranking of the eight types of place activities, a composite preference scale characterizing a group's overall place preference ranking was obtained through multidimensional scaling (Attneave, 1950: 516-556; Kruskal, 1968). The typical problem to be handle by multidimensional scaling can be roughly stated as follows: Given a set of stimuli, e.g., objects, people, places, and the like, the one can determine perceived distance between pairs of stimuli which vary according to some unknown dimension. The stimuli are represented by points on a scale in such a way that the significant features of the data about these stimuli are revealed in the geometrical relations among the points.

DISCUSSION

For a certain group of inmigrants who continue to identify with a rural "self," the setting for their social experiences and activities within the Bedford-Stuyvesant area appeared to be the communal church. The church provided these members with a "sacred space" within which they could reinforce and maintain a rural "self" that reflected a lingering past—a "self" that they were not willing to sacrifice, totally, in return for the urban way of life. The church has considerable reality potential, in that it continues to be relevant in terms of the motives and self-interpretations of its members in their social and spatial activities. The intensity of interpersonal relationship within the communal church often led to cohesive social and spatial networks outside the church. This intensity of interpersonal relationships is reflected in the sociospatial distance between the church and all other place activities (Table 12.2). This sociospatial relationship was found to be a major factor in the role that the church played in maintaining and reinforcing a "self" that served as a cushion between the inmigrants' past and present spatial experiences. The relatively compact and unique spatial extent of this group's behavior in space has probably contributed largely to the maintenance of this "self" (Figure 12.2).

TABLE 12.1   Number and Categories
of Place Activities
Composing Subjects'
Activity Space

No.	Place Activity
1	Job
3	Food marketing
3	Shopping
3	Entertainment
3	Organization, clubs, etc.
3	Associational, with relatives
3	Associational, friends
3	Worship
22	TOTAL

Not only was the church the most preferred place activity, but the perceived distance between it and the next most preferred place activity reflects the unique position that the church occupies in the group's social space (Table 12.3). For this group, the church presumably occupies a dominant role in the development of its members' self-images, and therefore adapts its functions to a variety of needs within the community. A majority of its members construed the church as being not only a place of worship, but a place of friendship. Church-related clubs and organizations were a major source of entertainment as well as friendship. This, again, is reflected in the small sociospatial distance between locations of entertainment, friendship, and the church. The psychological consequences would have been great if the communal group had been asked to substitute another type of place activity for the role of the church.

In contrast to the communal group, the associational church appeared to play a relatively insignificant symbolic role in the lived experiences of its members. The large sociospatial distance between the locations of the associational church and its members' residential spaces tend to reflect this insignificant role (Table 12.4). As portrayed in church participation, the associational group tended, for the most part, to sacrifice their rural past for what they thought to be a better way of life. Group members became socialized into the impersonal, segmented lifestyle and the pressures of city living. The group's social space reflected to a large extent this *genre de vie*. The group's place preferences (Table 12.3) and relatively dispersed patterns of behavior in space, reflected "selves" that were more urban than rural. Members exhibited a great deal of variance in their spatial patterns of behavior, and a lack of meaningful intragroup interaction. (Figure 12.3) A great deal of alienation and lack of individual freedom were detected in this group, because its members were trying to identify with "selves" that

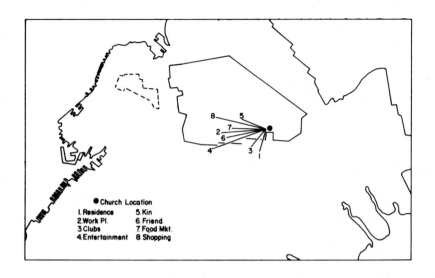

Church Location
I. Residence   5. Kin
2. Work Pl.   6. Friend
3. Clubs   7. Food Mkt.
4. Entertainment   8. Shopping

Figure 12.2: Mean Centers of Place Activities: Communal Group

TABLE 12.2   Interactivity Distance Matrix: Communal

	1	2	3	4	5	6	7	8
1								
2	.989							
3	.316	1.280						
4	.707	.800	.824					
5	1.420	1.810	1.280	1.020				
6	1.820	1.490	1.900	1.120	1.200			
7	1.560	1.560	1.550	.922	.640	.566		
8	2.550	2.500	2.500	1.920	1.310	1.070	1.000	
9	.565	1.550	.316	1.140	1.470	2.200	1.820	2.750

1 Matrix Unit = .50 Mi.

KEY:
1. Resident   4. Entertainment   7. Food mkts.
2. Work   5. Kin   8. Shopping
3. Clubs, organizations 6. Friends   9. Church

in no way reflected their past experiences. To its members the church was the least preferred of all place activities and was just one of the many specialized institutions that the city had to offer. The portrayal of work-place as one of this group's least preferred activity reflects also the associational lifestyle of its members. The alienation of self from work is a

TABLE 12.3   Composite Preference Scale: A Measure of
             Sociopsychological Distance Between Different Types
             of Activities

Communal Group's Preference

2	7	5	1	6	3	8	4

Most   Least

Associational Group's Preference

4	3	8	6	5	7	1	2

Most   Least

KEY:
1. Job   5. Kinship
2. Church   6. Friendship
3. Clubs, organizations   7. Food mkts.
4. Entertainment   8. Shopping

TABLE 12.4   Interactivity Distance Matrix: Associational

	1	2	3	4	5	6	7	8
1								
2	2.900							
3	.670	2.720						
4	.282	2.620	.640					
5	.509	3.180	.538	.707				
6	.894	2.050	.728	.632	1.140			
7	1.200	3.490	.806	1.330	.721	1.530		
8	3.620	1.560	3.710	3.360	4.050	2.980	4.510	
9	3.100	3.450	3.620	3.000	3.600	3.140	4.310	2.630

1 Matrix Unit = .50 Mi.

KEY:
1. Resident   4. Entertainment   7. Food markets
2. Work   5. Kin   8. Shopping
3. Clubs, organizations 6. Friends   9. Church

contributing factor to the low preference given to work. Relationships
which are not found at work or in other place activities are not sought in
church participation.

The significant difference in the two groups' sociospatial patterns suggests that the black community, from a geographical perspective, cannot
be studied as a monolithic group, as has been the case in past studies. More
microanalysis between and within black communities is needed to discern
possible variations in spatial processes and forms.

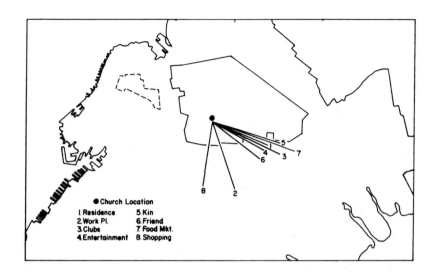

Figure 12.3: Mean Centers of Place Activities: Associational Group

SOME POLICY IMPLICATIONS

Although this study identified the associational church as playing a lesser role in its members' social and spatial experiences, the church as a whole is very much a part of the black community reference system. In areas of community development, policy makers have failed to take advantage of community's reference system. Impractical decisions are often made by planners, politicians, and so on, resulting in changes in the physical and socioeconomic structures of the community. Programs responsible for such changes have in most instances disrupted the social reference systems of communities.

Community people who share similar patterns of spatial behavior will most likely share the same community needs. Therefore, to solve community problems it becomes more practical to involve community groups whose members may share the same social spaces. A common sense of need must be present to allow community policy to function and for community people to reach a workable compromise. The black churches at the community level could be used to organize the community and define community needs. An example of this can be found in the work of the late Adam Clayton Powell, who was able to use the black church as a political base, which resulted in his identifying more realistically the community needs of Harlem. Therefore, it is argued that the only reliable way to discover the needs of different groups is to study their patterns of spatial behavior and to observe what choices or tradeoffs they tend to make. From the supply side of community development, such observations can contribute to better policy decision-making.

On the demand side, people can take advantage of their reference systems to organize themselves to gain greater discretion over choices of services and goods. Such an approach can maximize community participation and minimize alienation. By defining one's needs or one's sense of a problem in terms of the social reference system, one can deal with individual and community needs in a more realistic and more meaningful way.[6]

The Reverend Jesse Jackson of operation PUSH (People United to Save Humanity) and the Reverend Leon Sullivan of OIC (Opportunities Industrialization Centers) are cases in point. The success of these individuals lies mainly in their desire not to alienate the community when planning community programs. By taking advantage of a well-established reference system, i.e., the black churches, they were able to get the community actively involved in solving problems.

To solve these problems, they relied on some services that could be provided only by individuals on the supply side, i.e., planners, politicians, and so on, thus eliminating the possibilities of alienating certain decision makers. There has to be a certain amount of compromise and cooperation between both sides of the supply-demand model. For example, Jesse Jackson has negotiated contracts with certain large, predominant white companies that give certain groups within the black community the right to distribute company goods, thereby increasing black employment. The Reverend Leon Sullivan of OIC received money from the Nixon Administration. This was made possible as a result of multimillion-dollar manpower legislation that was signed by President Nixon.

In order for a community reference system to be used as a successful vehicle for community development, a sense of belonging and meaning, i.e., a self-concept, must exist among its members. The failure of the model city program can be attributed to a lack of identification with the community. A sense of community problems has to come from within the community rather than be defined by outside forces. The utilization of community reference systems would represent a more critical measure of community problems and needs. For a group of inmigrants in Bedford-Stuyvesant, the church tends to be a major component of such a system.

NOTES

1. A *place activity* is defined as an interaction point that incorporates a particular activity, e.g., work, shopping, or the like, at a specific place in space.

2. The same analogy as it is applied to the process of socialization is discussed by Berger and Luckerman (1966: 163).

3. Bedford-Stuyvesant is both a slum and ghetto, in that it is an area of overcrowded, poor-quality housing and is characterized by a distinct racial pattern including well-to-do members of a minority group, i.e., the gilded ghetto. Forman (1971) suggests that the concept, slum-ghetto, is a more realistic description of most situations involving a large concentration of segregated individuals of a single culture or racial group.

4. This figure is based on 71 census tracts that make up the area referred to as Bedford-Stuyvesant in this study, and includes both Black and Spanish-speaking persons. The breakdown is as follows: Approximately 83 percent are Black, and the remaining 12 percent Spanish. The figure is based upon the *1970 Census of Population and Housing* (Bureau of the Census, 1972).

5. The Bedford-Stuyvesant Restoration Corporation, a community-based organization, was organized under the leadership of the late Senator Robert F. Kennedy to make plans for the restoration of the Bedford-Stuyvesant area.

6. Examples of involving the people in the transformation of their community and society can be found in Freire (1970) and Friedmann (1973).

REFERENCES

ATTNEAVE, F. (1950) "Dimension of similarity." *American Journal of Psychology* 63.

BACHI, R. (1963) "Standard distance measures and related method for spatial analysis" *Papers of the Regional Science Association* 10.

BERGER, P. L. and T. LUCKERMAN (1966) *The Social Construction of Reality: A Treaty in the Sociology of Knowledge.* Garden City, NY: Doubleday.

BROWN, L. A. and J. HOLMES (1970) "Search behavior in an intraurban context: a spatial perspective." Discussion Paper 13, Department of Geography, Ohio State University.

Bureau of the Census (1972) *970 Census of Population and Housing.* Washington, DC:

BURTON, I. and R. KATES (1964) "Perception of natural hazards in resource management." *Natural Resource Journal* 3.

BUTTIMER, A. (1972) "Social space and the planning of residential areas." *Environment and Behavior* 4, 3.

DANIEL, V. E. (1940) "Ritual in Chicago's South Side churches for Negroes." Doctoral dissertation, University of Chicago.

ETZKOWITZ, H. and G. M. SCHAFLANDER (1969) *Ghetto Crisis: Bureaucracy vs. Progress in Bedford-Stuyvesant.* Boston: Little, Brown.

FAUSET, A. H. (1944) *Black Gods of the Metropolis: Negro Religious Cults of the Urban North.* Philadelphia: University of Pennsylvania.

FORMAN, R. E. (1971) *Black Ghettos, White Ghettos, and Slums.* Englewood Cliffs, NJ: Prentice-Hall.

FRAZIER, E. F. (1964) *The Negro Church in America.* New York: Schocken.

FREIRE, P. (1970) *Pedagogy of the Oppressed.* New York: Herder & Herder, 1970.

FRIEDMANN, J. (1973) *Retracking America: A Theory of Transactive Planning.* Garden City, NY: Doubleday.

HORTON, F. E. and D. R. REYNOLDS (1971) "Effects of urban spatial structure on individual behavior." *Economic Geography* 47.

JITODAL, T. T. (1964) "Migrant status and church attendance." *Social Forces* 43.

KRUSKAL, J. B. (1968) "How to use M-D Scal, a program to do multidimensional unfolding." Murray Hill, NJ: Bell Telephone Laboratories.

LAZERWITZ, B. (1961) "Some factors associated with variations in church attendance." *Social Forces* 39.

McNEAL, A. (1969) "The distribution of store-front churches in the greater Cincinnati Area." Master's thesis, Department of Geography, University of Cincinnati.

MEAD, G. H. (1934) *Mind, Self and Society.* Chicago: University of Chicago Press.

MYRDAL, G. (1944) *The American Dilemma.* New York: Harper & Row.

NELSON, G. K. (1971) "Communal and associational churches." *Review of Religious Research* 12.

New York Times (1955) "Our Changing City: Northern Brooklyn." July 23.

NOBLES, W. W. (1973) "Psychological research and Black self-concept: a critical review." *Journal of Social Issues* 29.

SHIBUTANI, T. (1955) "Reference groups as perspectives." *American Journal of Sociology* 60.

WIRTH, L. (1938) "Urbanism as a way of life." *American Journal of Sociology* 44.

13

BLACK CRIME: A REEXAMINATION OF THE ALCOHOL RECIDIVISM HYPOTHESIS

Kenneth A. Johnson

STRUCTURING THE PROBLEM

The thesis that blacks as a minority group are responsible for a disproportionate number of crimes committed in the United States—increasingly, crimes of violence—is an issue of serious debate. That blacks represent a sizable segment of offenders in our penal system can be said with little doubt. While they constitute less than 12 percent of the nation's population, they make up approximately half of the inmates in state and federal prisons.[1] Furthermore, criminal recidivism rates for blacks, who are frequently returned to prison upwards of three or more times for successive offenses, begin for most at a relatively early age.[2] These conditions suggest that black criminality deserves more research interest than it has received, specifically in regard to such a fundamental matter as the *cause* of black crime, which is basic to any systematic discussion of the recidivism problem.

AUTHOR'S NOTE: Data used in this study were originally gathered as part of a general Colorado prison survey by the Bureau of Sociological Research at the University of Colorado, Colorado Springs, and supported under Grant 75031094, Colorado Institute of Criminal Justice, 1975.

ALCOHOL AND BLACK CRIME

This research explores the hypothesis that alcohol abuse may be a considerable catalyst in the precipitation of criminal recidivism and also in the violent behavior evidenced by blacks in terms of homicides, criminal assaults, and conflict with the law in general (see, for example, Wolfgang, 1958; Strohm and Wolfgang, 1956; Roebuck and Johnson, 1962; Robins and Murphy, 1968; King et al., 1969; Conklin, 1972; Viamantes, 1972; Haberman and Baden, 1974; and Staples, 1976). Beginning with Wolfgang's work, in which a distinct association was discovered between violent homicides and the presence of alcohol in black male offenders, the role of alcohol and problem drinking in the occurrence of black crimes has come into new focus. Some observers, for example, rank it as the number one criminal offense and problem among blacks (Bourne and Fox, 1973; Harper, 1976; Staples, 1976).[3]

THE ALCOHOL-RECIDIVISM HYPOTHESIS

Several studies have attempted to test the proposition that alcohol abuse is related to criminal recidivism (Guze, 1964; Guze and Cantwell, 1965; Guze et al., 1969; Guze, 1972). These, however, provide us with little information on the magnitude of alcoholism among black felons, although they do indicate that the risk of recidivism is increased if the felon, black or white, has experienced previous problems with alcohol. In a eight-year follow-up of 51 blacks released from the Missouri State Penitentiary, Robins and Guze (1970) found that black offenders who had alcoholic histories undergo less alcoholic remission than whites. As a result, alcoholic blacks were also more likely to be reconvicted of a felony and reincarcerated than nonalcoholic blacks (see also Goodwin et al., 1971). Consequently, Robins and Guze take the position that alcoholism and problem drinking not only are primary factors in black recidivism, they are also crucial intervening links between pervasive ghetto problems, including family troubles. This study, then, is a replication of the issues suggested by previous analyses within the "alcohol-recidivism" conceptual framework. The same pattern of reasoning may be followed in retesting to determine the applicability of the findings to more homogeneous populations of black prisoners.

METHODOLOGY AND SAMPLE

Research data on the influence of alcohol factors and problem drinking in the perpetuation of black criminal recidivism were randomly selected as

part of a larger survey in 1975 of the inmate population in a maximum
security prison in the State of Colorado.[4] The sample of blacks (N = 159)
was composed of inmate males who were incarcerated at the time of the
study; 51 percent (N = 78) of the sampled cases were recidivists, having
been previously imprisoned in an adult correctional institution in the
United States. The social indicators of alcohol and recidivism convergences
in the offender's career cycle as reported in the official files or "jackets '
on personal characteristics and correctional and criminal history were
evaluated in each case, followed by extensive interviews with prisoners.[5]
This method combines case histories of apprehended offenders with their
personal reports in order to assess the extent of alcohol problems in the
past. One group of offenders whose criminal patterns are predominantly
alcohol-related are compared with others who do not exhibit this behavior
in their arrest records (Roebuck and Johnson, 1962).[6] Three measures of
possible alcohol-crime relationships were used in the process: (1) whether
the offender was drinking, intoxicated, or under the influence of alcohol
at the time he committed the crime for which he was imprisoned, (2) if
the offender had in the past been clinically diagnosed as having "chronic"
alcohol problems, and (3) if he had experienced an alcohol "blackout" at
the time the crime was committed.[7] As a fourth measure, relatively
common in criminological literature (e.g., McGlothlin et al., 1978), the
incidence of drug use in the life histories of black inmates was also
controlled as an outcome variable to weight its contribution as a motivat-
ing factor in the genesis of criminal careers.

Black felons in the sample, including recidivists, differ little descrip-
tively from the general population of black prisoners. A comparison
between Table 13.1 on the selected characteristics of inmates and Table
13.2 on the most serious offenses they commit provides the typical
profiles.[8] As can be seen, black prisoners are generally young, between the
ages of 20 and 24, and male. There were 68 percent of the black inmates
who were not high school graduates. Crimes of violence, particularly
robbery, 31 percent, and homicide, 11 percent, are most prevalent among
blacks; also high are economic crimes such as burglary, 10 percent, and
public order crimes like narcotics violations, 16 percent.[9]

RESEARCH FINDINGS

The relationship between alcohol abuse and criminal behavior may, in
some instances, be associated with several phases of the lives of individuals.
When crime occurs, it is usually the culmination of a series of social
interactions of life events (Tinklenberg, 1973). The social interaction that

TABLE 13.1 Selected Characteristics of Black Inmates

Characteristic	Colorado Black Inmate General Prison Population[a]		Colorado Prison Study Sample	
	Number	Percentage	Number	Percentage
Sex				
Total	361	100	159	100
Male	343	95	159	100
Female	18	5	0	0
Age				
Total	361	100	159	100
Under 18	1	(z)[b]	(z)[b]	(z)[b]
18	6	2	4	2
19	26	7	11	7
20–24	132	37	61	38
25–29	83	23	36	23
30–34	48	13	29	18
35–39	20	6	8	5
40–44	24	7	5	3
45–49	11	3	3	2
50 and over	8	2	2	1
Not reported	2	1	0	0
Median		25.9		22.1
Highest Grade Completed				
Total	361	100	159	100
Eighth grade or less	32	9	43	27
1–3 years of high school	138	38	58	37
Some high school (years unreported)	10	3	7	4
4 years of high school	54	15	42	26
Any college	18	5	9	2
Not reported	109	30	7	4
Median		11.3		11.1

NOTE: Percentage detail may not add to totals shown because of rounding.
a. Source: "Census of Prisoners in State Correctional Facilities, 1973" (Law Enforcement Assistance Administration, 1976: 36-37).
b. (z) Represents less than 0.5 percent.

takes place between consumption of alcohol and crime phenomena must be considered, explaining the effects of drinking alcohol while controlling for pressures to commit crime provided by the social environment. Because multiple factors may operate interdependently to influence these interactions, alcohol being but one antecedent, the basic methodological

TABLE 13.2   Most Serious Offenses by Blacks

Most Serious Offense	Colorado Black Inmate General Prison Population[a]		Colorado Prison Study Sample	
	Number	Percentage	Number	Percentage
Total	361	100	159	100
Crimes of Violence	210	58	94	59
Murder	26	7	18	11
Attempted murder	3	1	0	0
Manslaughter	14	4	0	0
Kidnaping	5	1	1	1
Rape	17	5	15	9
Statutory rape	1	(z)[b]	0	0
Sexual assault: force undetermined	5	1	0	0
Robbery	114	32	52	33
Assault	25	7	8	5
Crimes against property	96	27	38	24
Burglary	49	14	18	11
Larceny	23	6	8	5
Motor vehicle theft	3	1	1	1
Forgery, fraud, or embezzlement	20	6	10	6
Arson	1	(z)[b]	0	0
Stolen property	0	0	1	1
Crimes against public order	50	14	22	15
Drug offense	44	12	20	13
Weapons offense	2	1	2	2
Commercialized sex	1	(z)[b]	0	0
Other sex offense	2	1	0	0
Traffic offense	1	(z)[b]	0	0
Escape or flight	0	0	0	0
Other	5	1	4	2

NOTE: Percentage detail may not add to subtotals or totals shown because of rounding.
a.   Source: "Census of Prisoners in State Correctional Facilities, 1973" (Law Enforcement Assistance Administration, 1976: 36-37).
b.   (z) Represents less than 0.5 percent.

assumption in the research is that the criminal act cannot be explained by a unitary variable acting alone. Rather, it should be viewed as the consequence of a variety of variables. These variables are identified and their relative contributions assessed through means of multiple regression analysis.

MULTIPLE REGRESSION

In contrast to previous studies which used a small number of variables, the present study sought to increase the number of criterion variables having a potential effect on recidivism. There were 30 variables chosen as criteria, selected on the basis of past research in corrections—variables most relevant to, descriptive of, and predictive of recidivism. From these, 20 statistically significant predictors were identified and the data reanalyzed.[10] The secondary analysis was performed using bivariate correlations in describing a single variable relationship to the dependent variable. The results are presented in Table 13.3. The computation of zero-order correlation coefficients between the alcohol and drug measures and recidivism exhibited a positive low to moderate effect on recidivism in this stage of analysis ($r = .20, .21, .33$, and $.01$, respectively). What these analyses show is that with little exception, the measures are related in the direction in which the alcohol-recidivism hypothesis implied, but that the degree of relationship of each measure is generally small. On the other hand, as can be seen in Table 13.4, we find several facts of interest apparent in the regression model. After independent variable interaction effects are controlled, including type of crime, alcohol does not appear to be a significant factor in predicting the high reimprisonment rates of blacks.[11] Clearly, unemployment status at the time of arrest ($r^2 = .10$, $p < .03$), the age at first arrest, or the first police contact resulting in a police record ($r^2 = .24$, $p < .001$), and the number of arrests, defined as all previous arrests that resulted in court disposition or conviction ($r^2 = .23$, $p < .001$), are the best combination of predictors to estimate the probabilities of a black felon being returned to prison. T tests of beta coefficients are significant at the .01 level.[12] These three variables together explain nearly 60 percent of the variance in the regression model. On this basis alone our error in predicting the probability of recidivism in blacks can be reduced considerably. The above correlations show, simply, that the initial criminal experience comes to young blacks rather than to the middle-aged and that the older inmate has had more experience with the total correctional system from arrests and convictions to incarceration. This pattern appears to be consistent with the findings of other investigators and the data in criminological research showing that the age of an offender when first arrested, convicted, or confined for any crimes, the extent of his prior criminal record, the difficulty he has in procuring adequate financial resources when released from prison, and the likelihood of his becoming a recidivist are directly correlated (Dobbins, 1958; Glaser and Rice, 1959; Glaser, 1964; Miller, 1972; Pownall, 1975; Levine, 1975).[13]

TABLE 13.3　Bivariate Correlations
Between Black Recidivism
and Four Alcohol-Drug
Measures (N = 78)

Variables	r
Crime alcohol-related[a]	.208
Chronic alcohol problem[b]	.200
Alcohol Blackout[c]	.337[d]
History of drug use	.017

a. Offender was drinking, intoxicated, or under
the influence of alcohol at the time crime was
committed.
b. Offender has been clinically diagnosed as an
alcoholic.
c. Offender experienced an alcohol "blackout"
at the time of crime.
d. Significant at the .09 level.

DISCUSSION

To be sure, the observation that unemployment, or underemployment, is a crucial factor in the precipitation of new violations of the law by former black prisoners and that juvenile and arrest and conviction records act as barriers to obtaining public employment, is what blacks have known all along. A criminal record goes hand in hand with recidivism and is an obstacle to any job seeker, but it is harder on blacks. The quality of daily life and the succession of events that pattern the life cycle of most blacks make the phenomenon of arrest border on the routine. The relationship of early criminality with later recidivism is a result of the differential legal and penal treatment of blacks which leads to the development of multiple arrest records at a young age. Blacks are more likely to be indicted after arrest, more likely to be convicted in court, and more severely punished than other groups (Zax et al., 1964; Foslund, 1970; Green, 1970; Chiricos, 1972; Wolfgang et al., 1972).[14] Moreover, the probability of arrest, especially for black youth, is so blown out of proportion that one writer estimates, given a "steady state"—that is, if the current excessively high unemployment rates for blacks hold relatively constant (statistics vary but range between 40 and 60 percent, depending upon whether those who are discouraged, have given up looking for work, or never tried, are included [15])—over 90 percent of urban black males would, sometime in their lives, experience at least one nontraffic arrest (Christensen, 1967). These figures

TABLE 13.4   Multiple Regression Analysis Between Black Recidivism[a]
and Twenty Independent Variables[b] (N = 78)

Variables	r^2	P	Beta	T^c
Employment status (low scores associated with unemployment at time of arrest)	−.102	.03	−.10	−2.1
Age at first arrest (first police contact resulting in official record)	.244	.001	.31	2.9
Number of arrests (all previous arrests resulting in court conviction/disposition)	.239	.001	.48	6.0
		$R^2 = .58$		

a. Recidivism was not operationalized as a dichotomous variable; therefore, a multiple regression analysis with it as dependent variable is appropriate.
b. Other independent variables include: crime alcohol-related, number of juvenile commitments, number of family members with felony convictions, chronic alcohol problem, alcohol blackout, history of drug use, highest academic grade completed, previous court sentences other than prison, type of crime, military discharge, marital status, number of dependents, living arrangements, number of previous convictions, felony probations, and relationship to victim.
c. T values equal to or greater than 2.0 indicate significance at the .05 level.

are enhanced by the overrepresentation of blacks in the age group 14 to 24, the age group responsible for a disproportionately high share of crimes in all parts of the nation.[16] Furthermore, the rearrest probabilities for the black ex-offender are increased because of the likelihood of his being taken into custody for "suspicion" or "investigation" and reconvicted, regardless of actual criminal conduct. Given the pressures for plea-bargaining, an ex-convict who is prosecuted has little choice but to plead guilty, regardless of his actual guilt or innocence (Tittle, 1973).

On the strength of this and other studies, the "zig-zag" or ' oscillation" concept of recidivism is reinforced for blacks, wherein a developmental, cyclical, and sequential process becomes evident; if one situation holds— either unemployment, police contact and arrest resulting in an official record, or the offender is at a young age when officially recorded criminality occurs—it is highly probable that that situation will almost invariably be followed by one of the others (Glaser, 1964; Robins and Wish, 1977).

In other ways, the developmental cycle indicates that there is a tendency for blacks with progressively less favorable opportunity for the achievement of personal goals through socially legitimate means, to have, according to the "opportunity" theoretical scheme, an increasing proportion of criminals in their number. As a result, blacks that have positive and constructive aspirations may resort to crime if the opportunities of acquiring higher status and upward mobility are blocked (Cloward and Ohlin, 1960). This interpretation of the developmental process and opportunity nexus is analogous to what Davis defined with respect to another descriptive concept, the "unequal access to institutional participation" explanation for motivation or "justification" of crime throughout black communities. Of most importance for blacks is their perception of the "injustice of unequal access." As Davis (1974: 72) states,

> blacks did not feel that their full potential was being realized through the restricted avenues of institutional participation available to them. There was a general feeling of depressed opportunity relative to ability. The rules of the game (employment practice prerequisites) were seen as mechanisms for excluding blacks rather than standards for judging qualifications. The sense of injustice was experienced to such a degree by some that the entire social system was discredited and viewed as oppressive.

The same process can be stated differently. Many economic crimes such as robbery are used as "equalizers." Tired of the cycle of oppressive and often unwarranted arrests, of unemployment, of menial jobs at low wages, and of failure and lack of opportunity to compete on an equal basis, more than one young black man has decided that "the only way to get real money from him [whites in power] is to get a gun, go down there and put it to that mother-fucker's head and take it" (Brown, 1964: 284).

SUMMARY AND CONCLUSIONS

The prison study on black recidivism was undertaken to provide, if possible, an additional source of empirical evidence in support of the general hypothesis on crime and alcohol convergences in black criminal careers. Three major conclusions are drawn from analysis of the data:

1. Previous research suggests that the chances of being returned to prison are greater for blacks who drink heavily than for offenders who do not have such histories. This observation is not adequately supported in the study. Further, the findings fail to recognize a basic continuity

between alcohol and crime for black felons. Alcohol by itself is not shown to be significant as a cause of recidivism. Therefore, any problems resulting in its use appear to be consequences rather than effects in determining criminal behavior. These conclusions agree, essentially, with studies which examined the influence of alcohol on criminal activities in prison inmates and found that alcohol "abstainers" were proportionally greater among blacks; alcoholic felons were more likely to be white (see, for example, Blacker and Dermone, 1965; Roth and Rosenberg, 1971; Globetti et al., 1974). Moreover, in many cases where alcohol was involved, the criminal behavior mostly preceded the onset of heavy drinking in the lives of offenders (Goodwin et al., 1971). Because of this, one cannot give full credit to the assumption that alcohol is responsible for the majority of crimes committed by blacks.

2. This analysis gave grounds for a tentative rejection of the alcohol-recidivism postulate as it related to black crime. At the same time, it provided compelling evidence in support of a "developmental" approach to recidivism within the "opportunity" theoretical framework. The problem of recurrent and habitual criminal behavior among blacks appears directly related to various socioeconomic conditions that exist in our society. More specifically, it is characterized by the vicissitudes of unemployment and the low status of blacks in the labor market, long histories of trouble within the criminal justice system, and progressively increasing stigmatization from the frequent experiences of being shuttled in and out of juvenile reformatories and prisons. This process, and the circumstances that surround the lives of the average black felon when released from prison, are fittingly described by Colter (1976: 283):

> Except for a few uneasy relatives and uncertain friends, he is surrounded by suspicion, distrust, dislike, and hostility. . . . Proscribed from employment by most concerns and usually unable to find new friends or ways of earning a living, he tries to survive. He is a handicapped human being, one who needs all the things the rest of us need and a little bit more. He is encumbered not only by whatever made him commit a crime in the first place but by what the prison has done to him and what society is doing to him now. He has a heavy burden.

3. Finally, there is a critical need for more national baseline information on alcohol-related offenses and offenders in this too-long-neglected area in order to determine more comprehensively where and when alcohol is, in fact, involved in criminal offenses by blacks. The present research is only a first approximation of the task of independent variable specification in the etiology of black criminal recidivism.

NOTES

1. Black prisoners are so numerous that about 1 out of every 4 black men in his early twenties spends some time in prison, jail, or on probation, and estimates are that 1 out of every 20 black men between the ages of 25 and 34 is either in jail or in prison on any given day, compared to 1 out of every 163 white men of the same age group (Quinney, 1977: 138). Orland (1975) has argued that approximately two-thirds of the inmates in America's state prisons are black. See also the Law Enforcement Assistance Administration's *Sourcebook of Criminal Justice Statistics* (1977: 693).

2. While various investigators attach somewhat different meanings to it, the term *recidivism* is defined in the study to denote a prisoner who has previously been in an adult correctional institution.

3. Staples (1976) has pointed out that alcoholism (formerly known as the crime of public intoxication) accounted for about 20 percent or 280,706 black arrests in 1972. Public intoxication also accounts for the largest single category of offenders for which arrests are made in the United States.

4. For a complete description of the data collection and methodological procedures used, see Johnson (1976).

5. The proportion of blacks in the prisoner population of Colorado was higher than the proportion of blacks, as of 1970, in the general civilian population of the state. They comprised approximately 20 percent of the prison inmate population and only 3 percent of the civilian population. (See Law Enforcement Assistance Administration, 1976: 35-38.)

6. Criticisms of the method have shown that it may exaggerate the degree of recidivism, because repeat offenders receive longer sentences and are less likely to be paroled (Tittle, 1973). However, the proportions of repeat offenders and first-time offenders in the study are roughly equal.

7. These operational definitions were used to obtain comparability with the results of other studies on the drinking behavior of recidivist inmates. Of the collective case records of black felons, 27 percent directly or indirectly show implications of alcohol excess or number moderately among those offenders with chronic alcohol problems.

8. These are highly comparable to the characteristics of black jail inmates on the national level (see Current Population Reports, 1975: 162-176).

9. These crime patterns are frequently found to be alcohol-related. However, the crime of robbery is the only one of the crimes designated as violent in which alcohol shows only a minimum involvement. Alcohol appears to be more related to crimes against the person than to property crimes (Erskine, 1972: 9).

10. The conceptual framework in which the twenty independent variables are cast is compatible with regression coefficients as a measure of "effect." Preinstitutional variables are considered to be in the same "theoretical realm." See Gordon (1968: 592-594) for a discussion of the "partialling fallacy" problem in multiple regression analysis.

11. Roth and Rosenberg (1971), however, suggest that the culturally accepted phenomenon of heavy weekend or spree drinking among blacks could result in the underreporting of black alcohol problems in primary reports, such as presentence investigation and probation reports and the like.

12. The t test of beta coefficients is the criterion of statistical significance for correlation, particularly if the independent variables are weak. A t value equal to or

greater than 2.0 indicates significance at the .05 level. With a reasonable measurement error, say 2 percent, type 1 errors almost never occur (Hamblin, 1968).

13. The unemployment rate also appears to be a major determinant of the number of persons committed to federal prisons. See, for example, Congressional Budget Office, 1977. This Bureau of Prisons study shows a strong relationship between prior unemployment and recidivism on the national level (43 percent recidivism for those with no job, compared to 14 percent for those who had a job for more than four years). Hromas and Crago (1976) also reported a significant relationship between unemployment rates and "new" imprisonment rates at the Colorado State Penitentiary. When unemployment of males aged 20 and over goes up or down, the population of the prison follows the same pattern, allowing a 3-month time-lag, the time required from arrest to incarceration.

14. A few studies, however, contradict this conclusion (see, for example, Black, 1970: 744-746; Polk, 1978).

15. Vernon E. Jordan, in the Urban League's "The State of Black America–1978," reports that unemployment among black teenagers between 1967 and 1977 soared from 204,000 to 369,000, raising their jobless rate from 26.5 to 38.6 percent. Anderson (1978: 508), however, suggests that an increasing number of black youth have simply given up the search for work and have withdrawn from the labor market. If the discouraged youth were added to the unemployment statistics, measured by the standard definition, the black teenager unemployment rate would be closer to 60 percent.

16. The unemployment situation threatens to grow even worse as the very large number of black children now in big cities reach working age, and as today's teenage blacks grow older (U.S. Department of Labor, 1974).

REFERENCES

ANDERSON, B. E. (1978) "Jobs and income for Black Americans." *Labor Law Journal* (August): 506-512.

BLACK, D. J. (1970) "Production of Crime Rates." *American Sociological Review* 35: 744-746.

BLACKER, E. and H. W. DERMONE, Jr. (1965) "Drinking behavior of delinquent boys." *Quarterly Journal of Studies on Alcohol* 26 (June): 230-231.

BOURNE, P. G. and R. FOX (1973) *Alcoholism: Progress in Research and Treatment.* New York: Academic.

BROWN, C. (1965) *Manchild in the Promised Land.* New York: Signet.

CHIRICOS, T. et al. (1972) "Inequality in the imposition of a criminal label." *Social Problems* 19 (Spring): 553-572.

CHRISTENSEN, R. (1960) "Projected percentage of U.S. population with criminal arrest and conviction records," Appendix J in President's Commission on Law Enforcement and Administration of Justice, *Task Force Report: Science and Technology.* Washington, DC: Government Printing Office.

CLOWARD, R. A. and L. E. OHLIN (1960 *Delinquency and Opportunity.* New York: Free Press.

COLTER, N. C. (1976) "Subsidizing the released inmate." *Crime and Delinquency* 22: 282-285.

Congressional Budget Office (1977) *Federal Prison Construction: Alternative Approaches.* Washington, DC: Government Printing Office.

CONKLIN, J. E. (1972) *Robbery and Criminal Justice System.* New York: J. B. Lippincott.

Current Population Reports (1975) "The social and economic status of the Black population in the United States." Special Studies, Series P-23 *54: 162-176.*

DAVIS, J. A. (1974) "Justification for no obligation: views of Black males toward crime and criminal laws." *Issues of Criminology* 9 (Fall): 69-87.

DOBBINS, D. A. (1958) "Effects of unemployment on white and Negro prison admissions in Louisiana." *Journal of Criminal Law, Criminology, and Police Science* 48: 522-525.

ERSKINE, H. (1972) *Alcohol and the Criminal Justice System: Challenge and Response.* Washington, DC: Law Enforcement Assistance Administration.

FOSLUND, M. A. (1970) "A comparison of Negro and white crime rates." *Journal of Criminal Law, Criminology, and Police Science* 61: 214-217.

GLASER, D. and K. RICE (1959) "Crime, age and unemployment." *American Sociological Review* 24 (October): 671-686.

GLASER, D. (1964) *The Effectiveness of a Prison and Parole System.* Indianapolis: Bobbs-Merill.

GLOBETTI, G. et al. (1974) "Alcohol and crime: previous drinking careers of convicted offenders." Presented at the Midwest Sociological Society meetings, Omaha, Nebraska.

GOODWIN, D. W. et al. (1971) "Felons who drink." *Quarterly Journal of Studies on Alcohol* 32: 136-147.

GORDON, R. A. (1968) "Issues in multiple regression." *American Journal of Sociology* 73 (March): 592-616.

GREEN, E. (1970) "Race, social status, and criminal arrest." *American Sociological Review* 35: 476-490.

GUZE, S. B. et al. (1972) *Criminality and Psychiatric Illness: The Role of Alcoholism.* Rockville, MD: National Institute on Alcohol Abuse and Alcoholism.

——— (1964) "A study of recidivism based upon a follow-up of 217 consecutive criminals." *Journal of Nervous and Mental Diseases* 138: 575-580.

——— and D. P. CANTWELL (1965) "Alcoholism, parole observations and criminal recidivism: a study of 116 parolees." *American Journal of Psychiatry* 122: 436-439.

GUZE, S. B. et al. (1969) "Criminality and psychiatric disorders." *Archives of General Psychiatry* 20: 583-591.

HABERMAN, P. W. and M. BADEN (1974) "Alcoholism and violent death." *Quarterly Journal of Studies on Alcohol* 35: 221-231.

HAMBLIN, R. L. (1968) "Ratio measurement and sociological theory: a critical analysis." St. Louis, MO: Washington University.

HARPER, F. D. (1976) *Alcohol Abuse and Black America.* Alexandria, VA: Douglas.

HROMAS, S. and T. G. CRAGO (1976) "Colorado unemployment and commitment rates." Research Note 6, Office of Research, Planning and Information Systems, Division of Correctional Services, Colorado Department of Institutions, Denver, Colorado.

JOHNSON, K. A. (1976) "Technical report: information and records utilization—Colorado State Penitentiary." Colorado Springs: University of Colorado.

KING, L. J. et al. (1969) "Alcohol abuse: a crucial factor in the social problems of Negro men." *American Journal of Psychiatry* 125 (June): 1682-1690.

McGLOTHLIN, W. H. et al. (1978) "Narcotic addiction and crime." *Criminology* 16 (November): 293-315.

Law Enforcement Assistance Administration (1977) *Sourcebook of Criminal Justice Statistics.* Washington, DC: Author.

— — (1976) "Census of prisoners in state correctional facilities, 1973." National Prisoner Statistics Special Report SD-NPS-SR-3, National Criminal Justice Information and Statistics Service, Washington, DC.

LEVINE, J. (1975) "The ineffectiveness of adding police to prevent crime." *Public Policy* 23 (Fall): 136.

MILLER, H. S. (1972) *The Closed Door: The Effect of a Criminal Record on Employment with State and Local Public Agencies.* Washington, DC: Georgetown University, Institute of Criminal Law Procedure.

ORLAND, L. (1975) *Prison: Houses of Darkness.* New York: Free Press.

POPE, C. E. (1978) "Race and crime revisited." Presented at the meeting of Academy of Criminal Justice Sciences, New Orleans.

POWNALL, G. (1975) "Employment problems of released prisoners," in B. P. Perlstein and T. Phelps (eds.) *Alternatives to Prison: Community-Based Corrections.* Pacific Palisades, CA: Goodyear.

QUINNEY, R. (1977) *Class, State and Crime.* New York: David McKay.

ROBINS, L. N. and S. B. GUZE (1970) "Drinking practices and problems in urban ghetto populations," in N. K. Mello (ed.) *Recent Advances in Studies of Alcoholism.* Rockville, MD: National Institute of Mental Health.

ROBINS, L. N. and E. WISH (1977) "Childhood deviance as a developmental process: a study of 223 urban Black men from birth to 18." *Social Forces* 56 (December): 448-473.

ROEBUCK, J. and R. JOHNSON (1962) "The Negro drinker and assaulter as a criminal type." *Crime and Delinquency* 8: 21-33.

ROTH, L. and N. ROSENBERG (1971) "Prison adjustment of alcoholic felons." *Quarterly Journal of Studies on Alcohol* 32: 382-392.

STAPLES, R. (1976) *Introduction to Black Sociology.* New York: McGraw-Hill.

STROHM, R. and M. E. WOLFGANG (1956) "The relationship between alcohol and criminal homicide." Quar. J. Stud. Alc. 17: 411-425.

TINKLENBERG, J. R. (1973) "Alcohol and violence," in P. G. Bourne and R. Fox (eds.) *Alcoholism: Progress in Research and Treatment.* New York: Academic.

TITTLE, C. R. (1973) "Prisons and rehabilitation: the inevitability of disfavor." Social Problems 21: 385-395.

VIAMONTES, J. A. (1972) "Comparison of Black and white male alcoholics reveals some differences in drinking patterns." Presented to the Pan American Medical Association.

WOLFGANG, M. E. (1958) *Patterns in Criminal Homicides.* Philadelphia: University Pennsylvania Press.

WOLFGANG, M. E. et al. (1972) *Delinquency in a Birth Cohort.* Chicago: University of Chicago Press.

ZAX, M. et al. (1964) "Public intoxication in Rochester." *Quarterly Journal of Studies on Alcohol* 25 (December): 669-678.

PART IV
THE HISTORICAL ISSUES

The historical dimension to contemporary research is complete with its own new baggage of methods and interpretation. There exists a unity and diversity in the new approaches to history. The unity resides in the traditional principles around which historical data are organized; the diversity is to be found in the rise of new and sometimes competing norms and values.

Our authors believe that all historical inquiry should follow clear patterns of scholarship, precise canons of logic, and logically consistent interpretations. With this in mind, they attempt to explain those social phenomena which have impacted upon the world. They are convinced that radical interpretations of historical phenomena must include all recent data as well as bring added perspectives to explanations.

Fundamental to the discovery of new avenues for understanding historical events is openness. The scholars whom we have chosen to present their findings in this section have undertaken their work in the spirit of free inquiry. In this section, Palmer demonstrates the reasonableness of his approach to the question of slavery in America. He endeavors to present a review of the changing interpretations of slavery in the United States. His work succeeds in establishing not only the presence of changing interpretations but also in showing why those interpretations were necessary. Akpan shows that black nationalism in America influenced African liberation and vice versa. The issues of black historical development, as shown by Akpan, have a cyclical relationship. In Nyang and Vandi's chapter there is an emphasis on Pan-Africanism in the historical process. They relate the concept to politics and society, demonstrating how Pan-Africanism sparked African history. Furthermore, they categorize the different manifestations of Pan-Africanism into Global Pan-Africanism, Continental Pan-Africanism, Regional Pan-Africanism, and Micro-Nationalism. The historical element in these works is essentially openness to society.

14

AFRICA IN THE DEVELOPMENT OF
BLACK-AMERICAN NATIONALISM

Emmanuel Akpan

Africa is of great significance to the development of Black-American nationalism. Black Americans trace their roots to Africa, the place where, anthropologists tell us, the ancestors of today's people became differentiated from the other primates. Barrett (1974: 1) argues that the Black-American "soul" force comes from Africa, the source of the "soul" of every Black person, regardless of wherever that Black person resides. *Soul,* Barrett maintains, signifies the moral and emotional fiber of the Black individuals that enables them to see their dilemmas clearly and at the same time encourages and sustains them in their struggles. He sees *soul force* as that power of the Black person to turn sorrow into joy, crying into laughter, and defeat into victory. It derives its impetus from the ancestral heritage of Africa. The continent of Africa is the rallying point for Black people wherever they are found on earth. The Black American's rich, unique cultural heritage comes from there.

Africa is of significance to the development of Black-American nationalism because, contrary to what racist scholars would have the world believe, Africa is the continent where human civilization began. Egypt was one of the earliest places of learning and civilization. The civilization passed from Africa to Greece and Rome and then to Europe and America. The early Egyptians were Black. Information obtained from Moses, the patriach of sacred history, and Herodotus, the patriach of profane history, all go to show that the ancient Egyptians, Black and wooly-haired people, astonished the world with their arts and sciences, in which they reveled with unbounded prodigality. Their reports show that the Egyptians became masters of the East and the lords of the Hebrews (Auerbach,

1975: 125). The wife of Moses, the lawgiver, was from Africa. Solomon, the most renowned of kings, married an African (Pritchard, 1974: 104). His African wife was the most favored of Solomon's seven hundred wives and three hundred concubines. He even composed that beautiful poem called the Canticles to honor and praise her. Eloise Johnson, in her "Tutankhamun and Racism," also reports of the mighty power and fame of Pharoah Tutankhamun, a Black king. King Tutankhamun, along with all that he represents, is indeed a Black gift to the whole world. The civilization of Egypt, according to Banifeld (1968: iii) in his *Africa in the Curriculum*, lasted longer than any other civilization known to man—about 10,000 years. It reached its height and was in decline before Europe was born.

In addition to events in Egypt there were great empires in West Africa. There were the great kingdoms of Old Ghana, Mali, Songhai, and Kanem-Bornu, to mention just a few. The Ghana Kingdom extended almost to Timbuktu in the east. The kingdoms of the Western Sudan, Ghana, Mali, and Songhai were remarkable in the degree to which they were able to establish complex political structures that centralized the government of large areas of West Africa. Ghana could conquer its neighbors because it knew the use of iron even as early as then. The University of Sankore in Timbuktu became the center of Muslim learning in Africa. According to Wallerstein (1961: 18), the practice of medicine at the Timbuktu university was much advanced, and doctors performed some operations that were not known in Europe for another 250 years. Knowledge of science and literature was extensive.

Black-American nationalism is based on its strong affinity and direct relationship to that grandest of all the continents of antiquity, Africa. Regardless of how Black Americans have been changed by American culture, beneath them one can yet find sufficient patterns of commonality to show an interlocking and philosophical synonym with Africa.

Any discussion of the significance of Africa in the development of Black-American nationalism that ignores the significance of Black-American nationalism in the development of African nationalism would be not only incomplete, but unfair. Black-American nationalism has on its own part contributed greatly to the development of national consciousness in Africa. The rise of nationalism in Africa is one of the most important and certainly the most dramatic developments of the mid-twentieth century. Nationalist movements have freed most African countries from colonial rule. Today, millions of Africans are living in freedom and independence. They walk with their heads held up in full human dignity as Africa, for the most part, has been liberated.

The rhetoric of Black-American nationalism has been very instrumental in winning freedom for Africa. The Black-American rhetoric of nationalism was carried to Africa through Pan-African Conferences, African students, and the mass media. For several years Africans have studied in American colleges and universities. The United States provided a stimulating training school for these foreign black students; not only did they get formal education, but they were constantly rubbing up against racial discrimination which made them more receptive to the ideas of the intellectuals and proponents of Black nationalism. Legum (1976: 27) mentions a particularly significant example of cross-fertilization of ideas between Blacks of the United States and Africans. The episode of the Nyasaland Rising of 1915, led by John Chilembwe, stands out in the minds of most people. Chilembwe had been a student in the United States for some years. On returning to his homeland, he became deeply troubled over the poor conditions of his people under British rule. In 1915 he led a revolt against the British rulers. A commission of inquiry which investigated the revolt linked it to the American Black by indicating that one of its causes was the political notions absorbed by Chilembwe while in the United States in a Black Baptist seminary.

Independent Black churches—especially the African Methodist Episcopal Zion Church—and other Afro American churches established strong ties with African religious movements of a Pan-African character. Chilembwe's Church of Christ, which undertook the uprising against the British colonial authority, is credited to have had the best clarity of political vision in the whole of South Africa because of the expert coaching in revolution he had received from Black-American nationalists. Religious movements in Africa reinterpreted the Bible purely in terms of African resistance to white rule.

Another person who transmitted the spirit of Black-American nationalism to Africa was Edward Blyden, the brilliant and controversial West-Indian-born Liberian who, after his death, was referred to as one of the greatest sons of Africa. He had his early lessons in Black nationalism in America. He was born in the century when the myth of Black inferiority was very strong.

Blyden came to America through the hands of a white missionary friend. On reaching the United States he attempted to attend a theological school. He was refused admission to the Rutgers Theological Seminary because of his color. His stay in America put him in contact with prominent Black Americans. Martin Delaney was one of them. Although Blyden was very much interested in helping to build a great African nation in Africa, he accepted going to Liberia, and while in Liberia was gratified to find evidence of Liberian loyalty to the militant American Negro leader, Henry Highland Garnet, and his motto: "Better to die free men than to live to be slaves" (Lynch, 1970: 13). According to Lynch, Blyden became one of the most learned and articulate champions of Africa and the Negro race. He gave members of his race a new pride and hope, and inspired succeeding generations of African nationalists.

Just as Black-American nationalists did in the United States, Blyden established newspapers to represent and defend the interest of the Black race. He fostered cultural nationalism in West Africa based on pride in Negro history and culture. He is also said to have worked very hard toward the formation of a modern transtribal West-African nation. African nations remember him as a man who contributed a great deal to the effort to dispel the lingering myth of European peoples of the inferiority of the Black man.

World War II also brought Africans and Black Americans into close contact. During the war the African soldiers met Black-American soldiers who provided them with living examples of the noncolonized African. The more contact they had, the more the Africans became aware of their unequal status under colonial regimes. They returned to Africa with hard feelings. Thus the stage was set, and the cry for freedom began to thunder in most parts of Africa.

In truth, Black-American nationalism is not an isolated movement. Many Black Americans see their demand for equality as part of the African demand for equality and freedom.

One of the most prominent African nationalists after World War II was James Aggrey, a college principal from what was then known as the Gold Coast (now Ghana). Aggrey had spent several years in the United States. In keeping with the spirit of the time when he was in the United States, Aggrey was a moderate. He is best remembered in Africa for his statement that harmony on the piano requires both black and white keys—an ideology he must have gotten from the rhetoric of Booker T. Washington.

Aggrey was a boyhood hero of Kwame Nkrumah, who for several years was the Prime Minister of Ghana. Nkrumah led Ghana to freedom, and in 1957 Ghana became the first tropical African state to win independence. Nkrumah, too, studied in the United States. Life was not easy for him during the years of his stay; he was poor and Black. In order to support himself, his autobiography states that he had to sell fish on Harlem streets and wash dishes in ships. In his autobiography he acknowledges the influence the Black-American rhetoric of nationalism had on him. He states with gratitude that while in America he was influenced more by Garvey's ideas than by any thing in the United States (Legum, 1976: 25).

Nkrumah's political party's motto was simply, "Self-Government NOW," an imitation of the Black-American rhetorical style. According to Clark (1973: 30), when Nkrumah was sailing out of New York harbor, he looked at the Statue of Liberty and said, "I shall never rest until I have carried your message to Africa." The most significant thing about Nkrumah's work is that once Ghana broke loose from British rule, the rest of the colonial structure began to collapse. By 1966 most of Africa had independence.

Most African leaders, past and present, got their nationalistic inspiration through the influence of Black-American nationalists. Nnamdi Azikiwe of Nigeria, who later became the first African governor-general in Nigeria, studied in the United States. While in America he was one of those who helped to establish an African students' organization. DuBois was in frequent contact with Azikiwe. He was at one time asked by DuBois to take the initiative in preparing the Sixth Pan-African Congress. Most of the people at that conference were Africa's future leaders. Some of the resolutions at that conference included a demand for independence and autonomy for Africa. When Azikiwe returned to Nigeria he became actively involved in the struggle to win independence for Nigeria. He published numerous newspapers, all of which were channels for attack on colonialism. On October 1, 1960, Nigeria became independent.

Other important African leaders whose political views have been influenced strongly by Black-American nationalism include the Reverend Sithole, the late Jomo Kenyatta (he was associated with the Mau Mau Revolt which shook up British rule in Kenya), Modibo Keita of Mali, Kenneth Kaunda of Zambia, Amilcar Cabral of Guinea, the late Tom Mboya of Kenya, Albert Luthuli of South Africa, Julius Nyerere of Tanzania, and Leopold Senghor of Senegal. It was Senghor who set in motion the most prominent cultural movement of the nationalist period in Africa. The movement was centered around the concept of "Negritude." In a sense, Negritude has existed for several years, wherever Black men have been forced to live in a foreign culture and have attempted to preserve their dignity. Many Black-American rhetors of the nineteenth and twentieth centuries expressed negritudinist ideas, and today the idea is spreading throughout Africa.

The most important link between the literary and political streams of Pan-Africanism was William DuBois. For several years he dominated the Pan-African Movement. He demonstrated his idea of Pan-Africanism by organizing several Pan-African conferences. The Pan-African Congress established fraternal bonds between Blacks throughout the world. His greatest influence on African nationalism can be linked to a struggle for human dignity as well as national freedom; recognition of the community of interests and necessity for mutual assistance; and cooperation between people of African descent wherever they may be found in the world. He also introduced the idea of nonalignment into African politics with the Western world.

African nations owe a debt of gratitude to Marcus Garvey—a dreamer and a messiah, to some people. His interest in the Back to Africa Movement and the rallying cry of Africa for the Africans cannot be ignored. The Blacks in Rhodesia and South Africa are fighting hard today to keep Africa for the Africans. He is best remembered for his encouragement that African leaders should establish powerful governments to manage their affairs.

Black-American nationalism has reached Africa through books, articles, and published speeches from Black Americans—books like Frantz Fanon's *The Wretched of the Earth.* Carmichael's *Black Power,* the published speeches of Martin Luther King, the speeches of Malcolm X, and the works of Delaney, Douglass, DuBois, and several others are read and assimilated in Africa and transformed into more readily accessible messages for the masses by the African leaders and intellectuals.

Many good things have come out of the cross-fertilization between Africans and Black Americans. Apart from the attainment of independence in most of Africa, a spirit of unity is growing among African states. The Pan-African Movement today has developed into the Organization of African Unity (OAU). In addition, there are several regional economic communities. There has been a renewed interest in Black arts and culture. The dreams of DuBois, Garvey, Delaney, Malcolm X, and many others are being turned into realities today.

The significance of Africa in the development of Black-American nationalism should rightly be viewed as a two-way street. Africa is of significance to the development of Black-American nationalism, just as Black-American nationalism is of significance to the development of African nationalism.

REFERENCES

AUERBACH, E. (1975) *Moses.* Detroit: Wayne State University Press.
BANFIELD, B. (1968) *Africa in the Curriculum.* New York: Edward Blyden.
BARRETT, L. (1974) *Soul Force—African Heritage.* Garden City, NY: Doubleday.
CLARK, L. [ed.] (1973) *Through African Eyes: The Rise of Nationalism.* New York: Praeger.

LEGUM, C. (1976) *Pan Africanism—A Short Political Gudie.* Westport, CT: Green-wood Press.

LYNCH, H. R. (1970) *Edward Wilmot Blyden: Pan-Negro Patriot, 1832-1912.* New York: Oxford University Press.

PRITCHARD J. B. [ed.] (1974) *Solomon and Sheba.* London: Phardom Press.

WALLERSTEIN, I. (1961) *Africa: The Politics of Independence.* New York: Vint-age.

15

CHANGING INTERPRETATIONS OF SLAVERY SINCE WORLD WAR II

Colin Palmer

Few historians will deny the assertion that the study of slavery in the United States has made great advances since World War II. Not only have scholars devoted more time and energy to the study of the peculiar institution, but they have begun to ask new and more sophisticated questions of the records. There has not only been a change in the nature of the questions themselves, but the racial assumptions of the historians, at least some of them, have undergone a significant transformation.

There are several factors which explain this scholarly metamorphosis. Adolf Hitler's assertion of Aryan superiority and the genocidal program directed against the Jews served, in part, to prompt a reexamination of the foundations of racism in the United States. The disturbing similarity between the Jewish experience in Germany and white America's racial attitudes toward its black citizens was not lost on some of the more thoughtful scholars. The writings of Melville Herskovits, especially his *The Myth of the Negro Past* (1941), as well as those of other social scientists, challenged—if not undermined—some of the prevailing assumptions regarding alleged black inferiority. Herskovits (1941: 293) cited a wide variety of data to demonstrate that the black condition was "to be ascribed largely to the social and economic hardships that these folks have suffered, rather than to any inability to cope with the realities of life."

The civil rights struggles of the 1950s and the 1960s and the demand for the creation of black studies programs also had an impact on the scholarly community. History professors began to revise their courses, belatedly, to include the black experience. This new scholarly interest, what some historians have called "presentism," was manifested not only in the increasing number of books on black history—many of them of poor quality—but also in the reassessment of some of the larger issues of Afro-American historiography. The history of slavery, in particular, received a more dispassionate treatment, and significant documentary sources, chiefly those left by the slaves themselves, were exploited. The earlier notion that slave narratives and autobiographies could not be relied upon for an accurate picture eventually gave way to innovative uses of these rich and remarkable data. Postwar historians of slavery had finally begun to take note of Richard Hofstadter's (1944: 124) charge that "any history of slavery must be written in large measure from the standpoint of the slave."

Many of the historians who initiated the reconsideration of the slavery issue after the second world war had been exposed during their college days to the writings of Ulrich B. Phillips. Phillips wrote many articles on slavery, but his *American Negro Slavery,* first published in 1918, was his most important contribution. This work remained the most authoritative and comprehensive treatment of slavery in the United States, until it was superseded in 1956 by Kenneth Stampp's *The Peculiar Institution.* Although Phillips's work was painstakingly researched, it was seriously flawed by racist assumptions. As a southerner, Phillips reflected the racist temper of his time, which was probably the reason that his treatment of slavery received almost uncritical acclaim from his white peers but brought forth serious objections from such black scholars as Carter Woodson (1919: 102-103) and W.E.B. DuBois (1918: 722-726).

Phillips (1918: 328) described a benign slave system in which the treatment of slaves was "benevolent in intent and on the whole beneficial in effect." According to him (1918: 343), slavery had a salutary effect on the African, since the slave plantations were "the best schools yet invented for the mass training of that sort of inert and backward people which the bulk of American negroes represented." Phillips concluded that the slave was an unwilling and inefficient worker who was incapable of performing complex tasks. His analysis of the evidence indicated that the slaves' productivity was low, and that consequently the institution of slavery was quite unprofitable. In his judgment (1905: 259), although slavery had retarded the economic development of the South, masters retained the institution because without it "the savage instincts" of the blacks would come to the fore. In other words, southerners maintained an unprofitable slave system because it was indispensable for the social control of the black population.

Phillips's conclusions remained influential and dominant for the next quarter-century. Local studies of slavery by Charles S. Sydnor (*Slavery in Mississippi*, 1933) and Ralph Flanders (*Plantation Slavery in Georgia*, 1933) reinforced in varying degrees Phillips's conclusions regarding the unprofitability of the institution. In 1944 the Swedish scholar Gunnar Myrdal published a major study, appropriately titled *The Negro Problem and Modern Democracy: An American Dilemma*. This lengthy work was not a study of slavery per se; rather, it was a clinical analysis of white-American attitudes toward blacks as well as of the contemporary black condition. Myrdal's bold and suggestive work raised questions that could no longer be avoided. He saw "the Negro problem," as he called it, as primarily a moral issue, and he questioned the justification for the Afro-Americans' inferior place in society. Myrdal's sound scholarship helped to ensure that in the future white scholars would have to forego overt racist assumptions in their writings. Things would never again be the same. In 1946 a further dimension was added to the study of race and slavery when Frank Tannenbaum published his brief but important study of slavery in the New World, *Slave and Citizen: The Negro in the Americas*, a book which would launch the comparative school of slavery studies. Tannenbaum argued that slavery in the United States was quite different from its counterpart in Latin America: Slaves in Latin America were imbued with a legal and a moral personality; in the Spanish possessions they were protected from mistreatment by their masters through the operation of the Siete Partidas, a body of laws which defined their status and gave them certain rights and privileges, such as the right to have a family. In addition, according to Tannenbaum, the Catholic Church and the governmental bureaucracy acted as mediators between the masters and their slaves. In strong contrast to his Latin-American brother, Tannenbaum depicted the North-American slave as totally under his master's control. Slave owners in the United States considered the slave subhuman and treated him or her accordingly. Thus, when emancipation came, it was difficult for white society to change its unfavorable perceptions of the new black citizens and allow them equal rights. Tannenbaum opened a new era in the study of slavery by introducing the comparative school, and the questions he raised would be dealt with more subtly by others.

The publication in 1956 of Stampp's *The Peculiar Institution* proved to be the most effective challenge to Phillips yet undertaken by a historian. Although Stampp presented a picture of slavery markedly different from that of Phillips, he was apparently still influenced by Phillips, judging from the questions he asked and the organization of his material. Unlike Phillips, however, Stampp did not start with the assumption that blacks were innately inferior to the white man. On the contrary, he was con-

vinced (1956: vii) that "innately Negroes are, after all, only white men
with black skins, nothing more, nothing less," an observation strongly
criticized by several of his peers.

The Peculiar Institution has remained a landmark of American historiography because of the high quality of its scholarship and the wide-
ranging treatment of its subject. Whereas Phillips had found slavery a
benign institution, Stampp (1956: 141-191) found it cruel and repressive.
Stampp also broke with Phillips on the question of the slaves' reaction to
their status. Phillips had concluded that slaves were quite docile, but
Stampp insisted that they were a troublesome property and utilized both
violent and passive means to resist their oppression. Stampp also con-
tradicted Phillips on the issue of the profitability of the slave system,
coming to the conclusion that although slaves were reluctant and inefficient workers, the institution itself was profitable on the whole.

It was quite clear from the critical acclaim which greeted the book that
many scholars believed that Stampp had conclusively won the debate over
the nature of slavery, that he had said the last word on the subject. But
such judgments were premature. The debate was reopened in 1959 with
the publication of Stanley Elkins's suggestive work, *Slavery: A Problem in
American Institutional and Intellectual Life*. Elkins elevated the debate to
a new plane by investigating the impact of slavery on the black personality. Like Tannenbaum thirteen years earlier, Elkins was also interested in the differences between slavery in the United States and in Latin
America. His excursion into comparative history did not result in any
fundamental revisions of Tannenbaum's conclusions. Indeed, he vigorously
reinforced Tannenbaum's thesis that slavery in the United States was more
repressive than elsewhere in the hemisphere. He agreed with Tannenbaum
that slaves in the United States lacked the institutional protection of the
church and the state, and that this contributed to the harshness of their
treatment. In addition, Elkins (1959: 37-80) concluded that the operation
of "uninterrupted capitalism" in the United States made great and burden-
some demands on the labor resources of the slaves, further accounting for
their uneviable existence.

Although many of his peers found his comparative approach useful and
even provocative, it was Elkins's discussion of the impact of slavery on the
black personality that received vastly more attention. In essence, Elkins
made a bold comparison between the impact of slavery on the personality
of the slaves and that of the German concentration camps on the personalities of their Jewish inmates. Drawing upon a broad arsenal of insights
derived from social psychology, Elkins concluded that slavery and the
concentration camps both constituted closed institutions and that the
behavior of the inmates of the concentration camps was in many respects

similar to that of the slaves in the American South. As a result of their treatment, Elkins (1959: 98) continued, Afro-American slaves formed "a society of helpless dependents," and the personality type most evident among them was that of Sambo. As he put it (1959: 82), "Sambo, the typical plantation slave, was docile but irresponsible, loyal but lazy, humble but chronically given to lying and stealing, his behavior was full of infantile silliness and his talk inflated with childish exaggeration. His relationship with his master was one of dependence and childish attachment." Thus, a repressive and inhumane slave system so completely traumatized the slave that he became the happy, docile, and childlike Sambo.

If Phillips dominated the stage in the earlier years, Elkins and Stampp would share most of the spotlight in the 1960s. In many respects, their works complemented and reinforced each other. Both authors shared the view that slavery was indeed a brutal institution, but whereas Elkins maintained that it produced the docile Sambo personality, Stampp found that it created in the slaves a tendency to resist and reject oppression. Much of the scholarship since these works were published has centered around either the rejection or the amplification of the Elkins-Stampp findings. The twin issues of the impact of slavery on the personality of the slave and the slave's reaction to his or her status have been addressed with skill, insight, and sophistication by some of America's most distinguished scholars. Foremost among these is Eugene D. Genovese, who recently published his monumental study of slave life, *Roll, Jordan, Roll* (1974). Others include George Rawick, who edited a collection of slave narratives and wrote an introductory volume, *From Sundown to Sunup* (1972). Also to be commended is John Blassingame's *The Slave Community* (1972).

These three works in particular have effectively challenged Elkins's contention that Sambo formed the dominant slave personality. Genovese, Rawick, and Blassingame have demonstrated that to a large extent slaves were able to construct and maintain an autonomous existence for themselves. In other words, after the termination of the day's labor, slaves returned to their quarters and from "sundown to sunup" functioned as people able to love and hate and laugh and cry. According to these scholars, slaves created an underlife, or subculture, which enabled them to survive the pressures of the slave system without becoming the broken, dehumanized beings that Elkins depicted. Slaves maintained as best they could some sort of family life, despite the fact that slave marriages had no legal standing and could be broken up with impunity by the masters. Many slaves performed their own marriage ceremonies (Rawick, 1972: 77-94), one of which was called "jumping over the broom," a simple rite whereby two slaves formed a marital union through the process of jumping over a broom. Although this ceremony had no legal validity, it was one way for a couple to assert their humanity under oppression. As Herbert Gutman (1975: 213-215) points out, once the slaves were emancipated, many of those whose marriages had been broken up arbitrarily, now rejoined their spouses. Slavery had not been able to destroy these human bonds.

In addition to preserving some semblance of family life, slaves, according to these scholars, drew psychic strength and comfort from their religious practices. Africans had come from societies where religion permeated every aspect of life; hence, in the slave quarters in America, religion played a crucial role in the Afro-Americans' day-to-day existence. Rawick (1972: 30-52) and Genovese (1974: 161-284) have demonstrated that the slaves were able to retain some of their traditional customs, but they also drew heavily upon Christian beliefs and practices. Slave religion, then, represented a syncretic combination of African traditional religions and Christianity. Vincent Harding (1969: 182-190) has persuasively argued that religion was also used as a form of resistance by the slaves. As he put it, "the religion of some slaves could lead them to pray and kill." The leaders of slave rebellions were often slave preachers, and religious occasions lent themselves to the planning of subversive activities. Slaves, in particular, drew inspiration from the biblical tale of Moses leading the children of Israel out of bondage in Egypt to the promised land of Canaan.

In essence, these historians agree that the slaves were able to develop a separate culture which allowed them, in the main, to survive the trauma of oppression with their personalities intact. The conclusions further indicate that the slaves were not merely reacting to their masters but were asserting their own cultural integrity and identity. It was this assertion of cultural independence which allowed them to survive the shocks and pressures of the slave system.

The question of whether or not slavery was profitable is another major area beset by changing interpretations. An examination of the most significant works on this issue published within the last two decades indicates that a majority of scholars agree that the institution was profitable, although there is disagreement over the amount. It appears that there is some methodological fuzziness surrounding this complex problem. Stanley Engerman (1967: 71) has pointed out, correctly, that three fundamental issues must be considered in any assessment of profitability: (1) "The profitability of slavery to the individual slave-owner"; (2) "the viability of slavery as an economic system"; and (3) "the effects of the slave system on the economic development of the South."

Historians have not always observed these distinctions in discussing the economics of slavery. The failure to clarify a specific aspect of profitability has contributed to much of the confusion surrounding the issue. As has been noted earlier, Phillips was convinced that slavery was unprofitable. In one of his articles (1905: 269-270), he concluded that "Negro slave labor was expensive, not so much because it was unwilling as because it was overcapitalized and inelastic. The negro himself, by reason of his inherited ineptitude, was inefficient as a self directing laborer in civilized industry." In addition, according to Phillips (1905: 275), "slavery was an obstacle to all progress." A number of subsequent works somewhat modified Phillips's conclusions, but it was Kenneth Stampp who most effectively challenged Phillips' findings. In essence, Stampp (1956: 414) found that most masters reaped a profit from their investment in human chattel. As he expressed it, "on both large and small estates, none but the most hopelessly inefficient masters failed to profit from the ownership of slaves."

The debate on profitability was furthered in 1958 when two Harvard economists, Alfred Conrad and John Meyer, published "The Economics of Slavery in the Antebellum South" (1958). In this pathbreaking article the authors concluded that "slavery was profitable to the whole South" (1958: 103-110). They calculated that during the period 1830-1860 the annual rate of return on male slaves rested somewhere between 4 1/2 and 8 percent on a majority of Southern plantations, although annual returns of 10 to 13 percent were not unknown on the more fertile soils. Female slaves who bore five children yielded an annual profitability rate of 7.1 percent, and those who had ten children brought an average annual profit of 8.1 percent. Conrad and Meyer (1958: 121) claimed, furthermore, that slavery did not retard the economic growth of the South.

The findings of Conrad and Meyer did not meet with uncritical acceptance by their colleagues. For example, Yasukichi Yasuba (1961: 60-67) and Robert Evans, Jr. (1962: 214-227), used a different methodology but in general supported the conclusions of the Harvard economists. Evans found, for instance, that the range of profitability fell between 9.5 and 18.5 percent. Not only did slavery constitute a viable industry, according to Evans, but "it gave every indication in its latter years of being a strong and growing industry." A contrary view was expressed by Edward Saraydar (1964: 325-337), who not only questioned Conrad and Meyer's methodology but concluded that the institution of slavery was generally unprofitable.

The most controversial addition to the literature on profitability appeared in 1974. This was William Fogel and Stanley Engerman's *Time on the Cross: The Economics of American Negro Slavery*. The authors of this study represent a breed of economic historians who use computers and sophisticated mathematical techniques to resolve many historical questions. The purpose of their remarkable project (1974: vol. 1, 264) was to delineate "the record of black achievement under adversity." Starting from this premise, Fogel and Engerman proceeded to demonstrate (1974: vol. 1, 67-94, 192-223) that the average slave worked harder and was more efficient than his or her free white counterpart. The average general rate of return on a slave, whether male or female, was about 10 percent, a return which was "equal to or in excess of the averages which obtained in a variety of nonagricultural enterprises." Southern agriculture on the whole was, according to these scholars, "about 35 percent more efficient than northern agriculture in 1860." Indeed, "southern slave farms were 28 percent more efficient than southern free farms."

Fogel and Engerman (1974: vol. 1, 93, 247-251) maintain that slavery was not moribund on the eve of the Civil War. On the contrary, the institution was quite vibrant. The decade of the 1850s was "a period of sustained boom in profits for cotton planters." In fact, the authors demonstrate that cotton production doubled between 1850 and 1860 in response to an increasing world demand. Their findings further indicate that slavery did not hamper the economic growth of the South. Judging from its per-capita income, if the South had been an independent nation in 1860 it would have been the fourth wealthiest in the world—wealthier, for example, than France, Germany, and Denmark. The authors point out that in the period just preceding the Civil War, "per capita income was actually growing 30 percent more rapidly in the South than in the North."

As might be guessed, *Time on the Cross* has provoked an intense scholarly reaction. Many historians, unfamiliar with advanced mathematical techniques and suspicious of quantitative history, are unsure of what to make of the book. Others have pointed out serious methodological errors and have questioned the accuracy of the authors' conclusions (David et al., 1976). It is undeniable, however, that *Time on the Cross* is a major historical work and that its findings will continue to be debated for years to come.

Many more issues than the ones I have discussed have received the attention of historians over the last three decades. Herbert Aptheker, who first published his *American Negro Slave Revolts* in 1943, has examined the phenomenon of slave resistance with great insight. Philip Curtin (1969) has produced a systematic analysis of the extent of the slave trade in the Americas, coming to the conclusion that fewer than 5 percent of the slaves from Africa came to North America. And Peter Wood (1974) and Gerald Mullin (1972) have written important studies of slavery in the colonial period in South Carolina and Virginia, respectively.

Although it is true that the study of slavery currently represents one of the most vibrant areas of American historiography, one must be cautioned against any uncritical acceptance of the new interpretations I have discussed. Care must be taken, for example, not to exaggerate the degree to which slaves were able to lead normal, independent lives. No one has yet argued that black slaves were superbeings, but some people have come dangerously close. It is important to remind ourselves that slavery was not "the jolly old institution," and that it served to limit the potential and seriously circumscribe the behavior of its victims. The trend to depict the slaves as human beings who did not merely spend a lifetime reacting to their masters, but who created something for themselves out of their oppression is to be welcomed, but historians must be careful not to overdraw this portrait lest old myths and distortions be replaced with new ones.

Similarly, it must be recognized that the cliometricians have their limitations. Their computers and equations may overwhelm us, but their findings must still be subjected to rigorous critical examination. It is clear that the task of reconstructing the black past has barely gone beyond its formative stage. The next decade should add immensely to our understanding of slavery, as more scholarly works appear. It is particularly important that black historians undertake the kinds of research that must be done in this area. For it is our responsibility to bring our special insights to bear upon the interpretation of this aspect of America's past.

REFERENCES

APTHEKER, H. (1969) *American Negro Slave Revolts.* New York: International Publishers.

BLASSINGAME, J. W. (1972) *The Slave Community: Planatation Life in the Antebellum South. New York: Oxford University Press.*

CONRAD, A. H. and J. R. MEYER (1958) "The economics of slavery in the antebellum South." *Journal of Political Economy* 66 (April): 95-130.

CURTIN, P. D. (1969) *The Atlantic Slave Trade: A Census.* Madison: University of Wisconsin Press.

DAVID, P. A. et al. (1976) *Reckoning with Slavery: A Critical Study of the Quantitative History of American Negro Slavery.* New York: Oxford University Press.

DuBOIS, W.E.B. (1918) Review of *American Negro Slavery,* by U. B. Phillips. *American Political Science Review* 12 (November): 722-726.

ELKINS, S. M. (1959) *Slavery: A Problem in American Institutional and Intellectual Life.* Chicago: University of Chicago Press.

ENGERMAN, S. L. (1967) "The effects of slavery upon the southern economy: a review of the recent debate." *Explorations in Entrepreneurial History,* Second Series 4, 2: 71-97.

EVANS, R., Jr. (1962) "The economics of American Negro slavery," in Universities' National Bureau Committee for Economic Research, *Aspects of Labor Economics.* Princeton: Princeton University Press.

FLANDERS, R. B. (1933) *Plantation Slavery in Georgia.* Chapel Hill: University of North Carolina Press.

FOGEL, W. F. and S. L. ENGERMAN (1974) *Time on the Cross: The Economics of American Negro Slavery*. Boston: Little, Brown.

GENOVESE, E. G. (1974) *Roll, Jordan, Roll: The World the Slaves Made*. New York: Random House.

GUTMAN, H. G. (1975) "The world two cliometricians made: a review essay of F + E = T/C." *Journal of Negro History* 60 (January): 53-227. (Reprinted as *Slavery and the Numbers Game: A Critique of Time on the Cross*, University of Illinois Press, Urbana, 1975).

HARDING, V. (1969) "Religion and resistance among antebellum Negroes, 1800-1860," in A. Meier and E. Rudwick (eds.) *The Making of Black America: Essays in Negro Life and History, Volume 1*. New York: Atheneum Press.

HERSKOVITS, J. J. (1941) *The Myth of the Negro Past*. New York: Harper & Row.

HOFSTADTER, R. (1944) "U. B. Phillips and the plantation legend." *Journal of Negro History* 29 (April): 109-124.

MULLIN, G. W. (1972) *Flight and Rebellion: Slave Resistance in Eighteenth Century Virginia*. New York: Oxford University Press.

MYRDAL, G. (1944) *The Negro Problem and Modern Democracy: An American Dilemma*. New York: Harper & Row.

PHILLIPS, U. B. (1918) *American Negro Slavery*. Englewood Cliffs, NJ: Prentice-Hall.

——— (1905) "The economic cost of slaveholding in the cotton belt." *Political Science Quarterly* 20 (June): 257-275.

RAWICK, G. P. (1972) *From Sundown to Sunup: The Making of the Black Community*. Westport, CT: Greenwood.

SARAYDAR, E. (1964) "A note on the profitability of antebellum slavery." *Southern Economic Journal* 30 (April): 325-332.

STAMPP, K. M. (1956) *The Peculiar Institution: Slavery in the Antebellum South*. New York: Knopf.

SYDNOR, C. S. (1933) *Slavery in Mississippi*. Englewood Cliffs, NJ: Prentice-Hall.

TANNENBAUM, F. (1946) *Sliave and Citizen: The Negro in the Americas*. New York: Knopf.

WOOD, P. (1974) *Black Majority: Negroes in Colonial South Carolina from 1670 Through the Stono Rebellion*. New York: Knopf.

WOODSON, C. G. (1919) "Review of American Negro slavery." *Journal of Negro History* 4 (January): 102-103.

YASUBA, Y. (1961) "The profitability and viability of plantation slavery in the United States." *Economic Studies Quarterly* 12 (September): 60-67.

16

PAN-AFRICANISM IN WORLD HISTORY

Sulayman S. Nyang
Abdulai S. Vandi

The fifteenth and sixteenth centuries were very important landmarks in human history. The whole of humanity was rocked to its foundations by a series of social, political, and cultural explosions. Europe, in particular, having sucked enough intellectual and cultural nutriants from the old Mediterranean world, began to develop its scientific and technological structures for what the world was later to call the Age of Exploration or the age of Vasco da Gama. This emergence of Europe, the pupil of Greece, Israel, and Rome, was destined to alter the relationship between people and other *people*, people and *nature*, and people and their *God*. The emergence of Europe as the theater of international political and economic development was certainly very crucial to the relationship between European and non-European human beings. Not only did the European seafaring peoples, particularly the Portuguese, perfect their naval and seafaring techniques in their bid for world naval power status, but they also employed their newly developed science and technology to compete and overthrow of their Muslim and Arab rival states to the East. Though Europeans did not establish full hegemony during this period, their power and influence continued to grow and expand, and they soon began to elbow their way through all the corridors of power around the world. The series of victories they scored in the Mediterranean, Africa, Asia, and the Americas, inflated their egos until they began to define themselves as above and beyond the rest of humanity, which, in their view, has fallen behind in the race for civilization and economic development (Sachs, 1976).

The inherent tendency of Eurocentric peoples to conquer, dominate, and expand led them to consider themselves as the divinely chosen mentors and guides of "the uncivilized human race"; hence, they undertook to refashion the world in their own image. It was the chauvanistic insistence of Eurocentric peoples upon governing humanity that brought *woe* upon the human race. The truth of the matter is that the contemporary crisis in race relations, and the mounting, exacerbated tensions between East and West and between South and North, are clearly the results of earlier, erroneous Eurocentric views of the world.

In the poetic language of Frantz Fanon (1963), the dichotomous relationship between Europe and the rest of us created a Manichean world. Perhaps Fanon more than anyone else has been most eloquent and successful in showing the tremendous psychological and psychohistorical damages and injuries inflicted by the European expansionists in their ever acquisitive drive and instict to exploit and rule the entire globe.

Besides the alteration of the relationship between European and other peoples, there was also the changing pattern of the relationship between human beings and their nature. The rise of Europe as a beehive of scientific and technological innovations was destined to affect the ecological balance between people and their environments. The arrival of the Industrial Revolution, which took place several generations after the European exploration and colonization of many areas of the world, again spelled disaster, for the peoples of the Third World in particular. Europe was bent on conquering the world, and in her bid for domination, she hesitated little to tamper and tinker with the ecological systems of the conquered peoples. The scientific and technological encounter of industrial Europe with the ecological systems of the oppressed world wrought havoc, for in their frantic efforts to relentlessly exploit Third World resources, the colonizing and imperialist powers of Europe cared little about the consequences of their acts. They were only interested in accumulating wealth, and the best way to do so was to introduce technology and science so as to get the job done with little delay and at a cheap cost. As a result of this attitude, the Third World became the source of raw materials and Europe became the beehive of industrial production. The technological disparity between the peoples of Europe and the Third World became the symbol of inequality in the world, thereby leading to the differences in attitudes toward nature in the two antipodal zones of the world. Whereas the European application of science and technology in the natural world has led Europeans to take the position that nature is a self-replenishing quarry from which people can obtain the much-needed stones to sculpt and translate into reality the images fashioned by their perception, the unregretted absence of such scientific theories and technological innovation and sophistication in the Third World allowed its people to maintain their sanity and traditional view of nature. Asante (1979) has eloquently demonstrated how we can begin to view the world in the alternative paradigms of Afrocentricism and Asiocentricism. Rather than see nature as object of human activity and manipulation, the Afrocentric man, whose life is still governed by the dictates of ancient understandings, would venerate and propitiate the mystical forces believed to be lurking behind the natural elements. Hence, the Eurocentric man parted company with the rest of the world in the realm of psychological attitudes toward nature. Such fundamental differences in attitude, in part, account in Western colonial history for the ruthless exploitation and "thingification" of peoples who were not of European extraction (Chinweizu, 1975).

In our modest attempt to place Pan-Africanism in world history, we refuse to evade the circumstances that led to the deterioration and subsequent alteration of the relationship between Europeans and their God. During the glorious period of the Renaissance and the Industrial Revolution, the better-educated classes in Europe began to totter in their commitment to Jesus and the Church. The once *sine qua non* Eurocentric Christianity was questionable. The wavering Europeans' belief in the Supreme Being was largely due to their advancement in scientific knowledge. The series of scientific and technological discoveries by the inquiring minds of industrial Europe were without immediate consequences. Principal among these consequences was the dramatic denunciation of the Church's message by a good number of Europe's best-educated fellows, primarily because of the controversy surrounding morality, the wisdom of human kind, and the so-called value-free scientific inquiry. This growing doubt among the intelligentsia opened a pandora's box full of mythologies and commandments under the rubric of science to explain and justify the subjugation and oppression of the Afrocentric and Asiocentric people. This radical change in the European intellectual's attitude toward the Heavenly Kingdom and its early representative not only affected the manner in which the European colonialists treated their vanquished subjects in the nineteenth and early twentiety centuries, but also put the leaders of the Christian church on the defensive; and many a devoted Christian, paradoxically, found in the victory of capitalism and industrial Europe an opportunity to reaffirm the validity of Christ's message and the cosmic challenge to save non-European souls in anticipation of the Saviour's long-awaited return to the New Jerusalem (Mazru, 1974).

Pan-Africanism as an ideology grew out of the soil of sorrow and misery of the transplanted Africans in the New World. Though many scholars have correctly identified the movement with the intellectual stirrings among the early leaders of the newly liberated Blacks in North America and the Caribbean, there is also the fact that the idea itself was an expression of identity and emotional dissatisfaction among the early generations of Black leaders. Having experienced the atrocities of slavery and the blatant racism of their White coinhabitants of the American continents, many of these men felt that they must create a new start for themselves. In defiance of the condition of semiservitude and open discrimination in their new home, many thought that their final realization of freedom and liberty could only come about in their ancestral home. Africa, the land which was deliberately blotted from their minds and whose history was denied by their former slave masters, became psychologically the functional equivalent of what Zion had meant to the Israelites who followed Moses out of the land of Egypt. Taking this biblical parallel as an analytical point of departure, many of these Black intellectuals saw their ancestral home as the New Zion, where the Black race has a rendezvous with destiny (Geiss, 1974).

Pan-Africanism as an ideology was a vague idea at first glance. The biblical analogy was uppermost in the minds of most of those who wished to return to Africa and start a new life for themselves and their families. To them Africa was a mystical place which was beckoning them from across the Atlantic to come home and make a contribution. Among the numerous Blacks returning to their ancestral home and become part of the African rise to historical prominence were those who did not see themselves as Africans and therefore felt it necessary to dispel the "wrong notions" that Blacks should return to Africa (Foner, 1971). This indifference in attitude and belief to the problem of Black liberation in the early period of postslavery in America and the Caribbean, resulted to the two major categories of Black-American responses to the Pan-African ideology. These categories include, the Global Pan-Africanists and the Diasporic Pan-Africanists. The main bone of content between the two categories was in the identifiable nationality of the New World Black person. Whereas the Global Pan-Africanists were advocating the creation of a state system or a homeland for those willing and able to make the return to the African Zion (Blyden, 1862), the Diasporic Pan-Africanists were content with their newly acquired American nationality and thus decided to hitch their psychohistorical wagon to the American Dream and its main instrument—the United States of America. The Diasporic Pan-Africanists were not necessarily hostile to the interests and welfare of their contemporaries, who were opting for the creation of an African Zion across the seas.

Instead, they were opposed to the massive transplantation back to Africa of the newly liberated Blacks under a hypocritical philanthropic machine. The truth of the matter is that those who advocated the Black Dream, enveloped in the American Dream, were logically paying their former masters in their own coin. After having heard the Jeffersons and the Madisons echoed the words of Locke in the firmaments of their intellectual debates on independence from Britain, the Diasporic Pan-Africans felt that they also deserved a piece of the "American Pie." Afterwards, they were citizens by virtue of birth and suffering. Born into families that had labored hard to build America, and having themselves mixed their labor with the American soil, they found it politically unwise and historically dangerous to accept the resettlement policies and programs of the American Colonization Society (Foner, 1971).

These two schools of thought have dominated Black intellectual life since the end of the slave trade. But in the United States of America, the dominant intellectual current has always been the Diasporic Pan-African strain. Though such Black leaders as Frederick Douglass and Booker T. Washington were quite aware of the efforts of men like Delaney and Blyden, they never supported their endeavors. Rather than simply put their eggs in the African basket, many Black leaders in the United States decided to try their luck in America, and so they channeled all the emotional and psychological energies of their fellow Blacks toward the struggle for full citizenship. This position was to a large extent, that of W.E.B. DuBois. Furthermore, DuBois never associated with the Global Pan-Africanist movement. He was bitterly opposed to the transplantation of African Americans from the United States to the continent of Africa (Isaacs, 1960). Like a number of his contemporary Jewish intellectuals of the pre-World War II era, he was very optimistic about the eventual assimilation of Blacks in the mainstream of the American system. In addition, he believed that the social and economic advancement of Black Americans would eventually have drastic and significant impact in the struggle for Black liberation and development elsewhere. The logic of DuBois was that Black advancement in one corner of the Western world would generate advancement in other parts of the world. Indeed, he advanced this argument up to the time of the Manchester Conference.

However, there was to be found dissent among the major actors in the Diasporic Pan-Africanist group. Three major subcategories of the movement emerged as a result of individual differences of the role of the movement within the leadership.

1. The Assimilationist group had as its basic position, the reiteration in the American Dream. The membership strongly believed that the destiny of African Americans in the United States is inextricably linked to the

future of these United States of America. Furthermore, they were to employ every conceivable legal and constitutional weapon in their search and struggle for solutions to the problems of African Americans. Having totally rejected the position of their parent movement, that America was a hopeless case and that Blacks had no future in the American society, they took to the politics of pluralism and compromise, long institutionalized by the founding fathers of the American Republic. The Assimilationist group had an element of realism in their analysis of the world situation of the post-1860s. Deeply concerned that the Americans of African ancestry had been almost virtually cut off from their cultural roots and had recognized the rapacity of the European powers in their bitter and fierce struggle for control of African lands, the leadership felt that the blood, sweat, and tears poured out on the American soil was beginning to yield fruits which would be denied to them if they were not firm enough in pressing their claims as citizens. Returning to Africa was a wrong recourse and a bad proposition. The argument further was, if the founding fathers of the American republic were barely able to slough off the yoke of their imperial kin, how much more difficult would it be for the newly liberated Blacks to ward off the imperial designs of Britain, France, and other European powers bent on raping Africans and their resources? In addition, there was the reluctance of many Black leaders to take the necessary risk of resettlement.

Edward Blyden (1862) reproached the leaders of the Assimilationist group for their refusal to accept the challenge to serve their race and uphold the Black pride with dignity in Africa. Whereas Blyden's followers were crossing the Atlantic in the same spirit as the enthusiastic Zionists bound for Israel in the heyday of the Zionist movement, the Assimilationists committed their efforts to "making it" in the American culture and society. They could not reckon with the back-to-Africa drive. Following Booker T. Washington's strategy of survival within a hostile White power structure, they envisioned in a tactical compromise and reluctant segregation, an opportunity to plot for future gains in the larger American system. Blyden and others denounced such political strategies for the African American as doomed to failure. Unable to see or foresee the possibilities of change in the American attitude of racial bigotry, the Global Pan-Africanists called for an immediate departure, and suggested that any further delay in departure to the ancestral home would only impede the pace and rate of development for the newly liberated African Americans. The logic of the Global Pan-Africanists however, did not carry the day, and the Assimilationists won the argument and proceeded in organizing the unconvinced Blacks for the political struggles that characterized the Civil Rights Movement of the late fifties and the early sixties (Blyden, 1862).

2. The Simulationist group was the second major subcategory in the Global Pan-Africanist movement. The fundamental belief of this body was that segregation of the races would be here for a long time, and that Black leaders have the responsibility to organize major institutions similar to those existing in the dominant White society. To the Simulationist group, the principle of separate mobilization of group resources and manpower within the general framework of the national economic and political system constituted the second best chance of enhancing and uplifting the African American in a segregated condition. There was also a strong recognition and apparent agreement that the two races do enjoy certain racial peculiarities and these can best be preserved through the process of dichotomization (Hawkins, 1962; Meier et al., 1971; Spencer, 1955).

3. The Black Nationalist group emerged as the third of the subcategories in the Global Pan-Africanist movement. This school of thought believes that the Black American has to fight an incessant battle against the racist forces in the United States. Because of the nature of the struggle for liberty, freedom, and territorial integrity, Blacks should seek a state of their own out of the states constituting the United States of America. The major difference between this group and its parent movement is its emphasis on a piece of land for its members, somewhere within the geopolitical borders of the United States of America. Their nationality, it seems, was psychologically and psychohistorically inseparable from the geographical place called the United States of America. The Republic of New Africa and the now defunct Nation of Islam were the most vocal advocates of this ideology. The most recent is the "Kingdom of Oyatunge," established in Beaufort County, South Carolina, on a piece of land donated by the state of South Carolina, ten years ago. The residents, all African Americans, born and reared in the United States, maintain their own government with no interference whatsoever from either the state of South Carolina or the U.S. federal government. A sign that reads, "You are now leaving the United States of America and entering the Kingdom of Oyatunge," is arrogantly placed at a point just before one enters the "Kingdom." In short, the Black Nationalists are those African Americans who wish to create their own polity somewhere in the continental United States of America (Browne and Rustin, 1968), where they can realize their own national ideals and forge their own destiny without the familiar interference of the dominant White society.

Any attempt to place Pan-Africanism in the context of world history without thoroughly recognizing the subtleties and tendencies within the

Black Community in the United States will proof futile. In fact, we are inclined to argue here that the conflicts now evident in the Pan-African Movement are clear manifestations of the latent differences and contradictions that were either deliberately or myopically kept out of public view by the community of suffering created by the blatant and collective oppression of the Afrocentric people, regardless of class, place of origin and nationality, and social status. When we begin to look at the evolution of the Movement in this light, we would not be surprised by the train of recent events in the Black world. A proposition related to the ones advanced earlier maintains that the Assimilationist position was destined to give the Black Community the opportunity to carve a place for some of its members in the growing bourgeois classes of the American society, but in so doing, Blacks would be paradoxically sowing the future seeds of discord. After having stormed the citadels of White power, African Americans were soon to find out that the Assimilationist policy cannot benefit all at once. In order to play the game of compromise and pluralism, some of the members of the Black Community must have the lion's share of the gains at the battle for equality. Those who are deprived of the fruits and spoils of this temporary victory must either accept the rules of communal politics or wage a class war against their more successful and prosperous brethren. This state of affairs, we submit, is now before us, and therefore the inevitable war of words that is currently reverberating in the firmaments of Black literary and political debates is no surprise.

The development of Pan-Africanism in the continent of Africa may be viewed as occurring in three distinct stages. The first stage was the importation of what we may refer to as *West-Atlantic Global Pan-Africanism*. This idea was largely propagated by the New World Blacks, who in many instances cast themselves in the role of civilizers and harbingers of the Christian message of salvation. Perhaps, because of their American Christian orientation, they unconsciously internalized the prejudices and biases of Western man vis-á-vis the rest of humanity. Many of them unquestionably believe in the inherent inferiority of the African culture and tradition vis-á-vis the superiority of the American civilization. It is their uncritical acceptance of Western values and norms that gave their brand of Pan-Africanism a different taste. Edward Blyden, a forerunner during this era, also felt that a rejuvenated Africa would be the product of the maturation and cross-pollination of Christian ethics, with the Christian spiritual message on the one hand, and the traditional African culture on the other. He was also a pioneer of the Negritudist Movement of the Senghors, Ceasires, and Damases, but he simply could not extricate himself from the intellectual and cultural webs of his times. As a result, he accepted the racial theories and the scientific justifications of the leading scholars of his times. Painfully enough, he tried to give such theories different interpretations. Dr. Edward Blyden's significance and contribution, however, lie not only in the promotion of the archaic west-Atlantic brand of Pan-Africanism, but also in his intellectual watering and subsequent nurturing of what we refer to as *East-Atlantic Pan-Africanism*. This brand of Pan-Africanism was the ideological brainchild of the New World Blacks and their descendants, who assimilated themselves to the African continent and decided to provide themselves with the intellectual justification for their place and role in history. Arthur Porter, in his *Creoledom,* thoroughly describes the movement and its significant contribution in generating West-African unity. Furthermore, the writings of Casely-Hayford and Kobina Sekyi demonstrate the maturation of East-Atlantic Pan-Africanism and the willingness of its advocates to challenge both the Western missionaries and the zealots of West-Atlantic Pan-Africanism (Langley, 1973).

East-Atlantic Pan-Africanism was most successful in the abortive attempt to create the necessary unity among the westernized communities of Blacks scattered along the colonial settlements on the west coast of Africa. But Langley has demonstrated that the sense of West-African identity or unity was later replaced in West-African history by the strong assertion of territorial nationalisms. This is to say that the East-Atlantic Pan-Africanist idea really never took firm root. With the collapse of the newly established West-African National Congress, the westernized Africans along the British coast of West Africa began to grope for a new identity, to be found in the newly established colonial territorial units of the Gold Coast, Sierra Leone, and Nigeria. This willingness to embrace the colonial structure constituted a temporary setback for the Pan-African idea. The idea however, was to regain momentum only after the beginning of the nationalist movement for independence became a reality that the colonial rulers could ignore only at their own peril (Langley, 1973).

The arrival of the Nkrumahs, Kenyattas, and Azikiwes on the African political scene produced yet another brand of Pan-Africanism. This new concept was to be known as *Continental Pan-Africanism*. Absolute and total independence of Africa was the primary goal of the Movement. Prior to independence, one could argue, the Nkrumahs and the Kenyattas accepted in principal some form of the Global Pan-Africanist idea, which dangled the hope of eventual liberation of Africa from the tentacles of colonialism. It was indeed this hope of independence that later put an effective brake on the wheels of political unification for Africa. We are inclined to argue here that the granting of independence to Africa brought two significant changes in the strategy and operations of the Pan-Africanist Movement. The conferring of national sovereignty to the variegated territorial units of Africa heightened the latent contradictions which, as shown in the case of African Americans in the United States, were kept from the political surface by the offensive heat of collective suffering under colonial rule. Whereas during the struggle for independence the African leaders were commiserating with one another in the postcolonial era, personal and group ambitions displaced collective African interest, and soon the comrades of yesterday became the archenemies of today. This fragmentation, resulting from the competing elites' desire to consolidate power over their colonially inherited territories, opened yet another pandora's box. This source of trouble for the African societies let loose a host of tribalistic ghosts who defied the exorcistic powers of the ablest of African politicians and leaders (Legum, 1972; Wallerstein, 1968). Soon the Pan-Africanist dream turned into a nightmare, and Africa's new rulers, whose commitments to the concretization of the Pan-Africanist idea have always been suspected, found it to their advantage to institutionalize the concept of continental unity. Nyang (1975) articulated in *Islam and Pan Africanism* that the institutionalization of the Pan-Africanist idea triggered and engineered a united Arab Africa with Black Africa, but created a gulf between the Africans in the Diaspora and their brethren in the African continent. Such a political arrangement also granted legitimacy and sanctity to the colonial boundaries. The African leaders began to caution each other about the charter of the Organization of African Unity (OAU) and its ruling against the interference of other states in the internal affairs of their neighbors. This sanctification of the inherited colonial boundaries condemned the African leaders to a life very much like that of the ancient Hebrews, whom Moses ordered not to convert their neighbors' wives. Unlike the Hebrews, however, the African leaders were bound by treaty agreements not to covert each other's territory.

What is interesting about this new development is that the institutionalization of the Pan-Africanist idea not only isolated the Diasporic Africans from the mainstream of the Movement, but it also conservatized the Movement. The revolutionary and fiery Pan-Africanists of yesterday are now the rulers of an independent Africa, their radical rhetoric has been tempered by the comfortable surroundings of their countries, and their agitation for greater African unity has changed to a call for greater intratribal unity and harmony. This radical change in the African leaders' concepts has affected the course of Pan-Africanism in Africa. Because of this, a number of new attitudes and tendencies have surfaced in the Movement. Among these is *Continental Pan-Africanism*, a version of the

Movement close to what Sinclair Drake has called elsewhere *Residential Pan-Africanism*. Fundamental to this line of thought is that Africa is an integral whole and that the destiny of Africans in general lies in the political and economic unification of all' the territorial units. In the absence of this form of political and economic unity, they argue, Africa is doomed to be the tentacle of neocolonialism, and Africans will continue to be the drawers of water and the hewers of wood for the more united and integrated peoples and societies of Europe and the West in particular (Nkrumah, 1965).

In addition to the Continental Pan-Africanists are the *Pan-African Regionalists,* who expouse a different form of the Movement. They emphasize the concept of regionalism, where the level of unity and integration is of paramount importance. The conflict over the methods and level of unity has caused the greatest problem between Kwame Nkrumah and his presidential contemporaries. The Nkrumanists, for instance, called for the immediate unity of all of Africa; this was simultaneously dismissed as radical, utopian, and outrightly impractical. Some were willing to experiment with economic integration, few for limited political partnership, but the vast majority opposed any loss of sovereignty. Among the Regionalists were the *Negritudists* and the *Sub-Saharan Fighters.* These two subgroups in the Regionalist Movement share the common belief that the Sub-Saharan societies have a common cultural denominator which separates them from their Arab neighbors to the north. The *Negritudists* feel that Black-African values are separate and distinct from the Arabo-Berber's, and the quest for unity must and should begin in the Black-African Community first and should later be extended to the Arabo-Berbers. Whereas the Negritudists limit the scope of unity to those who belong to the community of Black or hardcore African culture and civilization, the Sub-Saharans' spokespeople, like Chief Obafemi Awolowo, wish to exclude from African unity any Arab elements whose loyalty to Africa is dubious (Legum, 1972).

Furthermore, there are the *Micro-Nationalists,* who have embraced the idea of territorial nationalism a la Europe. Having been made the highly rewarded successors of the former colonial masters, and seemingly reluctant to contract any greater political marriages with their next-door neighbors, many of the new African leaders have found in Micro-Nationalism an ideological instrument of rationalization. This ideology now rationalizes and explains the deeds and misdeeds of the leaders to the less sophisticated masses. Pan-Africanism, with all of its inherited problems and controversies, is given lip service and hence made toothless and ineffective. The Micro-Nationalists have emerged as powerful figures in

Africa. Furthermore, the assumption of political independence has led some of the Micro-Nationalists to pursue some reactionary policies that work against the original aims and objectives of the Pan-Africanist Movement.

The postcolonial attempts at continental unity underscore the contradictions that have since surfaced in Africa, and the manner in which they are being handled by the respective parties to the ideological conflict. As indicated above, the conflicts that plague the Pan-Africanist Movement today were incipient and embryonic at the early stages of the Movement. They had not matured largely because of the level of material and cultural development within the Black world. With greater material development, during both the colonial and postcolonial periods, many structural and psychological changes have taken place in all four corners of the Black world. Changes in the world economy and in the relationships between the overdeveloped countries of the West and the underdeveloped countries in the newly liberated Third World countries have combined to push to the fore all the contradictions that were previously swept under the thick rug of Black solidarity. With the sudden outbursts of these conflicts and contradictions, the Pan-Africanist Movement, especially as symbolized by the Sixth Pan-African Conference in Dar es Salaam, has now become the politically haunted house where the ghost of Karl Marx is battling that of Marcus Garvey for control and space for a spiritual rest.

The struggle over the future of Africa and Pan-Africanism hangs in the balance. This is largely because the Pan-Africanists must resolve a fundamental contradiction in their world views. The conflict lies not in what Africa will be, but whose ideas will rule the minds and bodies of Africa and, in turn, those of the Pan-Africanists in the United States and the Carribbean. This question takes us back to the initial argument. The Pan-African idea was the brainchild of the New World Africans, and its eventual realization will depend on how the American society fares in the world economy and how Africans are treated in the stock exchanges and trade and commercial centers of the world. If the scientific socialists in Africa and the Americas get their way, Pan-Africanism will metamorphose into an African version of the Marxist Dream, and the successors of Kwame Nkrumah will be comparable to the Leninist successors of the Russian Pan-Slavists, whose dream was finally realized but under totally different circumstances.

On the other hand, if the deracialization of the Pan-Africanist idea is not successfully carried out by either the Black Marxists or their cousins, the Socialists, then the legacy of Marcus Garvey will prevail. Africa will be a giant partner in the capitalist world, and the Diasporic Blacks who are committed to Assimilationism in the United States will see a partial fulfillment of their dream of active participation in American society. Such a participation will draw them into business and political partnerships with African capitalist governments that are working very closely with the centers of capitalism in the West. Liberia in West Africa and Kenya in East Africa are examples of such capitalist governments. Pan-Africanism, under the above arrangement, will not be what Marcus Garvey dreamed about, nor will it be the fulfillment of the Osagyefo.

Our attempt has been to assess and critique the evolution of Pan-Africanism that led Africans and the Africans in the Diaspora to a crossroad. The African peoples must now decide whether they can blaze a new trail which will make them free and independent from either of the two giant nuclear powers, or whether they are going to continue in the role of cheerleader, shouting feverishly at the actors whose power and unity have historically catapulted them into prominence and then granted them the right to shape their own destiny. In other words, the Pan-Africanist idea is currently in search of actors who can fulfill its destiny. The Osagyefo was the boldest of Africa's children to fill that role; he has failed. Will another son of the harassed continent appear in the person of a Leninist Garvey or a Ricardian DuBois?

REFERENCES

ASANTE, M. K. (1979) *Afrocentricity: The Theory of Social Change.* Buffalo, NY: Amulefi.
BLYDEN, E. W. (1862) *Liberia's Offering: The Call of Providence to the Descendant of Africa in America.*
BROWNE, R. S. and B. RUSTIN (1968) *Separation or Integration.* A. Phillip, New York: A. Phillip.
CHINWEIZU (1975) *The West and the Rest of Us.* New York: Vintage.
FANON, F. (1963) *The Wretched of the Earth.* New York: Grove.
FONER, P. S. (1971) *Selections from the Writings of Frederick Douglass.* International Pubs., New York: International Publishers.
GEISS, I. (1974) *The Pan-African Movement: A History of Pan Africanism in America, Europe, and Africa.* New York: Holmes & Meier.
HAWKINS, H. (1962) *Booker T. Washington and His Critics: The Problem of Negro Leadership.* Lexington, MA: D. C. Heath.
ISAACS, H. R. (1960) "DuBois and Africa." *Race* 1, 2.
LANGLEY, J. A. (1973) *Pan-Africanism and Nationalism in West Africa.* London: Oxford University Press.
LEGUM, C. (1972) *Pan Africanism: A Short Political Guide.* Westport, CT: Greenwood.
MAZRU, A. A. (1974) *World Culture and the Black Experience.* Seattle: University of Washington Press.
MEIER, A., E. RUDWICK, and F. I. BRODERICK (1971) *Black Protest Thought in the Twentieth Century: 1880-1915.* Indianapolis: Bobbs-Merrill.

NKRUMAH, K. (1970) *Africa Must Unite*. New York: International Publishers.
——— (1965) *Neo-Colonialism: The Last Stage of Imperialism*. New York: International Publishers.
NYANG, S. S. (1975) "Islam and Pan Africanism." *L'Afrique et Asie Modernes* 104.
SACHS, I. (1976) *The Discovery of the Third World*. Cambridge, MA: MIT Press.
SPENCER, S. (1955) *Booker T. Washington and the Negro's Place in America's Life.* Boston: Little, Brown.
WALLERSTEIN, I. (1968) *Africa: Politics of Unity*. London: Pall Mall.

PART V
THE EDUCATIONAL DIMENSION

No field of inquiry and practice has occupied contemporary social and behavioral scientists more than education. It is a field at once fraught with diversities, contradictions, and heresy. Yet it is through education that a society enculturates its youth. This means that the importance of the educational institutions extends beyond the mere material structures of one type or another which house classes of instruction. Studies in the philosophy of education, the place of the learning room in society, motivation, and potentialities have come to be addressed with regularity and vigilance. Significance in this area covers almost all of the behavioral and social sciences. Our authors concentrate on the phenomena which directly relate to African-American education. These works are valuable because of the freshness of their interpretations, based upon solid empirical research.

Harris brings us new information on the desegregation issue and its impact on the American educational system. Scott provides a new look at Black students on predominantly white university campuses. She reveals that the campuses are white not merely because the majority of the students are white but because the ideology of the universities is white. These works constitute a higher level of analysis in educational research.

17

DESEGREGATION AND
BLACK CHILD DEVELOPMENT

J. John Harris, III

It was the black masses who first perceived that integration actually increases the white community's control over the black one by destroying black institutions, absorbing black leadership and making its interests coincide with those of the white community. The international "brain drain" has its counterpart in the black community, which is constantly being denuded of its best-trained people and many of its national leaders. Black institutions of all sorts—colleges, newspapers, banks, even community organizations—are all losing their better people to the newly available openings of white establishments. This lowers the quality of the Negro organization and in some cases causes their demise or increases their dependence on Whites for survival. Such injurious, if unintended, side effects of integration have been felt in almost every layer of the black community [Browne, 1976].

Recently, considerable attention has been focused on the erosion of the American family[1] and on the short- and long-term impact of various institutions—namely, education, or the development of these children. Interestingly enough, current data indicate that more than one-sixth of all children in our country are living in single-parent families; over 50 percent

AUTHOR'S NOTE: This chapter was originally presented as a paper at the annual conference of the National Council for Black Child Development, held at Philadelphia, Pennsylvania, June 9-12, 1977.

of women with school-aged children are employed; and situations in which both parents are working are increasingly becoming the majority.

In this, the wealthiest nation in the world, we do not provide *all* children with the education necessary to function successfully in society. A tragic reminder of this is that there are 20 to 23 million citizens or more in this nation that are judged "functional illiterates." More specifically, within the educational arena much concern is being voiced relative to (a) the effects of desegregation on the educational development of black children, and (b) the impact of desegregation on the quality of life for black Americans. The black problem in America today can be viewed as a moral issue with basic judicial, educational, political, and social overtones (Conley, 1977: 1).

The purpose of this chapter is to examine the tripartite relationship among desegregation, social science research, and the judicial system. In addition, the chapter will provide a critical analysis of the role the courts played in providing black children with a "quality education." Further, it will provide an overview of educational policy and suggest some strategies to be utilized, which the author feels will effectuate positive changes.

DESEGREGATION–SOCIAL SCIENCE RESEARCH– THE JUDICIAL SYSTEM

PRECEDENTS TO BROWN

It is significant to note that this country's negative stance on desegregation did not commence with Brown v. Board of Education of Topeka, Kansas (1954) or Plessy v. Ferguson (1896), but it goes as far back as 190 years ago, when the Massachusetts Legislature established schools for the poor while ignoring a petition seeking special schools for black children (also see Roberts v. City of Boston, 1850).

Also prior to Brown, there were several cases which addressed inequality in educational facilities. This nation became legally bound to the dictum set forth in Plessy, which upheld a Louisiana statute permitting separate educational facilities for Blacks and Whites, as long as they were "equal." Three other cases emerged, examining whether intangible educational benefits were provided to both races equally. Those cases were Missouri ex rel. Gaines v. Canada (1938), Sipuel v. Board of Regents of the University of Oklahoma (1948), and Sweatt v. Painter (1949).

BROWN AND SINCE

In the Brown decision, it was unanimously held by the Supreme Court that public school segregation denied black children the equal protection of the laws, as guaranteed by the Fourteenth Amendment, when based solely on race and permitted or required by law. The impressive testimonies and arguments given by Kenneth Clark, James Nabrit, Jr., E. C. Hayes, Thurgood Marshall et al., and the history of the ratification of the Fourteenth Amendment, were considered. But the decision rendered by the nation's highest tribunal was a straightforward legal one: "Separate schools are inherently unequal." Although formally binding, the decision was not self-enforcing. In short, the courts were persuaded by social science research data in Brown, but administrators, school boards, teachers, community members, and others did not share this conviction. This provided the impetus for Brown II in 1955.

Rather than having a remedy which was uniform, the Court endorsed a "practical flexibility" approach to meet local school diversity. The task of policing and evaluating school authorities' efforts was left to the lower federal courts, with the following suggested guidelines:

(a) School authorities have the primary responsibility for elucidating, assessing, and solving the problems, incident to desegregation, 349 U.S. at 299.

(b) The courts will have to consider whether the action of school authorities constitutes good faith implementation of the governing constitutional principles, 349 U.S. at 299.

(c) The courts will be guided by equitable principles characterized by a practical flexibility in shaping its remedies. But it should go without saying that the vitality of these constitutional principles cannot be allowed to yield simply because of disagreement with them, 349 U.S. at 300.

(d) While giving weight to public and private considerations, the courts will require a prompt and reasonable start toward full compliance, 349 U.S. at 300. The courts should enter such orders and decrees necessary and proper to admit to public schools on a racially nondiscriminatory basis with all deliberate speed, 349 U.S. at 301.

Inretrospect, the national governmental leadership position, in reference to desegregation, was summed up best by then-President Dwight D. Eisenhower:

Now I am sworn to one thing, to define the Constitution of the United States, and execute its laws. Therefore, for me to weaken public opinion by discussion of separate cases, where I might agree or might disagree, seems to me to be completely unwise and not a good thing to do. I have an oath, I expect to carry it out. And the mere fact that I could disagree very violently with a decision, and would so express myself, then my own duty would be much more difficult to carry out I think [Eisenhower, n.d.].

More recently, on March 24, 1970, former President Nixon responded to the Alexander v. Holmes County Board of Education (1969) ruling, by asking Congress to allocate $1.5 billion over a two-year period to improve educational programs in "racially impacted areas, North and South, and for assisting school districts in meeting special problems incident to court-ordered desegregation" (Nixon, 1970: 317). Although this was never approved, the request was part of the larger Great Society compensatory programs, based on "separate but equal" rather than busing. Other moves much evidenced were: (a) Moynihan's recommendation of "benign neglect," (b) Jensen and Shockley's genetic racism, and (c) outcries for "ethnically pure" neighborhoods.[2] These actions and former President Ford's subsequent outspokenness against busing may have helped nurture the Senate's opposition to busing.

Commencing with Brown, social science research has had a profound influence on desegregation policy in the United States. It is not surprising that social science research is replete with instances of irrelevance and confusion, coupled with unsound methodology, resulting in little improvement of the educational process for black children. Since the majority of the children in this country attend public schools, educators frequently fail to ascertain *and* fully understand the views of their black constituency.

For more than a decade after the Brown decisions, the expectations were operationally thwarted by the "all deliberate speed" effort. In 1964, in Green v. New Kent County School Board (1968), the Court overturned a plan that allowed all students to choose among public schools. This rendered decision set the stage for a new era in school desegregation.

Though confronted with President Nixon's request for delays and with an appellate court ruling reversing a lower court decision in Alexander v. Holmes, the Supreme Court directed the involved Mississippi school districts to begin operating schools on a unitary nonracial basis immediately.

It was not until June 29, 1970, in Swann v. Charlotte-Mecklenburg Board of Education (1971), when the Supreme Court granted certiorari, that some of the complex problems raised in earlier court decisions concerning busing were addressed. Federal District Judge James McMillan rendered a decision which said, in part, that districtwide desegregation using extensive busing, if necessary, was an appropriate remedy in cities with previously dual systems.

However, it was not until 1973, that the Supreme Court would consider non-South school desegregation problems brought forth in Keyes v. School District 1, Denver, Colorado (1973). This case saw the dawning of the inevitable metropolitan school desegregation suits, which sought to eliminate desegregation by crossing school district boundaries but would also increase court-ordered transportation of students. In Keyes (with a 7-1 decision, Justice Rehnquist dissenting), it was held that "intentional" segregation, whether or not imposed by statute, was unconstitutional. This case, along with Milliken v. Bradley (1974) and Tallulah Morgan et al. v. John J. Kerrigan et al. (1974) represent only a few of the more controversial cases involving school busing.

Also since Brown, social science research has become fundamental in the determination of educational policy. With this in mind, many black scholars have caucused to dispell some mistruths raised by this research. There are several examples which could be cited. However, I will use desegregation and social science research as one such example of how educational policy is determined by the use of *selected* social science research.

Black communities need to be cognizant of how policy makers are using selected social science research data as a basis for far-reaching and significant legal and policy-making decisions. This trend for black communities is a tacit recognition of Emile Durkheim's contention that institutions (in this instance, those of education) can and do shape our behavior in very predictable ways also referred to as the power of "social facts" (Miller and Kavanaugh, 1975: 159-171). Examples which do not objectively recognize the limits of social science research and have had direct influence on educational policy abound in the literature.[3] Individuals such as these were anathema to educational officials a decade ago. At that time, educators felt that society should deal with social problems and leave the teaching to educators. These works range from methodological problems to the misutilization of data which have culminated in unjustifiable policy inferences, affecting the desegregation process.[4]

In addition, some scholars have reached global conclusions on the basis of hastily contrived data. Interestingly, such research data has been limited to minority learners and specific variables that are indigeneous to those geographical areas. Thus, some of the studies contain substantially different findings, resulting in a confusing spectrum of evaluation which is many times indiscriminantly bought at face value by policy makers.

At a time when social science research has the attention of educational policy makers, it is tempting for social scientists to become overzealous in generalizing the significance of their findings (Carter and Harris, 1976a: 491).

EDUCATIONAL POLICY DEVELOPMENT

The history of success and/or failure of black educators to attain key policy-making positions in education is a critical indicator of the gains made in this nation.

It is imperative to understand what is really important about policy-making. Social science research views three policy theories—i.e., elite, group, and rational—as working constantly in the everyday policy-making process. The elite stance holds that only a very few decide for the majority of the populace. Group theory implies that various groups are formed by interest so that their demands are met, either formally or informally. The rational theory maintains that policy is most efficient.

To this end, black communities must fully understand the process. More specifically, these theories have both historical and contemporary implications. It is significant to point out that these theories hold true. But how applicable are they to the issue at hand? We know that the fiber generic to all minorities is that of common discrimination, which has tended to bring about unity among minorities' civil rights, political power, housing, health, and so on.

Furthermore, one may know, as the National Advisory Commission on Civil Disorders concluded, that "our nation is moving toward two societies, one Black, one White—separate and unequal." This perception is viewed as "metro-core" versus suburbia, Black versus White; and most important are the implications for those bent on turning back the hands of time to the Plessy v. Ferguson era.

The organizational structure of educational policy-making, however unique, has not adequately met the voiced concerns of black communities. To better understand educational policy-making, it is necessary that one understand the educational organizational structure; so let's pause for a bit of background information.

Historically, the responsibility of public education in America rests with the state government. The Tenth Amendment states that "the powers not delegated to the United States by the Constitution, nor prohibited by it to the States, are reserved to the States, respectively, or to the people" (see Kirp and Yudof, 1974: 731). Since the Constitution does not specifically mention education, it logically follows that education is a function of the states, and the state constitutions have made provisions for educating its citizenry.

Within those state provisions comes the authorization for school boards, "to make reasonable rules and regulations for the government of local schools and the power to enforce such reasonable rules" (Baldwin, 1975: 11), herein referred to as "school policies." School policies, then, are those legally adopted rules and regulations which govern and control the school systems' daily operations. Such policies, because they are public, are published and made available in particular publications or locations (Baldwin, 1975: 12).

The structure of policy-making consists of many different and diverse components, but the main components are: the school board and the superintendent, appointed by the school board, to act as chief administrator for the school system. The superintendent is the overseer of operations. The superintendent, then, consults a variety of experts who assist him or her in meeting his or her operational obligations (American Association of School Administrators, 1971: 20).

The type of organizational structure into which these components fit is described as the central structure, because most administrative decisions and actions come out of the central office. As a result of these types of organizational structures, a strong central office staff is of prime importance. Each central office staff member must be a specialist in as many areas as the system can provide.

The central office often solicits advice from operational units throughout the system. However, the structure is such that the central office is still charged with the primary responsibility for designing educational programs and transmitting the required directives to operational administrators and supervisors at the local level to implement those programs. The key communication characteristic of this type of structure is the central office of local school units (American Association of School Administrators, 1971: 20). Exceptions to this would naturally be in large urban school districts that have decentralized. But even then, there remains control at the district/regional office, overseen by the main school system office.

As we look at the method whereby rules and regulations are communicated, we can make a striking comparison between what the school system is doing and what public policy-making is doing. Attempting to analyze the process of policy-making involves a great deal of research of the organizational structure which formulates its policy.

All too often, Blacks and other minorities are not provided the necessary experiences that will allow them to become policy makers. As the paradigm presented in Figure 17.1 indicates, the minority community impact is minimized because of this bypass. Therefore, educational policy has been and will continue to be the focus of what has and will occur in schools located in black and other minority communities.

EDUCATIONAL STRATEGEMS

It is time for innovation within the total black community, innovation which is immediate, wide-spread, and long range. The innovation we are speaking about in simple terms must be imaginative,

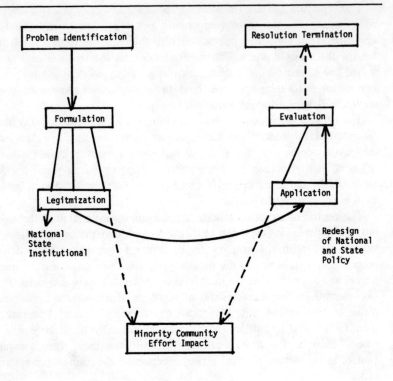

Figure 17.1: Educational Policy-Making Paradigm

NOTE: This paradigm moves the reader's attention along a linear direct path that requires the reader to associate the process with those theories that condition the process's substantive output.

grass roots and down to earth—based upon the very best thinking, planning and action. The existential alienation and "madness" of life is likely to wreak havoc upon the black American Community unless some well thought out and innovative efforts are made by black people themselves to control the situation before it gets out of hand [Marbury and Conley, 1976: 6-7].

The schools belong to the public and the public supports them. It then follows that the public is the authority to which educators are finally accountable for the manner in which they discharge their public trust. However, there is an inherent difficulty with our educational system. It must become more responsive to its black constituency. Educational history is replete with examples of this country's "benign neglect" of Blacks.

One may acknowledge the social, economic, and educational gains made by Blacks during the 1950s and 1960s, but these gains were soon to be lost because of such factors as national leadership policies, the recessions of 1969-1971 and 1974-1975, and, as mentioned, research conducted to place in the nation's consciousness the significant gains made by Blacks. There is and continues to be a great danger inherent in this belief. In 1974, Potomac Associates conducted a nationwide survey in order to ascertain those issues which were of concern to Americans. Two very crucial issues surfaced:

(a) The survey revealed that "improving the situation of black Americans" was next to the lowest problem area in rank, with regard to government spending, and

(b) the problems of black America ranked at the bottom of the list (Watts and Free, 1974: 278).

These data results reveal that the majority of the respondents felt that Blacks have arrived, and that white America can sit back and continue to foster periods of "benign neglect." When there continues to be a historical breakdown in addressing black educational concerns, then the cooperation between educational leaders and the black community will continue to erode.

Therefore, the operationalization of the following educational strategies for black child development are most necessary. First, it seems to me that, individually and collectively, we need to instill within ourselves a recognition of the need for knowledge acquisition. This may occur in a number of ways—e.g., through the griot method, sibling tutoring, and self-help. If one looks at the startling statistics of declining mean Scholastic Aptitude Test (SAT) scores over the past twelve years in general (American high school seniors being ranked seventh in science when compared to similar students in six other advanced nations), the more than 20 million citizens of this, the wealthiest nation in the world, who are judged "functionally illiterate," and the upward extremes of two-figure unemployment, then we can assuredly state that for low-income black youth these figures are much higher if not exponentially greater. There is no need in fooling ourselves with the "superfly," "hip," "boss," "ragging," and "styling-profiling" image when we do not even possess the basic skills necessary to communicate with each other or society at large. Perhaps through this realization we can begin to rethink and modify our practices to be more representative of street as well as nonstreet survival.

The next step is to proceed by initiating and facilitating action with and through the community and educational system. The black community, with organizations such as the National Council for Black Child Development (NCBCD), the National Association for the Advancement of Colored

People (NAACP), Operation People United to Save Humanity (PUSH), the National Alliance of Black School Educators (NABSE), the Association for Supervision and Curriculum Development-Black Caucus (ASCD), the American Educational Research Association-Special Interest Group on Black Concerns (AERA), and the Association of Black Social Workers (ABSW), to name a few, can help to improve the quality of education offered. In the absence of this, the majority of policy makers will continue to recklessly foster *their* own policies, with only a cursory consideration for black children.

A third strategy is to maintain an open line of communication with local, state, and national representatives in government. You may say that this is to follow a process that has not produced much speedy success among Blacks, and I concur. However, another response is that Blacks must continue to be schizoid to the extent of being able to work both within and outside the system; that is what I feel is *political* survival.

It is imperative that black communities be concerned about research, so as to make intelligent decisions. Emphasis should be placed on community good, rather than researchers' private amusement. Improving black community life through policy will require disruptive and revolutionary research from time to time as opposed to research tending to be centripetal (safe and recognized criteria—e.g., those dealing with sample adequacy are important, but many times very insufficient, with respect to the problems at hand). In short, standard criteria will produce standard research which is probably satisfying to the intended policy maker audience.

Fifth, the claim that "schools don't make a difference" cannot be substantiated by the black community. It is a cop-out. Even the most sophisticated multiple regression techniques are inadequate to the task of ferreting out the cause of educational achievement from cross-sectional data. The school is one of few vehicles, if not the only vehicle, available for Blacks to gain a fair share of the pie.[5] If one looks on a macro-level at the results of the fifteen-year effort (Purves and Levine, 1975) by the International Association for the Evaluation of Educational Objectives, surely there are meaningful implications for black community education in the United States on both the micro- and the macro-level.

Sixth, it is incumbent upon those researchers in the black community to begin and continuously conduct empirical research, and to synthesize other research (through organizations like IEA and the National Assessment of Educational Progress [NAEP]) critically, and put it in a more usable form for the black community. This step is not in lieu of, but, rather, is in addition to rebutting those social scientists who are committed to the intellectual degradation of Blacks.

Finally, there is the need to firmly understand what the desegregation/ integration/segregation process is all about.

Although the steps outlined here are listed separately, it is envisioned that in order to have a direct and significant impact upon the educational process, members of the black community and their supporters must take these steps and others concurrently, in order to have the greatest impact on the development of black children within the educational system.

A FURTHER PERSPECTIVE

As we reflect on the history of Blacks in this nation, undoubtedly there has been much change. For more than a century, many persons in this country held steadfastly to the illusion that if everyone would just sit still, time alone would solve the problems of race in these United States. On the contrary, it has been postulated that "the government's attention to the poor has gone from benign concern to malignant neglect" (Time Magazine, 1976: 77). Unfortunately, for Blacks and other minorities time has not been the problem solver:

> The historical reality of race relations in the Americas is that Whites have never altered their institutions primarily for the benefit of Blacks. Whether in the back country of Brazil or in the urban ghettos of New York, the hopes for racial justice have always depended upon the Blacks themselves. Only black hands and the Black determination to be truly free have managed to shape a future for black Americans out of the tragic shambles of the black past [McManus, 1973].

Although there are many critical issues that will affect Blacks in the future, the author feels that none is more crucial than that of educational attainment. For Blacks it may well be the only salvation. As expressed in Brown, "education is required in the performance of our most basic responsibilities, is the foundation of good citizenship, and is the principle instrument in awakening a child to cultural values." However, Blacks must not only be concerned about what Brown said; but also what the ruling did not say, or do. The case did not eliminate racism as a factor in lessening the quality of education afforded black children. What it did do was to assimilate black children into historically white educational systems. Desegregation has had adverse displacement effects on not only black students, but on teachers and administrators as well. But this need not be the inevitable result of desegregation (Carter and Harris, 1976).

In summation, if Blacks are truly committed and earnest in the concerns being voiced, about the effects of desegregation on the development

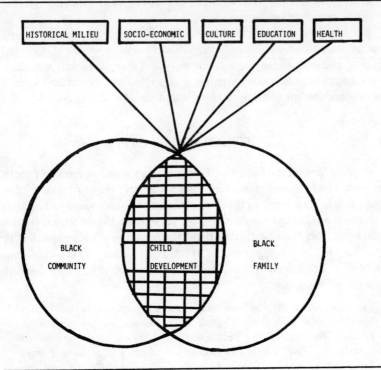

Figure 2: Black Child Development in Perspective: Conditional factors affecting Black child development

of black children, then Blacks collectively will share the responsibility. This means becoming and continuing to be integrally involved with our children, both in the home as well as in the schools (see Figure 17.2). In addition, Blacks must concentrate more on the student the school produces, at the end of the bus ride. Without this commitment, then our educational survival, in this nation, is questionable.

NOTES

1. For an interesting analysis of today's American family, see Bronfenbrenner (1977).

2. For an analytical discussion of "ethnic purity," that reinforces the assumption that color, not ethnicity, is the determining factor in America, see Tauber and Tauber (1965).

3. See Armor (1972a, 1972b), Jencks (1972), Coleman (1966, 1975), Jensen (1969, 1973), Eysenchk (1972), and Shockley (1972).

4. See Pettigrew and Green (1976a, 1976b) and Coleman (1976). For a very analytical and timely discussion of busing, see Carter (1976c).

5. For further edification, see Terry (1970).

CASES

ALEXANDER v. HOLMES COUNTY BOARD OF EDUCATION (1969) 396 U.S. 19
BROWN v. BOARD OF EDUCATION OF TOPEKA, KANSAS (1954) 347 U.S. 483.
GREEN v. NEW KENT COUNTY SCHOOL BOARD (1968) 391 U.S. 430
KEYES v. SCHOOL DISTRICT 1, DENVER, COLORADO (1973) 413 U.S. 189
MILLIKEN v. BRADLEY (1974) 418 U.S. 717
MISSOURI ex rel. GAINES v. CANADA (1938) 305 U.S. 337
PLESSY v. FERGUSON (1896) 153 U.S. 537
ROBERTS v. CITY OF BOSTON (1850) 59 Mass. 198, 206
SIPUEL v. BOARD OF REGENTS OF THE UNIVERSITY OF OKLAHOMA (1948)
   332 U.S. 631
SWANN v. CHARLOTTE-MECKLENBURG BOARD OF EDUCATION (1971) 402
   U.S. 1
SWEATT v. PAINTER (1949) 339 U.S. 629
TALLULAH MORGAN ET AL. V. JOHN J. KERRIGAN ET AL. (1974) 379 F.
   Supp. 410

REFERENCES

American Association of School Administrators (1971) *Profiles of the Administrative Team*. Washington, D.C.: Author.
ARMOR, D. J. (1972a) "The evidence of busing." *Public Interest* (Summer): 90-126.
——— (1972b) "School and family effects on black and white achievement: a reexamination of the USOE data," in F. Mosteller and D. P. Moynihan (eds.) *On Equality of Educational Opportunity*. New York: Random House.
BALDWIN, H. A. (1975) *School Law and the Indiana Teacher*. Bloomington: Beanblossom.
BRONFENBRENNER, U. (1977) "Comments." *Psychology Today* 10, 12: 41-47.
CARTER, D. C. and J. J. HARRIS (1976a) "Brown revisited." *Phi Delta Kappan* 57 (April).
——— (1976b) "Desegregation and the Black educator: a question of Black survival." Presented at the Third Annual Conference of thc Buffalo Education Association on Inner City Schools, Buffalo, New York.
——— (1976c) "Anti-busing legislation and society: reflections on the bicentennial." Presented at the National Organization on Legal Problems of Education annual convention, Atlanta, Georgia.
COLEMAN, J. S. (1976) "Response to Professors Pettigrew and Green." *Harvard Educational Review* 46.
——— (1975) "Racial segregation in the schools." *Phi Delta Kappan* (October): 75-78.
——— (1966) *Equality of Educational Opportunity Report*. Washington, DC: Government Printing Office.
EISENHOWER, D. D. (n.d.) *Public Papers of the President*.
EYSENCHK, J. J. (1972) *The IQ Argument*. Freeport, NY: Library Press.
FARLEY, R. (1975) "Residential segregation and its implications for school integration." *Law and Contemporary Problems* 39, 1: 134-149.
JENCKS, C. (1972) *Inequality: A Reassessment of the Effect of Family and Schooling in America*. New York: Basic Books.

JENSEN, A. P. (1973) *Educability and Group Differences.* New York: Harper &
Row.
—— (1969) "How much can we boost IQ and scholastic achievement?" *Harvard
Educational Review* 39: 36-123.
KIRP, D. L. and M. G. YUDOF (1974) *Educational Policy and the Law.* Berkeley,
CA: McCutchan.
MARBURY, C. H. and H. CONLEY (1976) "The bicentennial as a "Kairotic"
opportunity to improve counseling by understanding the Black child from a
historical prospect." Presented at the Quality of Life Conference–Year 2000,
Fisk University, Nashville, Tennessee.
McMANUS, E. J. (1973) *Black Bondage in the North.* Syracuse, NY: Syracuse
University Press.
MILLER, S. I. and J. KAVANAUGH (1975) "Empirical evidence." *Journal of Law
and Education* 4, 1: 159-171.
NIXON, R. M. (1970) "Statement about desegregation of elementary and secondary
schools." *Public Papers of the President* 91 (March).
PETTIGREW, T. F. and R. L. GREEN (1976) "School desegregation in large cities: a
critique of the Coleman 'white flight' thesis." *Harvard Educational Review* 46.
—— (1976b) "A reply to Professor Coleman." *Harvard Educational Review* 46:
225-233.
PURVES, A. C. and D. M. LEVINE (1975) *Educational Policy and International
Assessment: Implications of the IEA Survey of Achievement.* Berkeley, CA:
McCutchan.
SHOCKLEY, W. (1972) "Dysgenics, geneticity, raceology:" *Phi Delta Kappan* (Janu-
ary): 297-307.
STALVEY, L. M. (1970) *The Education of a WASP.* New York: Bantam.
TAUBER, K. E. and A. F. TAUBER (1965) *Negroes in Cities.* Chicago: AVC.
TERRY, R. W. (1970) *For Whites Only.* Grand Rapids, MI: Eerdmans.
Time Magazine (1976) 108, 19: 77.
Time Magazine (1975) "The busing dilemma." 22 (September): 1.
WATTS, W. and L. FREE (1974) *State of the Nation.* New York: Basic Books.

18

BLACK STUDENTS IN WHITE UNIVERSITIES REVISITED

Elois Scott

During the past ten years, much as been written about black students in white institutions. This chapter is another such effort. The intent is to review some of the issues involved in access to White institutions and to discuss some of the solutions. This will be done by (1) providing a literature review describing the barriers which have prohibited and continue to prohibit or circumscribe access; (2) discussing the impact that special admissions programs have had on access by describing the major objectives of these programs and identifying issues related to special admissions, and (3) describing one of the City University of New York's (CUNY) special admissions programs which appears to be working as means of looking at ways special admissions programs can address some of these issues.

BARRIERS

Crossland (1971) identifies five major barriers to access for minorities: (1) standardized tests, (2) poor preparation, (3) finances, (4) motivation, and (5) race. Because many of the barriers listed are inextricably embedded, it has been useful to collapse these categories. For example, in studies, race may or may not be a main effect, but it is always an interaction effect. Each of the first four factors Crossland identifies interacts with race. Consequently, race is assumed to be a factor and our discussion will be limited to (1) prior preparation and test performance, and (2) finances.[1]

PRIOR PREPARATION AND TEST PERFORMANCE

This issue, in terms of access to higher institutions, has to do with the relationship of prior preparation to the ability to perform well on the standardized tests that are required for entry into most colleges and universities.

Many black students are eliminated before they begin. According to a report by the National Advisory Committee on Blacks in Higher Education and Black Colleges and Universities (1979: 4), "more black students had dropped out of high school than had enrolled in college in 1977," and "one out of every four black persons between the ages of 18 and 24 had not attained the minimal educational goal—a high school diploma—and were not pursuing it."

Why are these figures so high? A frequent reason cited for the failure of large numbers of black students to complete high school is poor preparation. Boyd (1974) did a nationwide study of 785 black students at 40 colleges and universities in the United States in 1972-1973. One of the questions the students were asked was how well they felt they were prepared in several academic areas. Of Boyd's, 49 percent sample indicated that students had inadequate preparation in math, 37 percent in sciences, 34 percent in English, and 17 percent in all areas. It is interesting to note that students in Boyd's study also said they wished that more emphasis had been given in high school on the basic skills of spelling, vocabulary, and arithmetic. In addition, they expressed a need for more emphasis on reading more rapidly, expressing ideas better in writing and speaking, and the development of time management skills. If students who have already been admitted to college express this lack of preparation, how much more poorly prepared are other youngsters?

A study by Chandler (1974) found that 90 percent of high school seniors felt they needed more assistance in math and reading skills in order to succeed in college. Several other authors have also documented this lack of preparation (Grant and Hoeber, 1978; Cross, 1976a; Mulka and Sheerin, 1974; and Reed, 1979), to mention a few.

There is undoubtedly a direct relationship between poor preparation and the ability to perform well on the standardized tests required by most institutions. The literature abounds with data on the test performance of blacks. For example, the "Coleman Study" (Coleman et al., 1966) reported that blacks continue to fall behind grade level when their performance is measured by standardized tests. This varies from 1.6 below grade level in the sixth grade to 3.3 below grade level in the twelfth grade. This finding has tremendous impact in terms of high school completion but an even more profound impact in terms of the ability to perform well on college entrance exams.

In addition to poor preparation, what other factors affect the test-taking situation? Astin (1979: 21) describes the major controversy as being an issue over construct validity: "Do they accurately measure the academic abilities of people from other than white-middle class backgrounds?"

More recently, this issue was discussed by Fallows (1980), who points out that (1) the tests (SAT) tend to measure which students have had the best education—not which students have the potential for academic success; (2) preparation will improve performance; and (3) there is a certain ideology behind which is the "best" answer for all ETS tests and, further, this ideology is discernible. In describing his experience taking sample SAT, LSAT, and GRE tests, Fallows (1980: 46) said,

> In most cases, it was easy enough to guess the "right" answer—not by means of superior logic, but by knowing the way ETS thinks. Of all the forms of test bias, this may be the most insidious and deepest rooted: the shared assumptions about which logic is "compelling" and which merely "superficial" assumptions that derive from the social experiences that shape judgment and taste.

He further contends that test bias is more economic than racial. The 1974 College Board data on the relationship between economic status and test scores demonstrate a consistently direct, positive correlation between mean family income and student test scores: For instance, the mean family income for students with scores of 200-249 was $8,639; for students with scores of 450-499, $18,122; and for students with scores of 750-800, $24,124.

This information is particularly pertinent, since blacks tend to fall in the lower economic status. In fact, in Boyd's study (1974) of black students, 44 percent of the students enrolled in white institutions came from families with incomes of $9,999 or less. More recent data from the National Advisory Committee on Black Higher Education and Black Colleges and Universities (1979: xiii) show that "almost half of the black first-time freshmen were from families with incomes of $8,000 or less compared to 7 percent of white freshmen." Consequently, it is academic to say these tests have more socioeconomic bias than race bias, because most black youth fall in the lower socioeconomic bracket.

Another issue related to economics arises from the recent data which indicate prior test preparation can increase test scores. These studies, conducted by the Federal Trade Commission, looked only at the commercial test preparation schools and admittedly are open to sampling and methodological questions. However, it is indicated that students taking these courses score better. Since the cost of these workshops varies from $200 to $400, students from low-income families are less likely to be able to take advantage of them. Consequently, the "meritocracy" based on wealth continues.

Assuming, however, that these factors were not pertinent issues, what other factors might affect test scores? Cross (1976: 124) points out that

> another factor in the test environment that has been given little attention in research on test bias is the instructions given about guessing on the test. The cautious student who is afraid to give a wrong answer will make a score that may represent an underestimate of what he knows about the subject. Since there is evidence that the school situation has instilled fear-of-failure approach to learning for many low achievers, the question of guessing would seem to be a fertile and unplowed field for further research.... Students who fear giving a wrong answer on a test will be penalized more heavily than those who are willing to guess, because some of the guesses will prove correct.

Related to this is the factor of speed. Many black students proceed through tests too slowly. Failure to make students aware of the need to move more quickly frequently contributes to lower scores.

In addition, race of the test administrator and of the comparison group are additional factors. Katz (1970) found that the relationship of race of the test administrator to test scores was associated to students' perceptions of success. If students felt they had a high probability of being successful, the best performance occurred with a white administrator. However, if they felt their probability of success was low, or if they thought their performance would be compared to white norms, they performed better under a black test administrator.

FINANCIAL BARRIERS

Many factors relating to the financial constraints of students have already been discussed—a clear example of the confounding of these issues.

Because family income is considerably lower for blacks than it is for whites, college expenses must be met in a very different way. Table 18.1 compares the expected family contribution toward educational expenses

TABLE 18.1   Expected Parental Contribution Toward
              Education

Contribution ($)	Black Parents (%)	White Parents (%)
Less than 625	77	33
625–1,199	9	19
1,200–1,799	4	12
1,800–2,399	3	10
2,400–2,999	2	5
3,000–3,599	1	2
More than 3,600	5	21

SOURCE: Collapsed from "Minority Group Participation in Graduate Education"
(National Board on Graduate Education, 1976: 81).

by black and white parents. Of the black students in 1972, 79 percent
were receiving either scholarships, grants, loans, or some combination of
these. Indeed, according to the National Board on Graduate Education
(1976: 82), "overall, minority students comprised about one-third of the
total number of students assisted through these [BEDG and SEDG]
federal student aid programs."

The previous sections of this chapter have briefly described some of
the barriers and issues which limit access of blacks to white institutions.
The next section describes a special admissions program which attempts to
facilitate both access and success.

CUNY SEEK PROGRAM

SEEK (Search for Education, Elevation and Knowledge) is a program at
the City University of New York (CUNY) higher education system which
was enacted under the Higher Education Opportunity Act (HEOP) to
facilitate access to the CUNY system for minority students. SEEK provides counseling and guidance services, remedial and compensatory classes,
tutoring, and financial assistance to students who are economically disadvantaged (based on a sliding scale with consideration for the number in the
household, number of wage earners, and total income)[2] and educationally
disadvantaged students who received a general equivalency diploma (GED)
or students who graduated from high school with a score of less than 75 in
academic courses. This program, in addition to the institution of an open
admissions policy, has had a major impact on increasing minority enrollment in the CUNY system.[3]

The following is a description of an evaluation for the prefreshman
SEEK students.

PRE-FRESHMAN SUMMER SEEK

The students in this study were unique in the sense that they were
prefreshman SEEK students. Prefreshman students had to meet all of the
requirements of regular SEEK students (see previous section) in addition
to meeting the following criteria. (These criteria were described in a
memorandum to all SEEK directors.)

- "Participants in the Pre-Freshman Summer Program are to be
  students whose levels predict failure in college-level work [and]
  students who have failed the high school Basic Competency Tests in
  reading and mathematics."
- There will be "only noncredit learning instruction in basic skills
  areas: writing, math, reading, ESL (English as a Second Language)."
- "No tuition is to be charged."
- "Programs will operate for a six- to seven-week period."
- "Stipends . . . are to be provided for students who meet SEEK
  economic eligibility requirements."

In essence, this prefreshman program was an attempt to use the summer
session to provide remedial assistance *before* students were enrolled in
their regular college classes. In addition to attempting to ease the academic
transition to college life, counseling services were also provided to assist in
easing the social and psychological adjustment of students to college life.

During the summer of 1979, an evaluation of the Pre-Freshman Summer SEEK Program was conducted. The purpose of this evaluation was to
provide baseline information on the program, particularly in terms of
student perceptions. In order to accomplish this task, several types of
questions were asked. In general, however, there were three basic question
types. The first is demographic and provides a description of the students;
the second provides a description of student satisfaction of the program;
and the third provides information on student attitudes in a variety of
areas.

Some of the questions were formulated to be compatible with data that
were collected in the *SEEK Freshman Survey,* reported in June 1979. The
rationale for this was twofold. First, it allowed comparisons to be made
with students in last year's program to the students in this year's program.
Second, several of the questions on last year's evaluations were compatible
with the questionnaire developed by the American Council on Education
and the University of California. That questionnaire was used to collect
data on freshmen in a national survey. This, of course, permitted the
comparison of the incoming students with a national sample.

New questions were also added from two other questionnaires. One was developed by Richard R. Scott and Rupert Nacoste, to assess attitudes and characteristics of university students. The second was developed by Elois Skeen Scott specifically to evaluate perception of program satisfaction and effectiveness in special services programs, and to ascertain student characteristics.

QUESTIONNAIRE ADMINISTRATION

The questionnaire was administered by Mr. Joe Harris's office of the City University of New York. The staff person who administered the questionnaire was familiar with both the prefreshman program and the SEEK staff. The administration took place during regular class periods and no attempt was made to follow up on students who were not in class.

STUDENT CHARACTERISTICS

The following section describes demographic information on students who were administered the questionnaire. The data by college are displayed in Tables 18.2 and 18.3.

Of the 332 students who were in class during the administration of the questionnaire, out of a population of approximately 500, 241 were female and 90 were male. To further describe this group, Table 18.3 displays the enrollment by ethnicity.

The age of the students ranged from 16 to 43. The median age was 18.25, with a mean age of 19.29. The most frequently listed age was 18. The data which are reported in percentages correspond closely to last year's data (see Table 18.4).

What is immediately interesting about these data is the increase in the number of 17-year-olds and the slight decrease in the number of students 21 and older. Also of interest when comparing these data to national data is that students in this population are older. However, on the whole CUNY students tend to be older. The mean age in 1976 was 25.1 in the senior colleges and 25.6 in the community colleges.

Of these students, the largest number were 1979 graduates (253) with the next largest number being 1978 graduates (23). There were 19 who graduated in 1975 or earlier and 18 who received the GED.

When students were asked what their high school grade point average was, the largest number (90) responded, "B." In general, all of the scores tended to cluster around B+, B, and B-. Only six students said they had a C-. These data indicate that the students are fairly well prepared aca-

TABLE 18.2   Enrollment by College

College	Respondents
Baruch	109
Brooklyn	16
City	25
Hunter	82
Lehmans	34
Queens	31
York	10
Staten Island	0
John Jay	23
Total	332

TABLE 18.3   Enrollment by Ethnicity

Ethnicity	Respondents
Black	164
White	16
Hispanic	114
Asian/Pacific American	11
Native American	5
Other	15
No Response	7
Total:	332

NOTE: Here and in the tables that follow, totals below 332 are due to nonresponses.

TABLE 18.4   Comparison of Age of Students

Age of Students	Summer 1979 Pre-Freshman Students (%)	Seek (%)		National Freshmen (%)
17	15.7	3.3		3.3
18	42.8	45.2		75.3
19	20.8	21.8		17.2
20	4.2	7.4 ⎫		1.8
21–25	6.9	10.0 ⎬ 21–30		2.3
26–30	3.9	4.3 ⎭		
Over 30		3.7		

NOTE: The data referred to in the SEEK column of this table and all subsequent tables relate to the students in the SEEK Freshman Survey.

demically, at least by self-report measures. These data are compared by percentage to those in last year's evaluation, as shown in Table 18.5. What is immediately evident is that the students in the prefreshman group were less well prepared than the 1978-1979 group. Why this occurred is not known. It may, however, relate to the type of program in which the students were enrolled.

If we are to use Astin's (1970) data on predicting the effect of high school GPAs on dropping out of college, we get an idea of how well these students may do. Astin does suggest, however, that prediction is considerably improved when using high school GPA combined with standardized test scores. The grades reported by the SEEK students, do, then, give us a fairly good indication of possible persistence in college. Based on these data, most of the students should remain in school for their sophomore year.

These data are somewhat inconsistent with those of Friedman and Thompson (1971), who state that two-third of the students are in the lower half of their class and are not enrolled in college preparatory classes.

When the students were asked the type of high school program in which they were enrolled, the responses indicated the students were equally divided between having been enrolled in a college preparatory program (116) and a vocational program (117) while in high school. (Since a criterion for admissions under this program was a score of less than 75 on academic coursework, the self-reported high school GPAs may have been in vocational programs.)

Students were also asked to give their perceptions of their preparedness in several areas. The rationale for this question was that data by Franklin (1974) show the self-concept of students to decline after they have been enrolled in programs such as this one. The responses to this item provide us with baseline data from which to evaluate students' perceptions of prior preparation after having been exposed to a college curriculum for a period of one year. Table 18.6 displays these data by percentages.

Related to the question on preparedness, participants were asked how they would rate themselves as students. These data appear in Table 18.7. Although these data are self-report, they do not indicate the low self-concept that so many authors (Cross, 1976a; Mulka and Sheerin, 1974), among others, tend to describe.

At this point, students were asked in which areas they felt they needed academic help. They were requested to check all areas in which they felt they needed academic assistance. Table 18.8 displays the order in which students expressed this need. Clearly, these students felt they needed academic assistance even though they had previously described themselves as good students who were at least fairly well prepared. This may be

TABLE 18.5   Comparison of High School Grade Point Averages

H.S. GPA	Pre-Freshman Summer SEEK (%)	SEEK (%)	National Sample (%)
A	2.7	3.3	10.5
A–	4.2	5.0	12.8
B+	21.7	17.2	20.1
B	27.1	29.5	26.4
B–	16.0	17.5	12.7
C+	13.9	13.1	10.5
C	7.2	5.5	6.8
C–			
D	1.8	0.6	0.3

TABLE 18.6   Perceptions of Academic Preparedness (percentages)

Area	Poor	Fairly Well	Very Well
Mathematical skills	33.6	62.4	4.0
Reading and comprehension	25.2	58.6	16.2
Foreign languages	14.2	54.1	31.6
Science	43.3	32.8	23.9
History, social sciences	12.7	59.4	27.9
Vocational skills	9.0	53.5	37.4
Musical, artistic skills	22.6	51.6	25.8
Study habits	23.8	54.4	21.8

TABLE 18.7   Students' Views of Themselves as Students

Rating	Percentages
Excellent	4.2
Good	33.4
Average	56.6
Below average	2.4
Poor	0.9

TABLE 18.8   Areas of Academic
Assistance Needed

Areas	Respondents
Writing term papers	200
Mathematics	176
Vocabulary	154
Taking lecture notes	122
Critical reading	113
Study skills	98
Speech	74
Grammar	70

NOTE: Figures represent the number of
responses out of a total of 332.

partially explained by the Coleman et al. (1966) finding that minority
youth may lack an opportunity to evaluate their performances realistically. When they evaluate their work in comparison to that of their peers,
they do well; when they feel their work will be evaluated in comparison to
that of whites, they tend to feel they have done less well.

When students were asked the organizational procedure by which they
would like to receive this assistance, the majority said they would prefer
tutorial assistance rather than class instruction or individualized instruction. Individualized instruction was ranked second, and class instruction
was third.

A frequent question many educators in basic skills programs ask is
whether or not the student should receive academic credit for remedial or
developmental work. To measure the perception of students in this program regarding this question, they were asked if they would be willing to
take the courses listed in Table 18.8, assuming that they felt the need for
them, *without* receiving credit; 79 percent of the students said they would.

Although it is not possible to generalize from these data due to
numbers, sampling problems, and so on, the question of academic credit
appears to be more of an educator's concern than a student concern in this
study.

Related to their perceptions of what they could do to facilitate success
in their coursework, students were asked two questions pertaining to class
behavior. Both the questions and their responses appear in Table 18.9.

A follow-up question which probably should have been asked but was
not is, "How often do you attend class and how frequently do you
participate?" All this question has provided us with is perception of
important behavior, not *actual* behavior. These data are particularly inter-

TABLE 18.9   Student Class Behavior (percentages)

Questions	Very Important	Important	Somewhat Important	Not Important
How important do you feel daily class attendance is to your course grade?	78.3	17.5	2.7	1.5
How important do you feel class participation (speaking out) is to your course grade?	48.3	37.8	13.2	0.6

esting in light of an early study done at CUNY by Tormes (1969). He found that a major problem, at least in terms of instructors' perceptions of students, was their passivity. These CUNY students, ten years later, do not appear—from their own reports—to reflect passivity.

The next question asked students to rank the most likely reason they would have to drop out of school—if they were to drop out. The order, according to frequency, was: *grades* as the most likely reason, *personal* as the second most likely, and *money* as the least likely reason. These results may be due to the fact that most of these students receive some type of financial reward which enables them to come to school. In all likelihood, this is a finding which has occurred within the last ten years. Data prior to this has indicated lack of money as a major cause of attrition. In last year's report, 59 percent of the SEEK students did report financial problems to be a major concern and 55.6 percent reported academic problems to be a major concern. The data, however, are not comparable because of the difference in the format of the questions. The question in this year's evaluation requested students to rank, not check, all possible reasons for dropping out of school. Cross (1976b) reports that when administrators of remedial services in two-year colleges were asked what they felt the major obstacles were to learning, they ranked financial concerns as sixth out of a list of seven. These are clearly results of the federal programs which provide financial assistance to students.

The fact that these programs are providing considerable assistance can be demonstrated by comparing family income. Bayer and Boruch (1969) conducted a nationwide study of 243,000 college first-year students, 12,300 of whom were black. They found that 56 percent of the black students came from families with incomes of less than $6,000 in 1968. Comparing these data to data on the CUNY students ten years later, we find that the majority of the students still come from homes with incomes of less than $8,000. Considering inflation, these families are less well off than they were a decade ago. The fact then, that these students do not feel financial reasons will be the major reason for dropping out of college strengthens the notion of the major contribution financial assistance has played in the retention of college students.

Students were then asked what their reasons were for coming to college in general, and their reasons for attending their specific college/university. These data are shown in Tables 18.10 and 18.11.

It is difficult to interpret findings in Table 18.10. They were obviously all important. It is rather intriguing, however, to compare the responses of the prefreshmen on the item, "to be able to get a better job," and the item, "to be able to make more money." To make more money is clearly more important. What is unclear and impossible to discern from these data, is if students are aware of the relationship of money to specific jobs. One would suspect that they are, based on the information in Table 18.12 on anticipated undergraduate major. As Table 18.11 indicates, the two most important factors in students' selection of a particular college were its academic record and the programs it offered. (This is another slight indicator that these *are not* passive students.) Interestingly, the fact that colleges recruited them was of very little importance. This may be due to the fact that much of the recruiting was done while the students were still in high school; consequently, they may not have associated their recruitment with college recruitment.

Table 18.12 shows the breakdown of the students' intended majors. What is particularly interesting about these data is that they show a definite shift *out* of the social science and education areas and a significant increase in students interested in business degrees. Although it is speculation at this point, this may be attributed to better high school counseling.

The last column in this table provides the percentages from Boyd's (1974) data. It demonstrates, even more clearly, the shifts black students are making. In terms of political beliefs, most students (43 percent) consider themselves to be middle-of-the-road. These data are reflected in Table 18.13. Ten years ago, we would probably have obtained a much different response.

In terms of current issues, the same questions which were asked in the freshman survey were asked in this questionnaire. Prefreshman student responses, together with a comparison of responses on the freshman survey are found in Table 18.14. The categories "strongly agree" and "agree somewhat" have been collapsed to "agree." The two "disagree" categories have likewise been collapsed to "disagree."

It is quite interesting to note the shift that has occurred since Boyd (1974) collected his data. He reported that 60 percent of the students in his sample felt that less demanding standards were a good idea. The

TABLE 18.10   Reasons for Coming to College (percentages)

| | Very Important | | Somewhat Important | Not Important |
	National	SEEK	Summer '79 program	Summer '79 program	Summer '79 program
To be able to get a better job	80.0	75.4	54.2	10.5	16.3
To gain a general education	67.8	68.3	79.2	14.5	2.1
To be able to make more money	56.6	60.4	83.7	11.7	0.9
To learn about things that interest me	67.4	74.0	61.1	29.5	4.8
To prepare myself for graduate or professional school	61.3	44.2	74.4	19.0	2.1

TABLE 18.11 Reasons for Coming to This College (percentages)

| | Very Important | | Somewhat Important | Not Important |
	SEEK	National	Summer '79 program	Summer '79 program	Summer '79 program
My parents wanted me to go here.	10.5	5.8	9.0	25.0	56.6
My teacher/counselor advised me to go here.	12.2	11.5	10.2	29.2	52.4
This college has a great academic report.	55.1	50.7	53.6	29.8	9.6
Someone who attended here advised me to go.	15.5	13.9	14.2	24.7	51.8
This college has low tuition.	13.8	16.8	8.7	27.7	51.8
This college has strengths in my intended field.	72.6		69.0	21.7	4.5
A college representative recruited me.	7.2	4.2	3.9	15.4	68.4

TABLE 18.12   Anticipated Undergraduate Major (percentages)

Major Areas	Pre-Freshman Summer SEEK	SEEK	National	Boyd's Data, 1974
Arts, humanities	4.2	9.8	8.2	(English-4)
Physical sciences	1.2	4.3	3.2	2
Biological sciences	5.7	5.0	2.4	6
Business	33.4	21.7	23.9	15
Education	6.9	6.2	8.0	15
Engineering	1.5	4.0	10.0	4
Pre-professional	19.0	23.5	15.5	28
Social sciences	7.2	9.8	7.4	28
Technical	3.0	2.2	4.5	
Other	10.2	13.4	13.6	(Black Studies-1)

TABLE 18.13   Student Political Beliefs

Rating	Percentages
Very conservative	4.5
Conservative	19.3
Middle-of-the-road	43.1
Liberal	19.6
Very liberal	5.1

TABLE 18.14   Comparison of Current Issues (percentages)

Issues	Pre-Freshman SEEK		SEEK	
	Agree	Disagree	Agree	Disagree
Competing for grades should be a student's main concern.	66.2	20.4	65.3	30.4
Realistically, individuals can do little to bring about change in our society.	46.3	47.6	39.3	51.7
Faculty evaluations should be based, in part, on student evaluations.	79.8	11.1	64.6	24.4
If a college adopts an open admissions policy, the same performance standards should apply to all students.	79.0	13.5	66.3	21.5

students in this questionnaire, on the other hand, overwhelmingly felt that performance standards should not be lowered.

To round out the demographic data on these students, most (81.3 percent) listed their fathers as primary head of the household and 73.4 percent of these households have an annual income of less than an $8,000. This question, however, needs to be refined in subsequent questionnaires, since several students, although not a significant number, listed themselves as the primary head of household, even though this category was not provided in the questionnaire.

In terms of the educational level of their parents, 26.5 percent responded that their mothers had had some grammar school, while 49.4 percent responded that the mothers had had some high school or were high school graduates. These data are similar to, although slightly lower than, the educational level of the fathers. Of the fathers, 22.6 percent had some grammar school education and 37.7 percent had some high school education or had completed a high school degree.

Of the students, 50 percent are long-term New York residents, having lived in the area from 16 to 20 years; 17.5 percent have been in the area from 1 to 5 years; and 16.6 percent from 6 to 10 years.

The time these students have available will not all be devoted to education: 32.2 percent will be required to take care of children; 16.9 percent will be paying the rent; 31 percent will be contributing toward a portion of the rent; 22 percent will be paying the food bills; 79.7 percent will be buying their own clothing; and 34.3 percent will be paying other bills. Clearly, education and education-related activities will occupy only part of the students' time. It is the necessity to do these other activities which makes these students most different from the majority of white students. These other responsibilities also contribute in a major way to academic problems that students may encounter.

PROGRAM SATISFACTION

The following section looks at a series of questions specifically pertaining to the 1979 summer program. Each question has been listed and response percentages provided in Tables 18.15 and 18.16. The responses to these questions were very important. A major criticism of many programs similar to this is that the students are unaware that they are in a developmental program. Consequently, they are disillusioned and tend to express the feeling that "they don't need this," or "this isn't really college work." These students, however, are very receptive to this program.

In addition to the questions given in Tables 18.15 and 18.16, students were asked whether they would recommend this program to their friends; 95 percent responded affirmatively.

Another question asked students to respond to how they felt about being accepted into a program of this nature. The majority of students (86.1 percent) felt positively about it. This is extremely important. Data from some of the other studies on basic skills programs in higher education have found that students have resented being admitted as "special students in special programs." Related to these issues, students responded that the work they had done this summer had made them more positive (94.3 percent) toward their academic work and toward their ability to succeed in college.

To summarize, students in this program were very positive about the experiences they had, both programmatically and individually. In addition, they felt no negative stigma as a result of program acceptance and would recommend the program to their friends.

STUDENT ATTITUDES

This last section concerns questions of a general nature. The basic issue in all of these questions is locus of control. In other words, do these students feel they can affect their lives. These data are presented in Table 18.17 in terms of percentages, means, medians, and mode scores. The categories ranged from "strongly disagree" (1) to "strongly agree" (4).

The first five questions are basic locus of control items in a generalized setting. In almost all cases, this is particularly evident when the categories are collapsed to "agree" and "disagree." These students feel they exercise a great deal of control over their lives. In question 4, however, they do acknowledge that knowing the right people is helpful.

In questions 6 through 9, the students indicate a very positive perception of their academic abilities and their academic rewards. These feelings are substantiated in items 10 through 13, which show the students to have perceived themselves as having high worth and a strong self-concept.

Questions 14-15 begin to show mixed perceptions. The responses to item 14 are pretty evenly divided—48.5 percent disagree and 44.6 percent agree that opportunities generally go to whites, even when minorities have appropriate training. Item 15 blames the victim. If minorities do not do well, it is their own fault. It will be interesting to see how the students respond to these items in follow-up studies. The idea that they are already internalizing responsibility for failure without regard to institutional and

TABLE 18.15   Perception of SEEK Program (yes/no response set)

	Percentages		
	Yes	No	No response
When you entered the SEEK program, were you given adequate information about what the program entailed?	66.6	30.7	2.7
When you entered the SEEK program, did you know that some of your courses would be designed to help you do better in your regular classes?	72.9	24.4	2.7
Do you feel you needed the classes that were provided for you this summer?	92.8	5.4	1.8

TABLE 18.16   Perception of SEEK Program (very much-not at all response set)

	Percentages			
	Very much	Somewhat	Not at all	No response
Do you feel that the courses which were organized by the SEEK program met your *individual* needs?	56.3	40.7	1.5	1.5
Were your instructors available and helpful enough to you?	75.6	21.7	2.1	.6
Were the materials that were used interesting?	51.5	42.5	4.8	1.2
Were the materials useful in meeting your educational needs?	66.0	31.0	2.4	.6
Do you feel better prepared for fall semester as a result of this program?	68.7	28.6	1.5	1.2

TABLE 18.17 Locus of Control Items

Items	Strongly Disagree (1)	Disagree (2)	Agree (3)	Strongly Disagree (4)	Mean	Median	Mode
1. In almost any business or profession, people who do their jobs well rise to the top.	6.0	10.5	55.1	25.0	3.02	3.08	3.00
2. When I make plans, I am almost certain that I can make them work.	2.1	9.6	63.6	22.6	3.09	3.09	3.00
3. In my case, getting what I want has little or nothing to do with luck.	6.0	14.8	53.3	23.2	2.96	3.02	3.00
4. Knowing the right people is important in deciding whether a person will get ahead.	5.4	23.5	42.8	24.7	2.90	2.95	3.00
5. People who don't do well in life often work hard, but the breaks just don't come their way.	7.5	34.6	41.9	11.4	2.59	2.63	3.00
6. In the kinds of things we do in school, I am at least as good as other people in my classes.	2.7	9.3	67.8	15.1	3.00	3.02	3.00
7. I am usually proud of my grades.	2.7	23.2	59.3	9.0	2.79	2.89	3.00
8. School is harder for me than for most other people.	11.7	56.9	24.1	3.3	2.19	2.14	2.00
9. It seems that no matter how hard I try, I never get the grades I deserve.	9.3	55.4	25.6	4.5	2.27	2.18	2.00
10. I take a positive attitude toward myself.	1.8	11.1	49.4	34.3	32.0	3.22	3.00
11. I feel I am a sperson of worth, on an equal plane with others.	2.1	5.7	54.5	33.4	3.25	3.24	3.00
12. I am able to do things as well as most other people.	1.5	4.5	63.3	26.2	3.19	3.16	3.00
13. On the whole, I am satisfied with myself.	1.8	11.7	55.1	26.8	3.12	3.12	3.00
14. Many minorities who don't do well in life do have good training, but the opportunities just always go to whites.	9.9	38.6	29.8	14.8	2.53	2.45	2.00
15. Many minorities have only themselves to balme for not doing better in life; if they tried harder they'd do better.	9.9	19.3	40.4	24.4	2.84	2.94	3.00

NOTE: Columns 1 through 4 give percentages.

social constraints is disturbing. One would hope that as they mature, they will put effort into its proper perspective.

To summarize, we have seen how racial, financial, prior preparation, and test-taking skills have served as means to restrict the access of blacks to white institutions. Further, we have seen improvement since the institution of federally funded financial programs and special admissions programs. The fears that special admissions programs water down existing academic standards need not be actualized. Black students, when given the opportunity, can compete on an equal footing. Willie's study (1973) of black students at four white institutions in upstate New York demonstrates how successful black students can be when they persist. He found that black first-year students experienced the greatest academic difficulties, compared to white students. Second- and third-year students improved considerably but were still behind their white counterparts. Fourth-year students, however, had caught up with their white counterparts and in many cases were outperforming them. Studies like this tend to strengthen the notion that we should both facilitate access, and encourage persistence.

To conclude, although access has been considerably improved, there are still many factors which work to inhibit the success of black students in white institutions. Continued diligence and an advocacy position are required if we are to work toward alleviating these problems.

NOTES

1. It is assumed that many of the motivational problems young people are supposed to have would be alleviated with proper preparation and adequate finances, thus allowing students to perform better.
2. The program description is provided in the Final Report for the SEEK Program of the City University of New York 1976-1977, Part II student performance information. Unpublished report.
3. An excellent description is provided of the CUNY open admissions program by Lavin, Alba, and Silberstein, in Vol. 49, No. 1, 1979, *Harvard Educational Review.*

REFERENCES

ASTIN, A. and Higher Education Research Institute "Testing in post secondary education: some unresolved issues." *Education Evaluation and Policy Analysis* 1, 6: 21-27.
——— (1970) "Racial consideration in admissions," in D. Nichols and O. Mills, *The Campus and the Racial Crisis.* Washington, DC: American Council on Education.
BAYER, A. and R. BORUCH (1969) *The Black Student in American Colleges.* *American Council on Education Research Reports* 4, 2.

BOYD, W. (1974) *Desegregating America's Colleges.* New York: Praeger.

CHANDLER, M. (1964) "The longitudinal study of educational effects: design of the follow-up surveys." Presented at the annual meeting of the American Association for the Advancement of Science, San Francisco.

Office of Program and Policy Research (1977) *City University of New York Student Survey.* New York: City University of New York.

COLEMAN, J., CAMPBELL, HOBSON, McPARTLAND, MAUD, WEINFIELD, and YORK (1966) *Equality of Educational Opportunity.* Washington, DC: Government Printing Office.

College Entrance Examination Board (1975) *College-Bound Seniors, 1974-75.* New York: Author.

CROSS, K. P. (1976a) *Accent on Learning.* San Francisco: Jossey-Bass.

——— (1976b) *Beyond the Open Door: New Students to Higher Education.* San Francisco: Jossey-Bass.

CROSSLAND, F. (1971) *Minority Access to College.* New York: Schocken.

FALLOWS, J. (1980) "The tests and the 'brightest': How fair are the College Boards?" *Atlantic Monthly* (February): 37-48.

FRANKLIN, C. (1974) *The Open Admissions Freshman Program and Basic Skills Developmental Program.* Washington, DC: Educational Resources Information Center. (ED 090 841)

FRIEDMAN, N. and J. THOMPSON (1971) *The Federal Educational Opportunity Grant Program: A Status Report, Fiscal Year 1970.* Washington, DC: Educational Resources Information Center. (ED 056 253)

GRANT, M. and D. HOEBER (1978) *Basic Skills Programs: Are They Working?* Research Report 1, American Association for Higher Education, Washington, D.C.

KATZ, I. (1970) "Experimental studies of Negro-White relationships," in L. Berkowitz (ed.) *Advances in Experimental Psychology, Volume 5.* New York: Academic

LAVIN, D., R. ALBA, and R. SILBERSTEIN (1979) "Open admissions and equal access: a study of ethnic groups in the City University of New York." *Harvard Educational Review* 49, 1: 53-92.

National Advisory Committee on Black Higher Education and Black Colleges and Universities (1979) *Access of Black Americans to Higher Education: How Open Is the Door?*

National Board on Graduate Education (1976) "Minority group participation in graduate education." National Board on Graduate Education Report 5.

MULKA, M. and E. SHEERIN (1974) *An Evaluation of Policy Related Research on Postsecondary Education for the Disadvantaged.* 2 vol. Washington, DC: National Science Foundation.

NICHOLS, D. and O. MILLS (1970) *The Campus and the Racial Crisis.* Washington, DC: American Council on Education.

REED, R. (1979) "Increasing the opportunities for Black students in higher education." *Journal of Negro Education* 47: 143-150.

SAMUDA, R. (1975) *Psychological Testing of American Minorities: Issues and Consequences.* New York: Dodd, Mead and Company, 1975.

TORMES, Y. M. [ed.] (1969) "Some differences in dropouts and survivors in the College Discovery Program," in *Research Briefs.* New York: City University of New York.

WILLIE, C. and A. S. McCORD (1973) *Black Students at White Colleges.* New York: Praeger.

ABOUT THE AUTHORS AND EDITORS

MOLEFI KETE ASANTE received his Ph.D. from UCLA in 1968. He is Professor of Communication at the State University of New York—Buffalo. A Visiting Professor of Communication at Howard University, he has authored, coauthored, or edited fifteen books, including *The Handbook of Intercultural Communication* (Sage, 1979) and over fifty articles. He has chaired twenty-five doctorates, half in intercultural communication, serves on seven editorial boards, and appears in numerous reference works. He is editor of *Journal of Black Studies*.

ABDULAI S. VANDI received his Ph.D. from the State University of New York—Buffalo. He is Assistant Professor of Mass Communications and Telecommunications at the School of Communications, Howard University, Washington, D.C. A technological determinist, his interest areas include global information and cultural imperialism, communications and development, international communications organizations and policy, and he is an adversary of European concepts of civilization, mechanization, and development or advancement. He is a consultant with several international communications organizations and the author of numerous publications, including the book, *A Model of Mass Communications and National Development* (1979).

EMMANUEL AKPAN is a Lecturer in the Department of Mass Communications, University of Nigeria at Nsukka. His major research interest lies in the cultural and communication changes in the Nigerian society.

NJOKU E. AWA is Associate Professor of Communication at Cornell University. His research interests include communication and development, language and cross-cultural behavior, and transactional communication.

JOSEPH A. BALDWIN is Associate Professor of Psychology and Director of the Community Psychology Program at Florida A&M University. He specializes in the psychology of oppression, victimization, and racism.

DAVID R. BURGEST is University Professor of Social Work, Governors State University. He has a general research interest in social science, with specific emphasis in Black/White and minority studies.

J. JOHN HARRIS, III, is Associate Professor of Administration at the School of Education, Indiana University. He specializes in the innovation and strategies of educational administration and supervision.

JUANITA HOWARD is Assistant Professor in the Department of Sociology and Anthropology, Baruch College. Her research interests include the social concerns of the Black Community and the sociological implications of media processes.

295

KENNETH A. JOHNSON is Associate Professor of Sociology at the University of Colorado at Colorado Springs. He was Assistant Director of the research project on evaluation of the Colorado State Penitentiary, and consultant to the Governor's Task Force on Corrections.

SULAYMAN S. NYANG is Associate Professor of Political Science and Public Administration at the Center for African Studies, Howard University, Washington, D.C. A career diplomat, he was the Gambia's number two man in the Middle East between 1975 and 1978. He has published heavily on Africa, the Middle East, and Islamic issues.

COLIN PALMER is Associate Professor of History, Oakland University, Rochester, Minnesota. He has specialized primarily in the fields of slavery and the slave trade, and is the author of numerous publications, including the book, *Salves of the White God: Blacks in Mexico (1560-1650)* (1976).

DORTHY PENNINGTON is Associate Professor of Speech Communications and Human Relations at the University of Kansas at Lawrence. Her research interests include intercultural/interracial communication, human relations, strategies in public address, and a thorough concentration in temporality and cultural cosmology.

DONA RICHARDS is Assistant Professor of Africana Studies at Hunter College. She is a product of the New School for Social Research, and her primary concentration is in the critique of the dominant principles of Western-European thought.

ELOIS SCOTT is Director of The Reading and Writing Center, University of Florida, and holds a faculty position in the University's School of Education. Her publications include several books and articles. A recent chapter on communication competencies appeared in the NSFE *Yearbook*. She has done extensive work in program evaluation from elementary through postsecondary educational institutions.

THADDEUS H. SPRATLEN is Professor of Marketing and Associate Director of the Black Studies Program at the University of Washington, Seattle. He has written extensively on economic and business subjects relating to Blacks in the United States. He also serves as a consultant on a variety of projects pertaining to economic and business development in the Black Community.

BOBBY M. WILSON is Assistant Professor of Geography and Urban Studies at the University of Alabama at Birmingham. His principal research interests include environmental and social planning, and urban housing. He is the author of numerous publications.

INDEX